# CHASING
# SHADOWS

# KEN HUGHES

# CHASING SHADOWS

THE NIXON TAPES, THE CHENNAULT

AFFAIR, AND THE ORIGINS OF WATERGATE

University of Virginia Press

CHARLOTTESVILLE AND LONDON

University of Virginia Press
© 2014 by the Rector and Visitors of the University of Virginia, Miller Center
All rights reserved
Printed in the United States of America on acid-free paper

*First published 2014*

9 8 7 6 5 4 3 2 1

LIBRARY OF CONGRESS CATALOGING-IN-PUBLICATION DATA

Hughes, Ken, 1964–
    Chasing shadows : the Nixon tapes, the Chennault affair, and the origins of
Watergate / Ken Hughes.
        pages    cm
    Includes bibliographical references and index.
    ISBN 978-0-8139-3663-5 (cloth : acid-free paper)—ISBN 978-0-8139-3664-2 (e-book)
    1. United States—Politics and government—1969–1974.   2. Nixon, Richard M.
(Richard Milhous), 1913–1994—Political and social views.   3. Audiotapes.
4. Chennault, Anna.   5. Watergate Affair, 1972–1974.   6. United States—Politics
and government—1961–1963.   7. United States—Politics and government—
1963–1969.   I. Title.
    E855.H83 2014
    973.924092—dc23

                                                                    2014013429

To Alison
*of the greatest gifts*

# CONTENTS

# INTRODUCTION

What more could we possibly need to know about Watergate? Four decades have passed since Richard Nixon left the White House looking like a man whose worst fears were being realized. But he had not yet hit bottom. President Gerald Ford's blanket pardon soon relieved him of the fear of prosecution and imprisonment, but that was not the ultimate threat Nixon faced. His presidency had been ended by a handful of tapes, secretly recorded on his own orders via microphones hidden in the Oval Office and other locations where he conducted the people's business. Public exposure of the full collection of Nixon tapes could destroy much of what remained of his reputation. The 3,432 hours of recordings captured a pivotal time in his presidency and American history. During the time of his secret taping, February 16, 1971, to July 12, 1973, Nixon negotiated the diplomatic opening to China, the first nuclear arms limitation treaty with the Soviet Union, and a settlement of what was then America's longest war, while winning a landslide reelection that realigned American politics and (not coincidentally) committing the wide-ranging abuses of power known collectively as Watergate. Until his dying day, the former president waged a legal battle to keep the public from learning what was on the rest of his tapes. The reasons became clear after his death, as the federal government gradually released most of the Nixon tapes (while withholding material on policy, privacy, and national security grounds) over the next two decades, a process completed only in August of 2013. At the same time, the National Archives made public many of the 50 million pages of Nixon administration documents in its collection.

In an article reflecting on the fortieth anniversary of the Watergate break-in, Carl Bernstein and Bob Woodward, the two investigative journalists whose trailblazing articles in the days and months following the burglary started to expose the pervasive abuses of power behind it, marveled at the wealth of documentation now available: "Today, much more than when we first covered this story as young *Washington Post* reporters, an abundant record provides unambiguous answers and evidence about Watergate and its meaning." From this record, Woodward and Bernstein concluded that Watergate consisted of five wars waged by

Nixon: "against the anti–Vietnam War movement, the news media, the Democrats, the justice system and, finally, against history itself."

The Chennault Affair played an unacknowledged, largely unseen, role in all five of these Watergate wars, driving some of Nixon's most outrageous assaults on war critics, journalism, the opposition, justice, and history. The affair is a thread running through the Huston Plan, the Enemies List, and the Special Investigations Unit ("the Plumbers"), and it provides clearer answers to questions about some of the more outlandish decisions Nixon made. Why was his reaction to the leak of the Pentagon Papers so extreme? Why was he obsessed with getting his hands on all government documents related to his predecessor's decision to stop bombing North Vietnam in 1968? Why did he order the Watergate cover-up?

The Chennault Affair is not, however, the magical key to all of Watergate; it's part of a much bigger, complicated story. Many factors contributed to Nixon's fall, far more than I can fit in these pages. Wand-waving accounts that reduce the complexity of Nixon's downfall to a single cause are the preserve of Watergate revisionists. From time to time a new theory emerges placing the blame for Nixon's undoing on the scheming of a scapegoat (or, more marketably, a shadowy conspiracy of scapegoats). John W. Dean plays a recurring, featured role in these fantasies. Ever since Dean went from White House counsel to witness for the prosecution in the spring of 1973, Nixon and his defenders have tried to shift responsibility for Watergate onto his shoulders. Dean was a key figure in the cover-up, but not the central one. That was Nixon. The notion that the president was the victim of a criminal conspiracy rather than the perpetrator of one cannot survive the tape-recorded sounds of him calling the shots from the Oval Office.

"His secret tapes—and what they reveal—will probably be his most lasting legacy," Woodward and Bernstein wrote in 2012. The authors of two enduring classics on Watergate, *All the President's Men* and *The Final Days,* found that there was even more to the story than investigators uncovered at the time: "The Watergate that we wrote about in the *Washington Post* from 1972 to 1974 is not Watergate as we know it today. It was only a glimpse into something far worse."

Since 2000 I have studied the White House tapes as part of the Presidential Recordings Program founded by the University of Virginia's Miller Center. These years of research have convinced me that the origins of Watergate extend deeper than we previously knew to encompass a crime committed to elect Nixon president in the first place. *Chasing Shadows* tells the story of that crime and its role in the unmaking of the president.

# CHASING SHADOWS

**O** N ALL 2,658 hours of secretly recorded Nixon White House tapes that the government has declassified to date, you can hear the president of the United States order precisely one break-in. It wasn't Watergate, but it does expose the roots of the cover-up that ultimately brought down Richard Milhous Nixon. Investigation of its origin reveals almost as much about the president's rise as his fall.

June 17, 1971, 5:15 p.m., the Oval Office. None of the president's men knew what to do when he ordered them to burglarize the Brookings Institution, a venerable Washington think tank. Richard Nixon had gathered his inner circle to talk about something entirely different—the recent leak of the Pentagon Papers, at that point the biggest unauthorized disclosure of classified information in US history. The seven-thousand-page Defense Department history of Vietnam decision making during the administrations of Harry S. Truman, Dwight D. Eisenhower, John F. Kennedy, and Lyndon B. Johnson had nothing on President Nixon. The study stopped well before his election, climaxing with LBJ's surprise March 31, 1968, announcement that he would not seek a second full term.

In that same speech, Johnson created the issue that nearly sank Nixon's presidential campaign. LBJ announced that he was limiting American bombing of North Vietnam—and would stop it completely if Hanoi could convince him that this would lead to prompt, productive peace talks.[1] Throughout the fall campaign, Nixon worried that LBJ would announce a bombing halt before Election Day, a move that would boost the Democratic nominee, Vice President Hubert H. Humphrey. Johnson did, and it did. The president announced the bombing halt on Halloween, less than a week before the voting. The Republican nominee, who had begun the campaign 16 points ahead in the polls, watched his lead disappear. Nixon still won, but it was too close—at that point the second-closest race of the twentieth century, right behind the one he had lost in 1960 to JFK.[2]

"You could blackmail Johnson on this stuff, and it might be worth doing," said White House Chief of Staff H. R. Haldeman, a California public relations executive with blue eyes and a brush cut who spent years polishing Walt Disney's image before taking on the greater challenge of managing Nixon's.

"How?" the president asked.

"The bombing halt stuff is all in the same file," Bob Haldeman said. "Huston swears to God there's a file on it at Brookings." Haldeman was working with some bad information. Tom Charles Huston, author of the secret Huston Plan to expand government break-ins, wiretaps, and mail opening in the name of fighting domestic terror, claimed Brookings had a top secret report on the bombing halt, written under the direction of some of the same people who oversaw the Pentagon Papers project.

"Bob, now you remember Huston's plan? Implement it," the president said.

An aide began to object.

President Nixon: I mean, I want it implemented on a thievery basis. Goddamn it, get in and get those files. Blow the safe and get it.[3]

This wasn't what Haldeman had in mind. He wanted government officials to visit Brookings on the pretext of inspecting how it stored classified material and to confiscate the bombing halt file in the process.[4] No one in the Oval Office pointed out that the president's idea was illegal. National Security Adviser Henry A. Kissinger, a former Harvard government professor with a profound German accent, asked the obvious question: "But what good will it do you, the bombing halt file?"

"To blackmail him," the president said. "Because he used the bombing halt for political purposes."

"The bombing halt file would really kill Johnson," Haldeman said.

"Why, why do you think that?" Kissinger asked.

The timing, Haldeman said. Johnson stopped the bombing less than a week before the election.

"You remember, I used to give you information about it at the time," Kissinger said, reminding them of the secret role he had played as an informant to the 1968 Nixon campaign on Johnson's bombing halt negotiations.[5] Kissinger had worked as a consultant on a 1967 bombing halt initiative for LBJ, so when he visited the American negotiating team in Paris during the 1968 talks, members confided in him. He gained Nixon's trust by betraying theirs. "To the best of my knowledge, there was never any conversation in which they said we'll hold it until the end of October," Kissinger said. "I wasn't in on the discussions here. I just saw the instructions to [Ambassador W. Averell] Harriman."[6] (Years later, Kissinger denied having had access to information about the negotiations at the time; the instructions to Ambassador Harriman, LBJ's lead negotiator with the North Vietnamese, were, of course, highly classified information.)[7] If Kissinger was right, then even if Nixon got someone to break into Brookings and steal the bombing halt report, it was unlikely to contain the blackmail information he said he wanted.

Yet Nixon ordered the Brookings burglary at least three more times in the next two weeks. It was one of the reasons he took the fateful step of creating the Special Investigations Unit (SIU), an unconstitutional secret police organization better known as "the Plumbers" because one of its jobs was to plug leaks. The SIU recruited a former FBI agent with experience doing "black bag jobs" (that is, government-conducted break-ins) and a former CIA agent experienced in covert operations.[8]

Exactly one year to the day after Nixon first ordered the Brookings break-in, a different one planned by these two former government agents took place at Democratic National Committee (DNC) headquarters in Washington's Watergate apartment and office complex. Once Washington, DC, police arrested five men in dark suits and blue gloves at the DNC offices on the morning of June 17, 1972, President Nixon faced a stark choice. An unobstructed investigation of the crimes the two former government agents had committed would lead back to ones that the president himself had ordered. He could either order a cover-up or face impeachment.

So why did Nixon want the bombing halt file so badly in the first place? What good would blackmailing LBJ do, anyway? (At that point, Nixon just wanted the former president to hold a press conference denouncing the leak of the Pentagon Papers—not much of a motive to commit a felony.) The potential downside was enormous—impeachment, conviction, prison, disgrace—and the upside was questionable at best. If Nixon were the kind of president to conduct criminal fishing expeditions for dirt on his predecessors, his tapes would be littered with break-in orders. But Brookings is the only one.

There is a rational explanation. Nixon did have reason to believe that the bombing halt file contained politically explosive information—not about his predecessor, but about himself. Ordering the Brookings break-in wasn't a matter of opportunism or poor presidential impulse control. As far as Nixon knew, it was a matter of survival. The reasons why are not on Nixon's tapes, but on those of his predecessor.

# The Chennault Affair

October 30, 1968, 10:25 a.m., the President's Little Office. President Lyndon B. Johnson had a problem unlike any he'd ever faced. For guidance he turned to the last of his three great mentors. All were giants of Democratic politics. The first two were President Franklin D. Roosevelt and House Speaker Sam Rayburn, a fellow Texan. The third was Sen. Richard B. Russell of Georgia.

Johnson valued Russell's judgment above all others'. But on the two issues that dominated his legacy as president, civil rights and Vietnam, LBJ had defied his counsel. "In this job a man must set a standard to which he's working. In my case, it is what will my grandchildren think when I'm buried out there under the tree on the ranch," Johnson told a *New York Times* reporter writing about the twilight of his presidency. "I think they will be proud of two things: what I did for the Negro and seeing it through in Vietnam for all of Asia. The Negro cost me 15 points in the polls and Vietnam cost me 20."[1] Russell was the president's public opponent on civil rights and his private counselor on Vietnam. While he acknowledged that Johnson would suffer politically if he didn't fight in Vietnam, Russell told the president in 1964 that this was a war America didn't need to wage: "It isn't important a damn bit."[2] Other critics emerged as the war went badly, but Russell warned LBJ long before he sent in the first combat brigade. "I never did want to get messed up down there. I do not agree with those brain trusters who say this thing has tremendous strategic and economic value and that we'll lose everything in Southeast—in Asia if we lose Vietnam," Russell told the president. "I don't think that's true. But I think as a practical matter, we're in there, and I don't know how the hell you can tell the American people you're coming out. There's just no way to do it. They'll think that you've just been whipped and you've been run, you're scared. And it'd be disastrous."[3]

The president was on the brink of another Vietnam-related political disaster in October 1968. For months, Hanoi had demanded an unconditional halt to American bombing of North Vietnam before it would discuss any settlement of the war. Johnson, however, insisted that Hanoi meet certain secret military conditions before he would call off the aerial and naval bombardment of the North. Hanoi had finally accepted his demands, but just as LBJ was getting ready to order the bombing halt and announce the start of peace talks, he received a warning: the Republican presidential nominee was trying to sabotage the peace talks before they even began. Faced with an unprecedented problem, he turned, as he had so many times before, to Senator Russell.

President Johnson: Well, I've got one this morning that's pretty rough for you. We have found that our friend, the Republican nominee, our California friend, has been playing on the outskirts with our enemies and our friends both, our allies and the others. He's been doing it through rather subterranean sources here.[4]

The warning came from a source no president could safely ignore: Alexander Sachs. An economist at Wall Street's Lehman Corporation who had helped write campaign speeches for FDR, Sachs entered history when he warned Roosevelt on behalf of Albert Einstein and other leading physicists that Nazi Germany might build an atom bomb. An October 11, 1939, meeting in the Oval Office between FDR and Sachs led to the Manhattan Project.[5] Sachs had a pretty good track record of forecasting trouble. "Among the developments he was credited with having predicted," the *New York Times* wrote, "were the 1929 Depression, the 1933 banking crisis and the rise of Hitler."[6] Like these earlier warnings, the one Sachs gave Johnson concerned matters that could affect the future of America and the world.

At an October 28, 1968, working lunch on Wall Street, Sachs had heard from "a member of the banking community, a colleague, a man he has known for many years, and one in whose honesty he has absolute confidence" that Nixon was approaching the peace talks "like another Fortas case."[7] Conservative senators had successfully filibustered Johnson's nomination of Supreme Court Justice Abe Fortas to become chief justice earlier that month. Sachs wouldn't reveal the identity of his source, but told Under Secretary of State for Political Affairs Eugene V. Rostow what he'd heard:

> The speaker said he thought the prospects for a bombing halt or a cease-fire were dim, because Nixon was playing the problem as he did the Fortas affair—to block. He was taking public positions intended to achieve that end. They would incite Saigon to be difficult, and Hanoi to wait.
>
> Part of his strategy was an expectation that an offensive would break out soon, that we would have to spend a great deal more (and incur more casualties)—a fact which would adversely affect the stock market and the bond market. [North Vietnamese] offensive action was a definite element in the thinking about the future.

These difficulties would make it easier for Nixon to settle after January. Like Ike in 1953, he would be able to settle on terms which the President could not accept, blaming the deterioration of the situation between now and January or February on his predecessor.[8]

Mere hours after LBJ got this warning from Sachs, he learned that the South Vietnamese government was indeed going "to be difficult." South Vietnamese president Nguyen Van Thieu had started saying that three days between stopping the bombing and starting the peace talks just wasn't enough time for him to get a delegation to Paris. "Didn't he say *one* day originally?" Johnson asked his advisers. The president began to suspect Sachs was right.[9]

President Johnson: The next thing that we got our teeth in was one of his associates, a fellow named [John] Mitchell, who's running his campaign, who's the real [Eisenhower White House chief of staff] Sherman Adams of the operation, in effect, said to a businessman that "we're going to handle this like we handled the Fortas matter," unquote. "We're going to frustrate the President by saying to the South Vietnamese, and the Koreans, and the Thailanders, 'Beware of Johnson.'[10] At the same time, we're going to say to Hanoi, 'I can make a better deal than he has because I'm fresh and new, and I don't have to demand as much as he does in the light of past positions.'" [*coughs*] Now, when we got that pure by accident, as a result of some of our Wall Street connections, that caused me to look a little deeper.
Russell: I guess so.
President Johnson: And I have means of doing that, as you may well imagine.
Russell: Yes.[11]

The president didn't spell it out on the telephone, but US intelligence agencies were reporting Saigon's internal discussions of the bombing halt negotiations to him. The National Security Agency (NSA) was intercepting diplomatic cables from the South Vietnamese embassy in Washington, DC, to its home government; the Central Intelligence Agency (CIA) had a bug in the office of South Vietnam's president. It took decades for the US government to declassify the CIA and NSA reports, and even then the intelligence agencies redacted many passages with thick black markers. So heavily censored are the public versions of these reports that they do not include the next name Johnson mentioned, the central figure in what came to be known as the Chennault Affair.[12]

President Johnson: And Mrs. [Anna] Chennault is contacting their ambassador from time to time. Seems to be kind of the go-between.[13]

Anna Chan Chennault was the widow of Lt. Gen. Claire L. Chennault, the American leader of a volunteer air group, the Flying Tigers, that defended China against Japanese invaders in World War II. It was then that he met Chen Xiangmei (Plum Blossom), a beautiful young war correspondent. Once the war was over, Chennault divorced his American wife of thirty-four years.[14] In 1947, he married Chen Xiangmei, now Anna Chan, in Shanghai. He was fifty-seven; the press couldn't determine her age (twenty-two).[15] The Chennaults planned to live in China, where they ran a new airline, Civil Air Transport (CAT). Mao Zedong's Communist revolution disrupted their plans. When the Nationalist government of Chiang Kai-shek retreated to Taiwan while continuing to lay claim to all of China, CAT moved to the island as well.[16]

The Chennaults became fixtures of the "China Lobby." Not so much an organization as an alliance of conservative American politicians, activists, and Chinese Nationalists, the China Lobby blamed President Harry S. Truman and the State Department of the World War II general George C. Marshall and Dean Acheson for "losing" China. The China Lobby never really came up with a way Truman could have saved China from Communism. Nor did it have to—the rallying cry of "Who lost China?" was effective enough to help Republicans win the House and Senate in the 1950 midterm elections. Politicians tried to make their opponent's name the answer to the question "Who lost _____?" during the Cold War because the tactic paid off on Election Day. Successfully casting an opponent as the sort who would leave the nation vulnerable to foreign threats—due to weakness, failure to grasp the nature of the global challenge, cowardice, shortsighted political opportunism, even disloyalty—won elections.

Anna Chennault's narrative of her life story reflected and reinforced such attacks. In her account, Chennault lost her homeland to Mao's revolutionaries because a Democratic administration in Washington failed to support Chinese anti-Communists.[17] This was a tale Republicans loved to tell. Once Chennault moved to America, she rose rapidly in political circles. In the age of the "Washington hostess," Chennault made herself a renowned one ("Our China doll," in the words of another) for the parties thrown at her penthouse apartment in the capital's new and fashionable Watergate complex.[18] *Life* magazine sent photographers to shoot her party prep.[19] Chennault rose in business, too, as vice president of the Flying Tiger Line, founded by her late husband's World War II comrades and then the biggest freight airline on the planet.[20]

Chennault assembled a dazzling network of social, business, and political connections. With former First Lady Mamie Eisenhower, Chennault served as cochair of the women's advisory committee for the Nixon campaign.[21] She was the only Chinese American woman to attend the 1968 GOP convention as a delegate. Chennault raised a quarter million dollars for Nixon, making her his top woman fund-raiser.[22]

The men of the Johnson administration never knew what to make of her. To them she was "the Dragon Lady" (a name drawn not from Asian history or culture but from an American comic strip, *Terry and the Pirates*) or "the Little Flower" or "the Lady" or just "the woman." She was singular.

President Johnson: I know it's her.

Russell: Uh-huh, uh-huh.

President Johnson: Mrs. Chennault, you know, of the Flying Tigers.

Russell: I know Mrs. Chennault.

President Johnson: She's young and attractive. I mean, she's a pretty good-looking girl.

Russell: Certainly is.

President Johnson: And she's around town and she is warning them to not get pulled in on this Johnson move.[23]

The president had a great deal of information from the NSA intercepts and the CIA bug, but he was missing the central piece of the puzzle. Nixon had taken pains to keep it from him. One of his speechwriters, without realizing how important it was, kept the following memo from the foreign policy adviser Richard V. Allen to the candidate (referred to within the campaign as "DC").

3 July 68

To: DC

From: Dick Allen

Re: Possible meeting with South Vietnamese Ambassador

Talked with Mrs. Chennault, who is long-time friend of Saigon's Ambassador to the U.S., Bui Diem. He is now in Paris, designated official observer and representative of SVN government to the peace talks. He is due back in here (Washington) next week some time.

Mrs. Chennault has apparently asked him if he would talk to DC. I explained schedule tight, but possible to check on available time.

Meeting would have to be absolute top secret, etc.

Initiative is ours—if DC can see him, I am to contact Mrs. Chennault, she will arrange.

Near the words "top secret," Nixon scribbled, "Should be but I don't see how—with the S.S." Secret Service agents provided Nixon protection as a candidate, but their boss was President Johnson. "If it can be (secret) RN would like to see," the candidate wrote, referring to himself by his initials. The speechwriter who kept the memo thought the meeting hadn't taken place.[24]

The meeting had taken place, however; Nixon had managed to keep it secret.[25] On July 12, 1968, Chennault and South Vietnamese ambassador Bui Diem flew from Washington, DC, to New York City, where the Nixon campaign was headquartered, for a meeting with the candidate and his campaign chairman, John N. Mitchell. Chennault revealed this years after the fact in her 1980 memoir, *The Education of Anna*. Ambassador Diem provides a corroborating account of the meeting in his own memoir, 1987's *In the Jaws of History*.[26]

Chennault introduced Nixon to the South Vietnamese ambassador for the first time. Nixon designated her as "the sole representative between the Vietnamese government and the Nixon campaign headquarters," Chennault wrote. She quoted the candidate as saying: "Anna is my good friend. She knows all about Asia. I know you also consider her a friend, so please rely on her from now on as the only contact between myself and your government. If you have any message for me, please give it to Anna and she will relay it to me and I will do the same in the future. We know Anna is a good American and a dedicated Republican. We can all rely on her loyalty."[27]

So when President Johnson told Senator Russell that "Mrs. Chennault is contacting their ambassador from time to time, seems to be kind of the go-between," he was more right than he knew.

President Johnson: In addition, their ambassador is saying to him [South Vietnamese president Nguyen Van Thieu] that Johnson is desperate and is just moving heaven and earth to elect Humphrey, so don't you get sucked in on that. He is kind of these folks' agents here, this little South Vietnamese ambassador. Now, this is not guesswork.[28]

CIA reports on the bug in Thieu's office indicated that the South Vietnamese president thought Johnson was calling the bombing halt to help Vice President Humphrey win the election. Humphrey wasn't Thieu's candidate. Within the Johnson administration, Humphrey had opposed LBJ's decision in 1965 to escalate and "Americanize" the Vietnam War; Nixon, America's premier anti-Communist politician of the Cold War, had called for increased American intervention. Thieu realized that his own actions could influence the American presidential election—and shape South Vietnam's future. If it became clear that the South Vietnamese government didn't agree with LBJ's bombing halt deal, Thieu said, that "would be to the advantage of candidate Nixon."[29]

President Johnson: We don't think they're going to come in the light of the Nixon thing. We just—

Russell: I'm surprised at Nixon. I never did have any confidence in him, but damn if I thought he'd stoop to anything like that.

President Johnson: Well, we—it may be his agents.[30]

For months Johnson had gone to extraordinary lengths to secure Nixon's support for the US negotiating position. When Nixon was just the front-runner in the Republican race, still fending off challenges from Gov. Ronald W. Reagan of California on his right and Gov. Nelson A. Rockefeller of New York on his left, he received an invitation to the White House for a personal briefing from the president. "He says he is for our position in Vietnam," LBJ had told his advisers. "He thinks Democrats will go the other way." The president feared Nixon was right. "When he gets the nomination he may be more responsible," Johnson said. "The GOP may be of more help to us than the Democrats in the last few months" of the administration.[31]

The public knew that the president had launched a new initiative to seek "an honorable peace" the same night he revealed his decision not to run for reelection.[32]

Tonight, I have ordered our aircraft and our naval vessels to make no attacks on North Vietnam, except in the area north of the demilitarized zone where the continuing enemy buildup directly threatens allied forward positions and where the movements of their troops and supplies are clearly related to that threat.

The area in which we are stopping our attacks includes almost 90 percent of North Vietnam's population, and most of its territory. Thus there will be no attacks around the principal populated areas, or in the food-producing areas of North Vietnam.

Even this very limited bombing of the North could come to an early end—if our restraint is matched by restraint in Hanoi. But I cannot in good conscience stop all bombing so long as to do so would immediately and directly endanger the lives of our men and our allies. Whether a complete bombing halt becomes possible in the future will be determined by events.[33]

Johnson offered to stop the bombing of North Vietnam altogether if it would lead to prompt, productive peace talks. What that meant in practical terms wasn't exactly clear to the public. The ambiguity was purposeful. Hanoi demanded an "unconditional" bombing halt, and Johnson had conditions. If he made them public, his peace initiative would be dead on arrival, so they remained secret.

But the president did reveal them to the likely nominee of the opposition party. It was a calculated risk. Politicians were debating whether to stop the bombing. If Nixon or any candidate said he would stop it unconditionally, the North Vietnamese might just sit on their hands until after the election, hoping for a better deal from Johnson's successor. They might do that even if the candidate offered only slightly better terms in public than Johnson's negotiators were demanding in secret. LBJ took the candidates into his confidence to keep them from undercutting him. He was not about to let them destroy any hope of accomplishing the goal he set out in a speech that used the word "peace" thirty-one times. Johnson might have been a lame duck, but he was still president. He got the blame for dragging America into "Lyndon Johnson's War"; he wanted the credit for starting peace talks to get it out.

Sitting across the Cabinet Room table from the Republican front-runner on July 26, Johnson laid out his secret terms. American negotiators in Paris had told the North Vietnamese that the United States would stop the bombing only if Hanoi:

1. *Respected the Demilitarized Zone dividing North Vietnam from the South.* The tradeoff was obvious. Johnson was still bombing the area directly north of the Demilitarized Zone (DMZ) because that was one place where Hanoi amassed troops and trucks before infiltrating them into the South. The bombing didn't stop infiltration, but did slow it down. Unless Hanoi respected the DMZ, a bombing halt would allow it to move more soldiers and supplies into the South, endangering the lives of American soldiers.

2. *Stopped shelling South Vietnamese cities.* The North Vietnamese and Vietcong forces were using mortar and rocket fire to terrorize civilians.

3. *Entered peace talks with Saigon.* The only participants in the Paris talks at this point were the Americans and North Vietnamese. Hanoi refused to discuss any topic other than an "unconditional" US bombing halt; Johnson insisted on full-fledged peace talks that included the

South Vietnamese. In return, he was willing to let Hanoi bring the National Liberation Front (NLF), the Vietcong's political wing, to the bargaining table as well.

Johnson's negotiators didn't call these "conditions" in the Paris talks, since Hanoi maintained its position that the United States had to stop the bombing without "reciprocity" of any kind. The administration came up with creative synonyms for conditions, such as "understandings" and "facts of life"—as in, it was simply a fact of life that Johnson would have to end any bombing halt if the North Vietnamese crossed the DMZ. Privately, though, Johnson called them conditions.

Richard Nixon had no objections to any of them. The more conditions Johnson set, the less likely Hanoi was to accept them. That suited Nixon fine. Johnson's approval ratings had skyrocketed after he announced the end to most American bombing of the North in March. A complete bombing halt combined with the start of peace talks would help Nixon's most likely Democratic opponent, Vice President Humphrey. Nixon was against a bombing halt, although he didn't tell the president (or the voters).[34] "I understand that Hubert is under tremendous pressure," Nixon said. The chief remaining antiwar Democrat in the race following Robert Kennedy's murder, Sen. Eugene J. McCarthy, D-Minnesota, was calling for a bombing halt.[35] Robert F. Kennedy had announced his support for one the day he launched his candidacy.[36] Humphrey's liberal base was largely for a halt as a way to get negotiations started. "I think he'll have to come up with a bombing pause," Nixon said.

Johnson said he didn't think so. He'd spoken with the vice president the night before and said a bombing halt would be absolutely ridiculous. The president didn't mention that he'd threatened to repudiate his vice president if Humphrey crossed him on this issue. "In fact, he told me that it would endanger American troops like his son-in-law and cost lives. I would have their blood on my hands," Humphrey told a political adviser after the meeting. "He would denounce me publicly for playing politics with peace."[37] Johnson made it a point of pride and strict policy to give Humphrey's opponents the same information he gave his own vice president. The same day he had Nixon to the White House, Johnson also personally briefed a right-wing, third-party candidate. George C. Wallace had made a national name for himself by declaring his support of "segregation now, segregation tomorrow, segregation forever" in his 1963 inaugural address as governor of Alabama and had since developed a national following on the political right. Wallace positioned himself as the conservative alternative to both major parties, and the Gallup Poll showed his support among registered voters at 16 percent.[38] The late 1960s was a time of both large-scale antiwar demonstrations and the rise of the political Right; in part, the former fueled the latter. Wallace rallies always applauded his line about the demonstrator who had once lain down in front of LBJ's limousine: "I'll tell you this—if I were President and anyone lay down in front of my car, that'd be the last car he would lay down in front of."[39] The Left was gaining a lot of attention; the Right was gaining votes. Regarding the bombing halt, Wallace expressed as much support for LBJ as Nixon did. The president's negotiating position was a hawkish one.

Secretary of State Dean Rusk and National Security Adviser Walt W. Rostow joined LBJ in the Cabinet Room for the July 26 Nixon briefing. Outwardly, the secretary and the adviser had little in common. Rusk was the son of a rural Georgia preacher; Rostow, the son of a Russian Jewish immigrant to New York City. Rusk spoke in a slow, easy drawl; JFK complained that Rostow wrote memos faster than he could read them. Rusk's parents were Calvinists and Rostow's socialists, but both men were hard-line anti-Communists, Johnson's top two civilian hawks on Vietnam. Nixon especially admired Rusk, privately deeming him "a tower of strength."[40]

The secretary of state gave his international perspective on the talks: the bombing of North Vietnam was "the principal interest of the Soviet Union" as well as the United States at the moment. At this point, however, the Soviets couldn't tell President Johnson what Hanoi would do if he ordered a halt; Moscow was nervous about pressing the North Vietnamese on the issue for fear that would drive them into the arms of China, its own rival for leadership in the Communist world, Rusk said. He claimed Hanoi had hurt itself in international opinion by continuing rocket attacks on Saigon; it was hard to generate indignation at the American bombing of military targets in the North while its soldiers were firing explosives at civilians in the South.

Nixon questioned them regarding "the whole jazz about coalition government," one in which Communists and anti-Communists would formally share power. National Security Adviser Rostow said everyone in South Vietnam viewed a coalition government as a way for the Communists to take over; Saigon was dead set against it. On the other hand, he said, the South Vietnamese would allow the Communists to compete in elections.

"My best judgment is that we're not losing the war," Johnson said. "We're winning it. Now, my best judgment is we're very close to winning it."

The Republican front-runner said he didn't buy the idea that the war was lost. The president would have told him if it was, Nixon said.[41]

After the briefing ended, Nixon talked with reporters on the West Wing steps. He called Johnson's briefing "candid" and "forthright." These were valuable words for a president suffering from what the newspapers called a "credibility gap." Nixon told reporters that the president and secretary of state spoke to him "straight from the shoulder." He gave them no details of the classified briefing other than to say it covered the Paris negotiations on Vietnam and that he would not say anything to "jeopardize the chances for a settlement."[42]

Right before the Republican convention in August, Nixon outlined a position on Vietnam that appeared to justify LBJ's confidence. The Republican front-runner made a virtue of a candidate's silence on the central issue of the campaign.

> Anything he might offer as a candidate would become unavailable for bargaining when he became President. Anything he might say, any differences he might express, would be taken by Hanoi as indicating the possible new direction of the next administration. Our negotiators in Paris represent not only the present administration, but the United States. In the spirit of country above party, as long as they have a chance of success—and as long as the administration remains committed to an honorable settlement—they should be free from partisan interference and they should have our full support. The pursuit of peace is too important for politics-as-usual.[43]

This was exactly what Johnson wanted to hear. It left the negotiations firmly in his hands. Publicly, Nixon respected his constitutional role.

> The present administration's emissaries in Paris must be able to speak with the full force and authority of the United States. Nothing should be offered in the political arena that might undercut their hand.[44]

As for what he would do if elected, Nixon said it was time to seek a negotiated settlement. He warned this would require patience. In the meantime, he promised to wage the war more effectively. "But rather than further escalation on the military front, what it requires now is a dramatic escalation of our efforts on the economic, political, diplomatic and psychological fronts." It also required training and equipping the South Vietnamese to play a greater role in their own defense. "As they are phased in, American troops can—and should—be phased out." Gen. Creighton W. Abrams and the US Military Assistance Command,

Vietnam (MACV), were already making a push to train and equip Saigon's army.

> However cruel its military aspects, this new kind of war is not primarily a military struggle in the conventional sense. It is primarily a political struggle, with the enemy conducting military operations to achieve political and psychological objectives. It is a war for people, not for territory. The real measure of progress is not the body-count of enemy killed, but the number of South Vietnamese won to the building and defense of their own country. This new kind of war requires greater emphasis on small-unit action, on rooting out the Vietcong infrastructure, on police and patrol activities, on intelligence gathering, on the strengthening of local forces. This kind of war can actually be waged more effectively with fewer men and at less cost.[45]

As president, Nixon would learn the limits of these tactics. During the campaign, however, his statement offered voters the hope of leaving Vietnam without losing the war.

When the 1968 Republican convention nominated him for president and Gov. Spiro T. Agnew of Maryland for vice president, Richard Nixon got a call from the White House before he even delivered his acceptance speech.

President Johnson: Dick, I want to keep in close touch with you along the line we did—

Nixon: Wonderful.

President Johnson: —in our last talk, and I want to try to play this thing as much in the national interest as is humanly possible and as fair as possible and I have just one purpose and that is the best interests of the country, and I believe that your conduct has been very responsible.

Nixon: Well—

President Johnson: There are some developments that have not changed the picture, but that I think you would do well to know about.[46]

The president invited the Republican nominee and his running mate to the LBJ Ranch for another briefing once the GOP convention ended. Johnson would have Ambassador Cyrus R. Vance, chief negotiator W. Averell Harriman's deputy, fly from Washington to Texas for the briefing before he headed back to Paris for another round of discussions with the North Vietnamese. Secretary of State Rusk, Nixon's favorite Johnson administration official, would be there, too. LBJ mentioned that Humphrey was visiting the next day, but not that the vice president had requested the meeting just a few hours earlier.[47] The president said he was under great pressures, but wasn't going to succumb. "I appreciate very much your attitude on the whole picture," Johnson said. He offered the Republicans lunch.

President Johnson: And I got a note this morning, my son-in-law's company had 220 [and] is down to half-strength and he lost—had thirty wounded yesterday.

Nixon: Incidentally, I thought you should know that [Gov. Spiro T.] Agnew [R-Maryland], my running mate, the guy I selected, he has a boy that's been there for five months—

President Johnson: Well, I'll be damned.

Nixon: —in Vietnam, so we've both got a good interest in that.

President Johnson: Well, I'll—

Nixon: And my nephew's out there. [chuckles]

President Johnson: Well—

Nixon: So we're all looking for the same—

President Johnson: We're both supposed to be great political animals, but we both want to do what's best for our country, [Nixon acknowledges throughout] and I think it's awfully important dealing with these commies for the next four months for us to be completely informed with the same facts and then we can do whatever our judgment dictates.[48]

Nixon's acceptance speech included a reassuring line: "We all hope in this room that there's a chance that current negotiations may bring an honorable end to that war, and we will say nothing during this campaign that might destroy that chance."[49] The next morning, when reporters questioned the nominee about the phone call from the president, Nixon promised again not to undercut the negotiations. "I told him that that would be the policy of the party, it would be the policy of the candidates between now and the election, but that we had to be kept briefed on developments, and that we couldn't be in a position where the ground was cut out from under us," Nixon said. "He said, 'It's vitally important that on this issue, that as long as these negotiations go on, that we have a united front at home on those negotiations, and I'm going to play it straight down the middle with regard to intelligence on what is going on in Vietnam.' I take the President at his word and I think that it will serve not only our interests, but more important it'll serve the interests of the country." In full view of the TV cameras, Nixon sat down at the hotel piano. Noting that "Home on the Range" was the favorite song of Johnson's favorite president, FDR, and that the title captured where the president would soon be "unless he changes his mind," the nominee played and sang it at full blast.[50]

While Nixon was giving every appearance of supporting Johnson's negotiating position, Humphrey was at the LBJ Ranch showing the president a draft campaign speech calling for a bombing halt. His campaign had struggled to craft a statement Johnson would accept. This was draft number eleven. LBJ talked him out of it once more.[51]

For the following day's visit from Nixon and Agnew, LBJ produced CIA Director Richard M. Helms along with Ambassador Vance and Secretary Rusk. "What about Thieu's attitude?" Nixon asked. "He did not object to the Viet Cong being at negotiations."

"We and the South Vietnamese would be at the table on an our-side-your-side basis," said Secretary Rusk. Thieu himself had proposed the "our side/your side" formula for the peace talks.[52] The US side could bring anyone it wanted (including Saigon's representatives), and the North Vietnamese side could bring whomever it wanted (including the NLF). Officially, neither Saigon nor the NLF would participate as a separate delegation; at the bargaining table would just be "our side" and "your side." It was a semantic solution to a diplomatic problem. The NLF, however, wanted to be a separate delegation from Hanoi.

The United States rejected that idea. "They have no problem making their views known," President Johnson said.[53]

Neither did he. Johnson spent the rest of August using any means at his disposal to make sure the upcoming Democratic convention in Chicago didn't undercut his negotiating position either. It was tricky, since officially the White House denied that the president was playing any role in the convention at all. When McCarthy proposed that the party platform urge the next president to immediately halt the bombing of North Vietnam and negotiate a coalition government with the NLF in the South, Johnson called Nixon the next day with talking points from Secretary Rusk to use against a Democratic candidate.[54]

President Johnson: "He's in a fighting mood, and you may wish to unleash him at the right time." That's what the comment from my office said.

Nixon: Huh!

President Johnson: "One, some comments on the McCarthy platform should be found in the draft speech. Is this platform being submitted as an ultimatum to the platform committee: adopt it or accept a floor fight? What ultimatum have the proponents in mind, 'Surrender to us on Vietnam or we will bolt the party'? Is not all this contempt? Why do the proponents not say what they mean? For example, instead of saying, 'Halt the bombing of North Vietnam,' why don't they say, 'You should stop bombing men and arms?'" Now listen to this: "Why don't, instead of saying, 'Halt the bombing of North Vietnam—'" You can take this if you want to. I think it's a good phrase.

Nixon: I'll jot it down.

President Johnson: "Why don't they say, 'You should stop bombing men and arms moving southward across the DMZ to kill US and allied forces'?"

Nixon: Mm-*hmm*.

President Johnson: Now, that's what it means, Dick.

Nixon: That's the crux of the matter.

President Johnson: That's all. That's in one sentence.[55]

At 11:22 p.m. on August 20, Nixon got an urgent call from the White House. The president informed him that Soviet and Warsaw Pact forces had invaded Czechoslovakia. Nixon said the invasion gave the president a stronger hand in the Vietnam negotiations.

Nixon: Let me ask you this. Can you keep—just talking very candidly—can you keep your Vice President and others to keep them firm on this thing? 'Cause you know, the hell with the goddamn election. We must all stand firm on this.

"Very frankly, I don't know. That's the honest answer," Johnson said.

"Well, I stand firm," Nixon said.

Johnson had told Democrats that if they didn't stand firm, "you [Nixon] would murder them."

"That's true," Nixon said.[56]

The Democratic president said the Republican nominee could be proud of his party's platform on Vietnam. After hanging up, Johnson spent the next three-and-a-half hours with Humphrey in the Oval Office trying to secure the vice president's commitment not to weaken the administration's position on the bombing halt. The meeting went until 3:10 a.m.[57] Before Humphrey flew to Chicago, he publicly declared that Hanoi was "not going to get a better deal out of me" than from the current president.[58] But on the day the Democratic convention began, the president was on the phone to Chicago threatening to denounce the party's policy statement if it contained compromise language that Humphrey backed: "Stop all bombing of North Vietnam unless this action would endanger the lives of our troops." Stopping the bombing *would* endanger the troops, Johnson told the chairman of the platform-writing committee (through intermediaries—the White House was still pretending LBJ was above it all). The president dictated the only words he would accept: "Stop all the bombing of North Vietnam when this action would not endanger the lives of our troops in the field; this action should take into account the response from Hanoi." Humphrey yielded. The alternative for him, once again, was public denunciation by the president himself. It took a bitter floor fight with the doves, but Johnson won by a vote of 1,567¾ to 1,041¼.[59] It was one of the prices Humphrey paid for the presidential nomination.

Once he had it, though, Humphrey started edging away from LBJ. "If there is any one lesson that we should have learned, it is that the policies of tomorrow need not be limited by the policies of yesterday. My fellow Americans, if it becomes my high honor to serve as president of these states and people, I shall apply that lesson to the search for peace in Vietnam as to all other areas of national policy," Humphrey said in his acceptance speech.[60] "Hubert Hints Shift on Viet," as the *Chicago Tribune* put it.[61] Humphrey started out far behind. The next Gallup Poll showed Nixon leading by 12 points.[62]

## Johnson v. Humphrey

Johnson and Humphrey appeared at odds as the campaign kicked off. The Democratic nominee made an offhand remark on September 9 that he hoped the first American troops could start coming home from Vietnam in 1969. The next day, the president told the American Legion convention in New Orleans, "We yearn for the day when our men can come home. No man can predict when that day will come, because we are there to bring an honorable, stable peace to Southeast Asia, and no less will justify the sacrifices that our men have died for."[1] It sounded like the president was correcting the vice president. Nixon seized the opportunity. He accused Humphrey of hurting the US negotiating position by allegedly promising to cut combat troops.[2] The Republican held a big lead in the Gallup poll: Nixon: 43 percent, Humphrey: 28 percent, and Wallace: 21 percent.[3]

On the afternoon of Monday, September 30, 1968, a news ticker in the White House spat out Lyndon Johnson's nightmare. A wire service story datelined Salt Lake City reported that at 7:30 that night, Vice President Humphrey would make a nationwide address on the NBC television network promising a bombing halt.

As President, I would stop the bombing of the North as an acceptable risk for peace because I believe it could lead to success in the negotiations and thereby shorten the war. This would be the best protection for our troops. In weighing that risk and before taking action, I would place key importance on evidence—direct or indirect—by deed or word—of Communist willingness to restore the demilitarized zone between North and South Vietnam. Now if the Government of North Vietnam were to show bad faith, I would reserve the right to resume the bombing.[4]

Humphrey's speech placed just one condition on the bombing halt; Johnson still had three. At 6:45 p.m., an aide told Johnson that Richard Nixon was on the line. The president interrupted a meeting to take the call.

Nixon: The only reason I bother you is that I'm going in very shortly to be on a television program, and there just came over the wire this statement by Hubert with regard to saying that he would have a bombing pause if elected. And the only purpose of my call is to determine whether there's any change in our own policy at this time with regard to what position the administration is taking.

President Johnson: No, there's not. I have not read his speech, and it has not been discussed with me. I say this in strict confidence.

Nixon: I understand.

President Johnson: I don't want you to quote me or repeat me, so I'll talk freely.

Nixon: I won't, I won't. I'm not even letting anybody know I called you.[5]

LBJ did know what the US military commander in Vietnam was saying about a bombing halt and freely shared that classified information with the opposition party's nominee. At this point, General Abrams said, stopping the bombing would give the enemy an opportunity to position troops, tanks, and artillery due north of the DMZ "in a position to initiate a large-scale invasion of South Vietnam with minimum warning time." It took eighty thousand North Vietnamese soldiers and up to two hundred thousand laborers to maintain Hanoi's air defenses; a bombing halt would give the North several options for redeploying them, "any of which would increase the threat to American forces." Johnson handed Nixon material for the strongest possible attack: a bombing halt at this time would aid the enemy and jeopardize American lives.

The president made it clear he was not backing down from any of his three conditions. "So in effect, we have said we are interested in what you have to say on these three subjects: DMZ, GVN presence, shelling the cities," Johnson said.

"Yeah," Nixon said. "But you don't insist on all three, just—"

"Well, we'd like to have all three," the president said. "But we ask them to make their commitment to us, tell us what they would do."[6]

Nixon remained deferential to Johnson throughout. Humphrey's speech "will be interpreted, as I'm sure you know, as a dramatic move away from the administration. It's my intention not to move in that direction," Nixon assured the president. "I just wanted to be sure that I was up to date on everything."[7]

There are two versions of Humphrey's next conversation with Johnson: the one in Humphrey's memoirs and the one on Johnson's tapes. Humphrey comes off a lot stronger in his book:

> About fifteen minutes before I began my speech, I called President Johnson from the studio. I told him what I intended to say and he said curtly, "I gather you're not asking my advice." I said that was true, but that I felt that there was nothing embarrassing to him in the speech and certainly nothing that would jeopardize peace negotiations. I said we had been in direct contact with [Johnson's chief negotiator in Paris, Ambassador] Averell Harriman and that [former UN ambassador] George Ball was there with me.
>
> Johnson said tartly and finally, "Well, you're going to give the speech anyway. Thanks for calling, Hubert." And that was that.[8]

The tapes and documents tell a different story.

1. Humphrey didn't call fifteen minutes before the speech. He waited until literally the last minute. The White House Daily Diary recorded his call coming in at 7:30 p.m., exactly when his prerecorded address began to air nationwide. If not for press reports, Johnson would have had no advance warning. The timing of Humphrey's call denied the president any opportunity to talk his vice president out of it—or to threaten him out of it, as he had done before.

2. Both LBJ quotes in Humphrey's story are inaccurate. The president did not grudgingly recognize his number two's independence with such words as "I gather you're not asking my advice" or, "Well, you're going to give the speech anyway." Johnson did not say these things "curtly" or "tartly," since he did not say them at all. (He did, to be fair, say, "Thank you, Hubert.")

3. Humphrey didn't mention Ambassador Harriman. When LBJ found out three days later that the Humphrey campaign had discussed the bombing halt speech in advance with Johnson's own negotiators in Paris, he was outraged.

On tape, Humphrey sounds a little apologetic. "I just thought I should have called you a little earlier," he said. When he read the one condition in his speech, Johnson said, "We have three."

President Johnson: Now, we don't want to divide up North or South Vietnam without both of them being present. So that ought to be understood before we give up our hole card—that if we bring them in, they wouldn't walk out. Negotiate in good faith with whom? With both of us, you see. The second thing is, we couldn't very well keep the bombing stopped very long, I think, from a practical standpoint, if they shell the cities.

Humphrey: Yeah, well, that's what we would mean by good-faith negotiations, Mr. President.

President Johnson: Mmm, all right. OK.[9]

While Humphrey was assuring the president that his speech covered all three conditions, his aides were telling reporters that he wouldn't even insist on the one he'd mentioned. "One of the Vice President's key foreign policy advisers said later that in mentioning the demilitarized zone Mr. Humphrey had meant only to give an example of the kind of sign that might be forthcoming, not a quid pro quo," the *New York Times* reported. "The Vice President was reported to feel that his new public stance on the bombing, one of the central issues in the presidential campaign, was noticeably softer than that of President Johnson. Mr. Humphrey's advisers hope that his statement will be interpreted by the peace faction in the Democratic Party as a break with the Johnson Administration."[10]

Humphrey tried to make Johnson (and LBJ supporters who might be favorably inclined toward his vice president by association) think that he was standing with the president. At the same time, he tried to make doves, LBJ's biggest critics within his own party, think that he was breaking with LBJ. He was straddling the issue, a much more complex and dangerous maneuver than mere flip-flopping. All it takes to execute a flip-flop is to move from one position to another. To straddle, however, a politician must take two opposite positions at the same time. The chances of catastrophic exposure are that much greater. Politicians caught in flip-flops can at least claim they've changed their minds. A politician caught in a straddle must claim to be of two minds. Humphrey was straddling the biggest issue of the 1968 presidential campaign in its final days, the moment of maximum media scrutiny.

The president didn't like this one bit. He intervened in the campaign against his party's nominee. LBJ's old colleague from across the aisle, the Senate minority leader since LBJ had been majority leader, Everett McKinley Dirksen, R-Illinois, knew him well enough to sense opportunity. He called the president and gingerly asked a question.

Dirksen: Are you at liberty to make some comment on Hubert's speech last night?[11]

It took the president less than an hour to call back with some expert advice on how to go after his vice president.

President Johnson: On this subject you called me about, I've had a good going over and I would say that the best position on it is, "What does he mean?"

Dirksen: Yeah.

President Johnson: That's up to him to say what he means. [*Dirksen acknowledges throughout.*] If he means, unilateral without any conditions, that's one thing. If he means they've got to re-institute the DMZ, well, then, that's another thing. Now, what does he mean? That's not quite clear and we don't want to be critical, and just wait until you hear further from him. And that's the way—I think that the other fellows oughtn't to get involved until that's clear. If he has a condition that you have to close up that DMZ where people can't come down there, well, then I don't think anybody—everybody would be for that. We want it closed. We've been urging it all along. But the question is, does he make that a condition, or does he unilaterally pull out first? Do you get that clear?

Dirksen: Yes, I do.

President Johnson: Now, I'll have the staff—the [National Security] Council—elaborate on each one of these points—there are four or five of them—and tomorrow or the next day, I'll give you a little, short, succinct briefing so you can be positioned not to let your people be irresponsible and talk to your other fellows around the country so that they'll know exactly how we analyze the thing.

Dirksen: OK.

President Johnson: And you can—I'll just use you as the transmittal belt.

Dirksen: OK.[12]

What did Humphrey mean? It was a clear, simple question, and Johnson knew that his vice president dared not answer it. For Humphrey to give any substantive answer—that he would insist on restoring the DMZ or not, that his position was the same as LBJ's or not—would throw him off his straddle. Thus did the Democratic president of the United States advise the highest-ranking elected Republican in the country regarding the best way to campaign against the Democratic vice president and presidential nominee. (Offering the services of the National Security Council [NSC] staff to furnish talking points to the opposition party—that was just gravy.)

Either Dirksen was a well-oiled transmittal belt or Nixon came up with the same idea as Johnson independently, because at a press conference that morning the Republican nominee asked his opponent for the thing he dared not provide: clarification. Nixon called Humphrey's speech his "fourth and possibly fifth different position on a bombing halt."

Humphrey had to choose, Nixon said. "He either has to be for the bombing halt, as some of his prospective supporters and present supporters want him to be, or he has to support the negotiators in Paris." Nixon mocked his opponent for saying he would take "a risk for peace" by stopping the bombing. "I would respectfully submit that the risk is not his. The risk that is taken is to the thousands of Americans in the DMZ whose lives would be threatened in the event that a bombing halt occurred and the North Vietnamese forces were able to attack them in greater numbers than presently is the case." This was the ammunition Johnson provided Nixon from the latest classified cable from General Abrams. Finally, the Republican sounded the president's favorite theme. Calling a bombing halt "the trump card" in the hands of American negotiators, he said, "Now, if that trump card is played by either of the presidential candidates by indicating that we in January might do something that the negotiators have refused to do in Paris, it means that all chance for those negotiations to succeed will evaporate."[13]

Asked to clarify his position, the Democratic nominee took a firm stand against taking a firmer stand. He told reporters that his televised statement "speaks for itself." He dismissed attempts to pin down what he was for or against. "Let me put it this way: What I have said is my position. I haven't tried to equate positions with the administration or with the critics. If this happens to agree with some parts of administration policy, well and good; if it disagrees, that's the way it has to be. If it agrees with some position somebody else has taken, well and good; if it disagrees, so be it." Humphrey somehow managed to make ambiguity sound bold, brash, even defiant. Bereft of answers, the *Times* resorted to printing its own questions. Would Humphrey require any kind of signal from Hanoi before he stopped the bombing? "Would the signal have to be associated with the demilitarized zone, or was that mentioned only as an example?"[14] Humphrey wasn't saying.

Ambassador Harriman, however, answered Nixon. He had a spokesman tell the press that, contrary to Nixon's pointed suggestion, the leader of the American delegation to the Paris talks saw no reason whatsoever to think that Humphrey's speech would hurt the negotiations.[15] The president was furious with his chief negotiator.

President Johnson: He's a damn fool. He's been playing politics.[16]

## Nixon v. Nixon

Exactly one week after Humphrey's speech, Nixon reversed course. The Republican nominee chose the most public forum possible for the maneuver: the annual conference of United Press International editors and publishers in Washington, DC, on October 7. No mere press conference, this was a convention of newspaper executives from across the nation. Nixon's sharp break with the past could not go unnoticed. "Always before," the *Times* noted, "he has said that he hopes that the negotiations in Paris will succeed and that while the prospects for success do not look too bright, he will say nothing to jeopardize the talks or to lead the North Vietnamese to believe they can get better terms from him than from the Johnson Administration." Now, he said things might be different in January 1969. "We might be able to agree to much more then than we can do now," Nixon said.[1] No straddle for Nixon, just a pure, simple flip-flop. The message was impossible for North Vietnam (or anyone else) to miss: if elected, President Nixon might be able to concede more than President Johnson.

Johnson and his hawks were caught off guard. Secretary of State Rusk had briefed Nixon before his UPI appearance, repeating the administration's bombing halt conditions. "He seemed to agree with all that," Rusk told Johnson at 10:02 a.m. on October 7, before Nixon spoke to the editors and publishers. "He then spoke rather thoughtfully about Vietnam. He said that he thought that the decision to make a fight for it was the right decision, that he thought we had had a bad deal on the public support for that basic decision, which he thought was right."

"That's comforting, that's comforting," Johnson said. "I was real concerned that he might be wobbling like our other friends had."

"Well, I saw no evidence of it today," Rusk said. "Now, I don't know what he's going to say in a speech [*chuckling*] in the next two weeks. But today he couldn't have been more solid and wanted to be helpful on Vietnam."[2] The day, of course, wasn't over.

After his UPI appearance, Nixon called the White House. He spoke of visiting Eisenhower in the hospital, where the former president was resting after his latest heart attack.

"It's the longest visit he had," Nixon said. "He just looks great."

"Didn't he?" Johnson said. LBJ had seen Eisenhower three days earlier. "Did he tell you what he tried to do to me?"

"No, no," Nixon said, laughing.

"Well, now, you must not tell this."

"No, I won't. Deep secret."

"He said that he thought what we were doing was absolutely right," Johnson said. "Just hold to it and not to give an inch, and we got through talking about Vietnam and he said, 'You know what happened?' I said, 'No.' Said, 'Mamie [Eisenhower] came in here a while ago and said that she's going to put on a robe—while you're visiting me, she's going to go down and put a Nixon sticker on your car.'"

Nixon and Johnson both laughed.

"Yeah, well, he told me the same thing," Nixon said.[3]

LBJ then shared a factoid: It had taken only seventy-four days to negotiate the Indochina (Vietnam, Laos, and Cambodia) part of the Geneva Accords in 1954. By coincidence, from the day after the presidential election to the day before the next president's inauguration was also seventy-four days. Johnson, however, was not hopeful. The president didn't criticize Nixon's statement directly. He hadn't done that with Humphrey, either. But he made an analogy with a clear point.

President Johnson: I don't think they're going to do anything until the election. I think they read all these statements and they see the *Times* and I just don't much believe if I could buy the [*Washington*] *Evening Star* for $10 million today, and I thought I might get it for $8 million if I waited a couple months, I just don't believe I'd do it unless I was in an awful big hurry. So my judgment is [*Nixon laughs*] there's not going to be much movement.[4]

The president was mistaken. Hanoi started to move. On Wednesday, October 9, during a tea break in Paris, North Vietnamese negotiators gave a little ground. They'd be willing to discuss allowing the South to participate in negotiations the day after America stopped the bombing.[5] Friday, October 11, at a private meeting between both sides' top negotiators, the North Vietnamese asked if Johnson would stop the bombing in return for their allowing the South to participate in peace talks.[6] That night, the Russians got involved. Valentin Oberemko, minister-counselor of the Soviet embassy in France, contacted Ambassador Harriman with "a very urgent matter" to discuss. On Saturday, October 12, he presented Harriman with a statement: "I have good reason to believe that if the U.S. stops unconditionally and completely the bombardments and other acts of war against [North Vietnam], the delegation of North Vietnam will agree to the participation of the representative of the Saigon government in the talks on the problem of political settlement in Vietnam. Thus these talks would be held by the representatives of the DRV, of the United States of America, of the NLF, and the Saigon government." Oberemko invited Harriman to take the statement down verbatim.[7] It clearly came from the Soviet government. Hanoi's top supplier of military aid was vouching for the offer.

This was a breakthrough. Hanoi had backed away from its demand that the bombing halt be "unconditional." Why? The short answer is that we don't know. While Americans can listen to LBJ's tapes and read many of his White House documents, Hanoi is far less open. According to the Vietnamese government's official account of the negotiations, North Vietnamese leaders thought LBJ wanted to halt the bombing to help elect Humphrey president and considered the preelection period "a propitious time to make the US de-escalate the war."[8] Apparently the Communists, as well as Republicans and many Democrats, misread LBJ. In Paris, Hanoi's negotiators still insisted on calling the halt "unconditional," but they had agreed tentatively to one condition. Johnson could order a bombing halt and have something to show for it: peace talks that included Saigon. If he wanted to help Hubert Humphrey win the presidency, this was his chance. He didn't take it.

That day, the president ordered a clampdown on all intelligence reports related to the bombing halt negotiations. No one could read them without his personal approval. He kept a tight grip. Only the "Tuesday Lunch Group"—LBJ's secretaries of state and defense, chairman of the Joint Chiefs, CIA director, national security adviser, and a couple of other key aides—got to see the reports. Not even analysts and senior aides could. The intelligence community called this "the freeze."[9]

On the day that Oberemko privately met with Harriman, McGeorge Bundy, Johnson's national security adviser until February 1966, broke his long public silence on Vietnam. "We must begin to lift this burden from our lives," Bundy told a symposium at DePauw University in Indiana. Bundy called for America to start withdrawing from Vietnam unilaterally in 1969.[10] Although President Nixon would do just that, Bundy was out on a limb in November 1968. Even the "peace plank" put forward by Democratic doves at the Chicago convention called for *mutual* withdrawal of American and North Vietnamese forces, as did Humphrey in his televised bombing halt speech.[11] Bundy also added his voice to those calling for a bombing halt. LBJ would blame much that went wrong in the next few weeks on Humphrey and Bundy's speeches.

McGeorge Bundy's speech proved awkward for his brother, William P. Bundy, who was still LBJ's assistant secretary of state for East Asian and Pacific affairs. Bill Bundy had to call South Vietnamese ambassador Diem to say his brother's speech did not reflect the Johnson administration's views.[12] Johnson didn't trust the Bundy brother who remained in his employ, where he had access to the most highly classified diplomatic cables on Vietnam. "You be sure Bill Bundy's not talking to anybody," the president warned Secretary of State Dean Rusk.

"Oh, I'm sure he's not," said Rusk, but Johnson's suspicion was correct. After LBJ cut off his vice president's access to classified cables on the war, Bundy invited a Humphrey campaign adviser into his home to read them.[13]

Before responding to Hanoi, Johnson made sure he had South Vietnamese president Thieu's support. On Sunday, October 13, General Abrams and Ambassador Ellsworth F. Bunker briefed Thieu on Hanoi's proposal—peace talks including Saigon and the NLF to commence after Johnson ordered a bombing halt—and on LBJ's response. Talks alone wouldn't be enough for Johnson. He would continue to insist on his two military conditions. North Vietnam would have to respect the DMZ and stop shelling civilians in South Vietnamese cities, or Johnson would start bombing again. South Vietnam's president agreed as long as the United States continued to press its offensive against Communist forces in the South and "so long as we are prepared to resume the bombing if they violate the DMZ or attack the main cities," Ambassador Bunker reported. He quoted President Thieu, who said, "we must try this path to see if they are serious."[14]

Johnson had many reservations. Did Hanoi understand the three "facts of life"?

Secretary of State Rusk assured LBJ that Ambassador Harriman would read them out loud to the North Vietnamese in Paris. If they insisted on no conditions, they had no deal. If they accepted the "facts of life" in silence, the United States could assume they knew that violating the DMZ or shelling the cities would trigger new US bombing.[15]

Johnson worried about appearances. People would call a bombing halt a month before the election a "cheap political trick."

But if he didn't stop the bombing, Rusk said, he'd be destroyed by his own record. How would it look if Hanoi accepted his military conditions and agreed to sit down with Saigon at the bargaining table, but LBJ kept bombing anyway?[16]

The president was already hearing rumblings from the Republicans. Nixon used Sen. George A. Smathers of Florida as an intermediary with the White House. Smathers was a Democrat, but a conservative one. He came to the White House on Monday, October 14, and told the president that word was out he was trying to throw the election to Humphrey. The Nixon campaign considered it a political trick; Nixon himself feared the administration was being misled, Smathers said.

LBJ gathered his national security team in the Cabinet Room that night. "I can understand how Mr. Nixon feels," Defense Secretary Clark M. Clifford said. "He doesn't want anything that could possibly rock the boat." The Republican was still ahead in the polls. Clifford said he doubted the bombing halt would affect the election. He quoted Mark Twain's sly proverb: "When in doubt, do right."

The president put the question to them all. Gen. Earle G. "Bus" Wheeler said all the Joint Chiefs were in favor of a bombing halt under his conditions. So was General Abrams. Secretary Clifford said he had no doubt it was the right thing to do. Johnson asked Secretary Rusk, one of his two staunchest hawks, "Do you know this is what we ought to do?"

"Yes, sir," Rusk said.

"I do not want to be the one to have it said about [me] that one man died tomorrow who could have been saved because of this plan." The president gave the execute order.[17]

That day in Paris, Ambassadors Harriman and Vance put LBJ's three "facts of life" to the North Vietnamese. Johnson could not stop the bombing unless they (1) entered peace talks with Saigon, (2) respected the DMZ, and (3) stopped shelling South Vietnamese cities. The North Vietnamese negotiators did not object to that. They did, however, raise an unexpected objection related to a minor logistical matter. At Johnson's instructions, the US ambassadors insisted that the peace talks with Saigon and the NLF start the day after the bombing stopped. The North Vietnamese said they couldn't get the NLF to France in just one day.[18] Although they had accepted the three points Johnson had pursued for months, they called the demand for next-day peace talks a new condition. In that case, Johnson said, tell Hanoi that if it could give him a date when the NLF would be ready to talk in Paris, he would stop the bombing twenty-four hours earlier.[19] For the time being, however, there was no deal.

"They welched on it," Johnson told Senate Majority Leader Mike Mansfield, D-Montana, the next day, October 16. In Johnson's telling, Hanoi had agreed to start peace talks with the NLF and Saigon the day after he halted the bombing, then turned around and accused the United States of imposing a new condition. The president also blamed McGeorge Bundy's troop withdrawal speech and an offhand comment that Humphrey made on the campaign trail that he was for a bombing halt "period, not comma or semi-colon."[20] He didn't, however, fault Nixon's flip-flop.

In a conference call with all three presidential candidates supposedly to brief them on the negotiations, Johnson didn't mention the one-day dispute at all. He said McGeorge Bundy's speech "didn't do us any good," but didn't criticize Humphrey by name while the vice president was on the line. Johnson told the three men vying to succeed him that the US government's position remained unchanged. He repeated his three conditions and said Hanoi hadn't "signed on" to them. This was technically true, there being no written agreement for Hanoi to sign. He asked the candidates to keep the conference call in "absolute confidence, because any statement or any speeches or any comments at this time referring to the substance of these matters will be injurious to your country." When Humphrey asked if they could tell reporters the president had given them "our regular report," Johnson provided a cover story instead. They could say the president read them the statement his press secretary had issued that day, which he then did: "There has been no basic change in the situation—no breakthrough." This wasn't true. Hanoi's acceptance of LBJ's three conditions was a major breakthrough, followed by a setback in the haggle over how soon the peace talks had to start. The president told the candidates none of this. He signed off without providing a clue as to why he'd called them in the first place.[21]

Rumors of a bombing halt led all three network newscasts that night. CBS, NBC, and ABC mentioned the candidate conference call, and all three repeated the false "no breakthrough" line.[22]

New minor issues delayed a bombing halt. The North wanted a joint communiqué announcing that the United States was stopping the bombing without any conditions. Johnson refused. On the question of how soon peace talks had to start after the bombing stopped, LBJ showed some flexibility. If Hanoi gave him a date when the NLF would be in Paris, he could stop the bombing two or three days in advance, instead of just one.[23] The North wanted at least a week.[24]

Meanwhile, South Vietnam started to wobble. While Hanoi was finally willing to accept Saigon at the negotiating table, South Vietnamese president Thieu started to say that permitting the NLF to take part in peace talks would produce disastrous consequences.[25] Saigon threatened not to take part in the peace talks if the NLF participated "as a separate entity."[26] Thieu had already solved this problem with his "our side/your side" formula, but now he balked. Aggravating things, Hanoi proposed to call the peace talks a "four-power conference" in the proposed joint communiqué. That would make the NLF sound like a separate entity indeed. The United States refused.[27]

If Hanoi couldn't get a joint communiqué, it wanted a "secret minute." It, too, would say that Johnson was stopping the bombing "without conditions." It didn't use the phrase "four-power conference," but it listed all four separately, including the NLF.[28] Johnson feared that if he agreed to the minute, it wouldn't stay secret.

The negotiations remained prominent on the front pages and the evening news. Publicly, the Republican nominee gave LBJ his full support. "If a bombing pause can be agreed to in Vietnam, one which will not endanger American lives, and one which will increase the chances for bringing a peaceful and honorable solution to the war, then we are for it. And the one man who can make that determination is the President of the United States," Nixon told a campaign rally in Johnstown, Pennsylvania. "Let's let him make that determination. And if he makes it, we will support him, because he wants peace and we do not want to play politics with peace."[29] This was exactly what LBJ wanted to hear.

The president was much less happy when Humphrey went on CBS's *Face the Nation* and said the bombing halt was for President Johnson to decide, not President Thieu. "Obviously we'll take into consideration many things. But this is an American mission. I believe there is very little bombing if any done by the South Vietnamese and this matter must be something over which the government of Vietnam—South Vietnam—cannot exercise a veto," the vice president said. "Humphrey Bars Thieu Veto on Bombs," the headlines read.[30] This did not help Johnson with his unhappy ally in Saigon.

The North Vietnamese were still insisting on a week to get the NLF to Paris. Johnson turned once more to his mentor. "I don't want to look bad in history and say I was offered something and I just was hardheaded and obstinate," Johnson told Sen. Richard Russell on October 23. The president said he wasn't sure Saigon could last seven days. "Now, if they wait a week, it may not be in existence," he said. LBJ was preparing for the worst. During the bombing halt, General Abrams would still have the authority to retaliate automatically if Hanoi violated the DMZ. "Now, the danger of that is they may want me to stop and then start again," Johnson said. "And that worries me because I'd look like a boob before election, to call it off one day and start it two days later."[31]

Johnson faced a political dilemma. If he ordered the bombing halt, it would look like he was helping Humphrey; if he didn't, it would look like he was helping Nixon. "I know that a lot of folks say, 'You had five years. Why'd you do it in five days beforehand?' On the other hand, if I put it off they'd say, well I could've done it and I wouldn't do it because I didn't want Humphrey," Johnson said. "And I think I've just got to do what I think's right when I get it in shape where I think it's right."

Russell offered little help. "I rather sympathize with you on this thing," he said, "because when you get down to it, I don't know what to do and I haven't even got a suggestion what to do."[32]

Johnson sought political cover. With his national security adviser, he questioned Gen. William W. Momyer, head of the Tactical Air Command, about the military impact of a bombing halt. Monsoon season made it a bad time to bomb north of the DMZ anyway, General Momyer said. Besides, if Hanoi wanted to violate the DMZ substantially, it would take two months just to get its troops into position. For the time being, the general said, US airpower would get better results targeting battlegrounds in South Vietnam and on the Ho Chi Minh Trail through Laos, whose border areas the North used to infiltrate men and war materials into the South. Johnson asked him directly: If you were president, would you halt the bombing? "Yes, sir," Momyer said.[33]

The president told his top advisers that he wanted maximum military and civilian support.

The Republicans continued to worry. "I had a call from Nixon," Senate Minority Leader Dirksen told Johnson on October 23. "He was rather upset." Campaign aide Bryce Harlow claimed to have an inside source who said:

> The President is driving exceedingly hard for a deal with North Vietnam. Expectation is that he is becoming almost pathologically eager for an excuse to order a bombing halt and will accept almost any arrangement. . . .
> Clark Clifford, [Joseph] Califano, and Llewellyn Thompson are the main participants in this effort. [George] Ball is in also, though somewhat on the fringe.

Careful plans are being made to help HHH exploit whatever happens. White House staff liaison with HHH is close. Plan is for LBJ to make a nationwide TV announcement as quickly as possible after agreement; the object is to get this done as long before November 5 as they can. . . .

White Housers still think they can pull the election out for HHH with this ploy; that's what is being attempted.[34]

Although Nixon said this came from "a source whose credibility was beyond question," indeed "from someone in Johnson's innermost circle, and, as events turned out, it was entirely accurate," Harlow didn't even claim to know the identity of the source. "My contact had a contact, and I don't know who that was," Harlow said. "He started to tell me and I told him, 'I don't want to know.'"[35] In other words, Harlow said he knew a guy who said he knew a guy. His source's source provided misinformation. Ball was no longer part of the administration, Thompson's role in the negotiations as US ambassador to the Soviet Union was peripheral, and Califano didn't even attend any of the meetings. ("Joe Califano can't spell Vietnam," LBJ said.)[36] Any attempt Clifford made to soften LBJ's conditions had failed. At this point the president had passed up more than one excuse to stop the bombing. He told Dirksen his position was unchanged. When he had something to tell the candidates, he would.[37]

Nixon didn't wait. His lead in the Gallup poll had fallen to 8 points—Nixon 44 percent, Humphrey 36 percent, and Wallace 15 percent.[38] In an October 25 statement to reporters in New York, the Republican nominee cast doubt upon the whole bombing halt negotiation in a minor masterpiece of insinuation.

I am told that officials in the administration have been driving very hard for an agreement on a bombing halt, accompanied possibly by a ceasefire, in the immediate future. I have since learned these reports are true. I am also told that this spurt of activity is a cynical, last-minute attempt by President Johnson to salvage the candidacy of Mr. Humphrey. This I do not believe.[39]

Those last five words—"This I do not believe"—recast an attack on the president as a valiant defense of him.

Johnson wasn't having it. During a luncheon speech at New York's Waldorf-Astoria on Sunday, October 27, the president dismissed the charges as "ugly and unfair" and Nixon as "a man who distorts the history of his time in office." The president then repeated every Cold War attack he'd made as JFK's running mate in 1960, blaming the Eisenhower/Nixon administration for losing Cuba and more.[40]

That day, Johnson ran out of excuses not to halt the bombing. The North Vietnamese dropped their demand that a secret minute say the halt was "without conditions."[41] As for the gap between the start of the bombing halt and the start of negotiations that included Saigon and the NLF, they split the difference—three-and-a-half days. Johnson's relentlessness had yielded results.

Not that he was happy. Over dinner with his foreign policy advisers at the White House that night, the president picked at his own success. Why did he have to yield and accept a gap of a half day more than three? Every minute of delay endangered the United States and South Vietnam, he said. LBJ suspected the Soviets of trying to influence the presidential election. Was there time to talk to them? He wanted Moscow's assurances on the DMZ and the cities. He'd rather be seen as stubborn and adamant than as a tricky, slick politician. And before he ordered a bombing halt, he was going to call General Abrams in from Vietnam and make damn sure he was ready for it.

The hawks around the table disagreed. Gen. Maxwell D. Taylor, JFK's chairman of the Joint Chiefs and LBJ's former ambassador to Vietnam, said he was for the bombing halt—and General Abrams would be, too. Secretary of State Rusk said the Soviets understood LBJ's three conditions: he said he smelled vodka and caviar in the deal. The president said they sounded like they'd been living in another world with a bunch of doves.[42]

The dinner meeting didn't end until 10:00 p.m., but National Security Adviser Walt Rostow went to see Dobrynin that night. He handed the Soviet ambassador a letter from LBJ to Chairman Alexei N. Kosygin. The letter spelled out LBJ's three conditions in writing. It stated plainly that any failure by Hanoi to respect the DMZ or South Vietnamese cities would trigger retaliation by General Abrams. The president wrote that he was "very anxious" to hear "any comments or reaction Mr. Kosygin may have to these three points" and concluded by saying he would weigh Kosygin's response *before* deciding whether to stop the bombing.[43]

It was midnight when Rostow finished writing up his meeting with the Soviet ambassador for LBJ. The national security adviser added a personal note:

> I understand well your reaction to the likelihood that Moscow and Hanoi are playing politics.

I understand well the certainty that some will accuse the President of playing politics.

But the tragic dilemma is that you will also be accused of playing politics if you let this slide—and politics against the party you lead. [Ambassador] Harriman and the Russians will see to that.

I am not even sure the deal will be there to pick up after the election.

Rostow subtly reminded LBJ that the men around the dining room table urging him to stop the bombing were Vietnam hard-liners, the strongest supporters of the war. "All of us know that, with all its uncertainties, we have the best deal we now can get—vastly better than any we thought we could get since 1961," he wrote. "And none of us would know how to justify delay."

If Johnson didn't stop the bombing now—after Hanoi accepted his three substantive demands, dropped its procedural objections, and met him halfway on a date to start peace talks—not even his hawks could defend him.[44] As long as the weather made hitting the North impractical and Hanoi respected the DMZ and the cities, it made more military sense to stop the bombing than to continue it.

On Monday, October 28, everything appeared to be falling into place. Ambassador Bunker cabled that President Thieu had agreed on a joint American–South Vietnamese announcement. The key line: "The two Presidents wish to make it clear that neither the Government of the Republic of [South] Vietnam nor the United States Government recognizes the so-called National Liberation Front as an entity independent of North Vietnam." Vice President Nguyen Cao Ky had told Bunker, "I think it is better that we openly recognize that the NLF will be there." The South seemed to be onboard, ready to sit across the negotiating table from the NLF as well as Hanoi.

The Soviet Union responded to LBJ's letter in under twenty-four hours. The North Vietnamese had assured his government of the seriousness of their intentions, Chairman Kosygin wrote. Their recent actions in Paris showed they were doing everything possible. "In this connection," Kosygin wrote, "it seems to us that doubts with regard to the position of the Vietnamese side are without foundation (groundless)."

Taken altogether, Kosygin's statements didn't amount to a great deal, Rostow wrote LBJ, but "for the first time, Moscow is responsive to our request that they commit themselves about the intent and integrity of Hanoi."[45]

Johnson, however, would not make a decision until the next morning. That night before bed, he left a 2:00 a.m. wakeup call—"even for him, that is bizarre behavior," Lady Bird Johnson wrote in her diary. A C-141 cargo jet was secretly flying General Abrams from Vietnam.[46] He would arrive at the White House in the middle of the night. "At 2 the phone shrilled and Lyndon jumped up, quick as a fireman, and was in his clothes and downstairs," the First Lady wrote.[47] Over the next half hour, Johnson's advisers assembled in the Cabinet Room for the decisive meeting.

The president noted that every single military and civilian adviser he had advised him to stop the bombing. Then he began to question General Abrams:

"Do you think they will violate the DMZ and the cities?"

"I think they will abide by it on DMZ," Abrams said. "On cities, I am not sure. I am concerned about Saigon." The advisers questioned him about the threat to the South's capital. It was a half dozen rockets or twenty-five to fifty sappers, the general said.

"If the enemy honors our agreement, will this be an advantage militarily?"

"Yes."

Would it compensate for the lack of bombing?

"Yes, sir, it will."

"Can we return to full-scale bombing easily if they attack?"

"Yes, very easily."

In August, General Abrams had said that stopping the bombing would increase enemy strength several-fold. What changed?

The enemy had moved out of I Corps, the part of South Vietnam closest to the DMZ. "He cannot cause the mischief he could have caused in August," Abrams said.

"I am going to put more weight on your judgment than anybody else. Can we do this without additional casualties?"

"Yes, we can."

What would he do with American airpower?

Hit the Ho Chi Minh Trail in Laos. The weather was changing there and in North Vietnam. Even without a bombing halt, he could only bomb the North one day or two per month until the end of LBJ's presidency. The weather would all but stop the bombing of North Vietnam, even if Johnson didn't.[48]

Did General Abrams have any reluctance to stop the bombing?

"No, sir."

"If you were President, would you do it?"

"I have no reservations about doing it. I know it is stepping into a cesspool of comment," Abrams said. "I do think it is the right thing to do."

It was unanimous.

At 5:00 a.m., the president and the general and a couple of aides went to the White House mansion and waited in the sitting room to hear from Ambassador Bunker, who in turn was waiting to see South Vietnamese president Thieu. They waited another hour.

At 6:04 a.m., Secretary of State Rusk called. Thieu said three days was not enough time to get a delegation to Paris. Now *South* Vietnam was saying the gap between the start of the bombing halt and the start of the peace talks should be longer.

Saigon's balk came mere hours after President Johnson received warning from Alexander Sachs that Republicans were trying to sabotage the peace talks. At this point, LBJ said there might be something to what Sachs said.

At 6:15 a.m., the president returned to the Cabinet Room for another meeting with the same group of advisers. Could you imagine what people would say if they found out Hanoi had met all his conditions for a bombing halt, but Nixon's conniving with Saigon kept the peace talks from happening? the president asked. It would rock the world. He read the group the warning from Sachs and said, "It all adds up."[49]

Around 8:00 a.m., the First Lady watched her husband return to their bedroom, put on his pajamas, and crawl back into bed. "I asked few questions," she wrote in her diary.[50]

## On the Case

Before long, Johnson was back up and putting together information from Sachs with diplomatic intelligence. Old reports took on new meaning.[1] One NSA intercept of a cable from the South Vietnamese embassy in Washington, DC, stood out. "I explained discreetly to our partisan friends our firm attitude," Ambassador Diem reported to President Thieu. "The longer the situation continues, the more we are favored, for the elections will take place in a week and President Johnson would probably have difficulties in forcing our hand. I am still in contact with the Nixon entourage, which continues to be the favorite despite the uncertainty provoked by the news of an imminent bombing halt. [*Excision*] informed that if Nixon should be elected, he would first send an unofficial person [*excision*] and would himself consider later going to Saigon before the inauguration." The "Nixon entourage" to which Ambassador Diem referred included Madame Anna C. Chennault.[2]

LBJ wanted to know if Cyrus Vance could tell him anything about John Mitchell, Nixon's campaign chairman. "He said he just knew who he was," Secretary of State Rusk said. "He said he wouldn't put it past him at all to do something like this, but he didn't have any real knowledge of him."[3]

Rusk wanted to delay the bombing halt a day to give them a chance to keep the deal from falling apart. "I feel myself that this thing could blow up into the biggest mess we've ever had if we're not careful here," Rusk said. If it got out that they stopped the bombing against the wishes of their allies, "this would confirm in everybody's view that the only reason we insisted on going ahead under these circumstances was because of domestic politics. I mean, I think that would confirm that to a fare-thee-well," Rusk said, "and we can't use the information we have because of its classification to rebut any of that."[4]

National Security Adviser Walt Rostow argued that it would be dangerous to reveal the information the White House had, since "the materials are so explosive that they could gravely damage the country whether Mr. Nixon is elected or not. If they get out in their present form, they could be the subject of one of the most acrimonious debates we have ever witnessed." Rostow made a crucial point: "There is no hard evidence that Mr. Nixon himself is involved. Exactly what the Republicans have been saying to Bui Diem is not wholly clear, as opposed to the conclusions that Bui Diem is drawing from what they have said."[5]

Johnson didn't know if Nixon was involved, but he aimed to find out. The Logan Act of 1799 prohibits as treasonous activity any interference by American citizens with the negotiations of the US government.[6] Nixon, Mitchell, and Chennault were all American citizens. With the election exactly one week away, the president directed the Federal Bureau of Investigation (FBI) to:

1. place a wiretap on the South Vietnamese embassy;
2. report on everyone who entered or left the embassy;
3. tail Chennault and report on her movements; and
4. tap the phone in Chennault's Watergate penthouse apartment.[7]

The FBI immediately did the first three.[8]

LBJ routinely met with his foreign policy advisers on Tuesdays at lunchtime to discuss Vietnam, so they all gathered at 1:00 p.m. for what was by then their third meeting of the day. The South Vietnamese may really see the bombing halt as a political deal to help Humphrey, Johnson said. "They know the Vice President would be softer." The Republicans had been working on them, saying Nixon would give them a better deal, he said, but "Nixon will doublecross them after November 5."

General Abrams was angry at Thieu. He'd been in the room with Ambassador Bunker when the South Vietnamese president made the decision to support LBJ's bombing halt position. "It was unequivocal. He took it, understood it, marched right up to the plate and swung," Abrams said.[9]

The first FBI report on the South Vietnamese embassy phone was intriguing. At 7:30 a.m. on Wednesday, October 30, a woman who did not identify herself called Ambassador Diem, who recognized her voice. He told her something "is cooking" and invited her to stop by that afternoon. She agreed to meet after a luncheon for Judy Agnew, the wife of the Republican vice-presidential nominee, Spiro T. Agnew.[10]

That afternoon FBI agents observed Madame Chennault visit the South Vietnamese embassy in Washington for approximately thirty minutes.[11]

That same day, LBJ instructed Ambassador Bunker to deliver a message to Saigon: "If President Thieu keeps us from moving at this moment of opportunity, God help South Vietnam, because no President could maintain the support of the American people." Johnson said he'd consulted with Thieu every step of the way during the bombing halt negotiations. "If President Thieu makes himself responsible for preventing the very peace talks which have cost so much to obtain, the people of this country would never forget the man responsible. No American leader could rescue the position of such a person with the American people."[12] LBJ was going forward with the bombing halt.

He would make sure journalists knew about the two military concessions he had wrung from Hanoi, too. While he couldn't announce them publicly, his aides would brief the press on background, or just leak the conditions, so word would get into the newspapers and on television.[13]

The White House arranged a second conference call with the three presidential candidates. This time Johnson had something to tell them. He would also drop a pointed comment on them about partisan interference with his peace talks. No names, nothing specific, but they'd all know something was rotten.

To make sure the message got through to the Republicans, the president called Senate Minority Leader Dirksen first. Some of Nixon's supporters were "getting a little unbalanced and frightened," the president said on October 31, and they'd started contacting Hanoi and Saigon with a message that interfered with the negotiations. "The net of it, and it's despicable, and if it were made public I think it would rock the nation, but the net of it was that if they just hold out a little bit longer, that he's a lot more sympathetic and he can kind of—they can do better business with him than they can with their present President," Johnson said. "Now, I rather doubt Nixon has done any of this, but there's no question but what folks for him are doing it. And very frankly, we're reading some of the things that are happening." The delay, he said, was proving fatal.

President Johnson: But they've got this question, this new formula put in there—namely, wait on Nixon. And they're killing 4[00] or 500 every day waiting on Nixon. Now, these folks, I doubt, are authorized to speak for Nixon, but they're going in there and they range all the way from very attractive women to old-line China lobbyists. And some people pretty close to him in the business world.

Dirksen: Yeah.

President Johnson: I was shocked when I looked at the reports, see?[14]

The president scattered morsels of information throughout a rather long and rambling recitation of his recent difficulties: "I really think it's a little dirty pool for Dick's people to be messing with the South Vietnamese ambassador and carrying messages around to both of them and I don't think the people would approve of it if it were known." He named a name. Nixon "better keep Mrs. Chennault and all this crowd just tied up for a few days," the president said.

Johnson took a moment to complain about Nixon's "This I do not believe" attack: "I thought Dick's statement was ugly the other day, that he had been told that I was a thief, and a son of a bitch, and so forth, but he knew my mother and she really wasn't a bitch. I mean you set up a statement like that and then deny it, it's not very good, because he knows better, and that hurt my feelings. You damn Republicans get mean when you get in politics, and I think it's cost him a lot of votes," Johnson said. "And to me when Nixon's saying, 'I want the war stopped, that I'm supporting Johnson, that I want him to get peace if he can, that I'm not going to pull the rug out of him,' I don't see how in the hell it could be helped unless he goes to farting under the cover and getting his hand under somebody's dress."

Dirksen said that "the fellows on our side get antsy-pantsy about" a bombing halt.[15]

By 6:05 p.m. that day, the White House operator found Nixon at his New York apartment, Humphrey in Newark, New Jersey, and Wallace at Norfolk, Virginia's Golden Triangle Motor Hotel. On speakerphone in the Oval Office with Secretaries Clifford and Rusk, General Wheeler, CIA Director Richard Helms, National Security Adviser Rostow, and a stenotypist taking it all down, the president gave the candidates his version of the bombing halt negotiations. LBJ emphasized the fixed, steadfast, and unyielding nature of his three demands. His Paris negotiators had told Hanoi at least a dozen times that he could stop the bombing only as long as it (1) respected the DMZ, (2) accepted Saigon at the peace talks, and (3) refrained from attacks on civilians in South Vietnamese cities. He'd gone to the Soviets with "doubts—repeat doubts—that the North Vietnamese would stop shelling the cities or would stop abusing the DMZ," Johnson said. "The Soviet Union came back to me on Tuesday or Wednesday and said that my doubts were not justified."

"Now, since that time with our campaign on, we have had some minor problems develop. First, there have been some speeches that we ought to withdraw troops, or that we'd stop the bombing without obtaining anything in return, or some of our folks are—even including some of the old China Lobbyists—they are going around and implying to some of the embassies and some of the others that they might get a better deal out of somebody that was not involved in this. Now, that's made it difficult and it's held up things a little bit." The vague reference to the China Lobby was the closest LBJ came to mentioning Chennault—just enough to strike the fear of God, Lyndon Johnson, and the US intelligence community into a guilty heart. "I know that none of you candidates are aware of it or responsible for it," the president added.

In a few hours he would announce the bombing halt and "set a date for a meeting where the Government of [South] Vietnam will appear," Johnson said. "But in the light of these overtures that have been surreptitiously made—the gossip that's gone on by some of the lobbies and the campaigners—I don't know just what will come out of that situation. We're in touch with it. We're on top of it. We're watching it."

Once Hanoi accepted his demands, Johnson noted, he couldn't say, " 'No, I've got to put it off because I'm concerned with an election.' I'm not concerned with an election. Y'all are concerned with an election."

Nixon was the first candidate to speak: "With regard to the talks, if they begin, and as I know, you've made it clear that they may not, but you think they may," would the president stop any other military action besides the bombing?

"Dick, the talks will be held. We have a firm agreement that the North Vietnamese will bring the NLF in and the South Vietnamese will be permitted to attend. We will stop the bombing only in the North where—in the confidence of the family, the American family—we practically have stopped it already anyway. We will take that same bombing that's taking place in the North today and apply it in Laos and in South Vietnam where we need it much more than we do in the North," Johnson said. And "we told them that if they shelled the cities or abused the DMZ, we would be back bombing tomorrow morning."

"But you are not going to state that publicly?" Nixon asked.

"No. We can't state that publicly because they will consider it [an] 'ultimatum' or 'threat' or 'reciprocity' or 'condition.'"

"The only thing you are going to state publicly is that the other people will be allowed to come to the conference," Nixon said.

"You are right," the president said.

Nixon could use Johnson's self-imposed silence on the two military conditions. For now he promised to back up the president, as did Humphrey and Wallace.[16]

Afterward the president briefed congressional leaders and met with his NSC. When it was over, he called the only statutory member of the council who couldn't attend, Vice President Humphrey. He gave the Democratic nominee a lot less information about the Chennault Affair than he'd given the Republican Senate minority leader. He didn't mention Chennault's name. He didn't even use a feminine pronoun. (Referring to a member of the China Lobby as "her" or "she" in 1968 would have narrowed the possibilities.)

President Johnson: And in the last few days the China Lobby crowd has been in it some.

Humphrey: Mm-hmm.

President Johnson: And they've been telling him that if—that Humphrey wouldn't stick with them at all, so they better put off and not let Johnson make any kind of peace because they'll do a much better job. They'll be much tougher. And their ambassador's been sending that word back, and they've got Thieu and them upset about the speech that you'd stop the bombing, [no] semicolon, comma, period, you know. And they've had—we've been watching it very carefully, and I know of what I speak. I'm looking at hole cards.

Humphrey: I know that.

President Johnson: So I had Thieu on board two weeks ago, and he signed up, and we agreed on the text of a joint announcement, and then [McGeorge] Bundy's speech came along, and they decided that they'd have to go back to Hanoi, and they went back and considered it, and Abrams won a few more victories, so they decided to go along. And when they did, in the meantime, Nixon's folks—I don't know whether he had anything to do with it or not. Don't charge that he does. I can't prove it. But some of the people supporting him told Hanoi that they could—he had no connection [with] this war, wasn't involved, and that he could be more reasonable—didn't have any commitments—than somebody that had been fighting them for five years. [*Humphrey acknowledges.*] And on the other side of the tack, they told the South Vietnamese that if they don't sell out—let Johnson sell them out here at the conference table and bring them in—the NLF—that Humphrey's going to get beat and they'll have a bright future.[17]

Johnson kept Humphrey on a tight rein. Not only did he keep Chennault's identity from his vice president, he also told Humphrey not to accuse Nixon of being involved, since LBJ lacked proof.

A televised presidential address interrupted America's Halloween. As promised, Johnson did not mention the military concessions Hanoi had made in return for his ordering "that all air, naval, and artillery bombardment of North Vietnam cease as of 8 a.m., Washington time, Friday morning." All he could do was hint at them: "We cannot have productive talks in an atmosphere where the cities are being shelled and where the demilitarized zone is being abused." Johnson did mention one result of the bombing halt, but it benefited the North as well as the South. "A regular session of the Paris talks is going to take place next Wednesday, November 6th, at which the representatives of the government of South Vietnam are free to participate. We are informed by the representatives of the Hanoi government that the representatives of the National Liberation Front will also be present," he said. "I emphasize that their attendance in no way involves recognition of the National Liberation Front in any form."[18] It was possible to come away from his speech with the false impression that all the United States got in return for a bombing halt was Hanoi's agreement to sit and talk with Saigon.

The Republicans had their own television broadcast that night from Madison Square Garden. Standing before nineteen thousand cheering supporters, Nixon pointed at his running mate, Spiro Agnew, and declared, "Neither he nor I will destroy the chance of peace. We want peace." The presidential nominee said he hoped the bombing halt would "bring some progress" toward peace.[19] News coverage took Nixon's broadcast at face value. "Nixon Hopes Johnson Step Will Aid the Talks in Paris," said the *New York Times*.[20]

President Johnson's broadcast, however, inspired skepticism. Even worse for LBJ, soldiers interviewed by NBC in Saigon voiced outright opposition. "Well, I disagree with it 100 percent. I believe President Johnson made a wrong decision there," said one man in uniform. Another said he didn't think it was a good idea. "We're still fighting in the South and we're still going to lose a lot of lives this way," said a third. "I think we should go bomb." Another soldier, asked if he thought it would work, said only that he sincerely hoped so. At least there was one who took a wait-and-see stand on the announcement, if not on the president himself.

"Well, I think it's a feather in President Johnson's cap if it works out," he said. "If it doesn't, it's not going to look too good for him."

"Do you think he had politics in mind?" a reporter asked.

"Probably," the soldier said. "Yeah, I really think so."

The background briefings had an effect, just not the one Johnson hoped. The NBC coanchorman Chet Huntley said LBJ "made it clear that if the bombing halt is to continue, the demilitarized zone must be restored and the shelling of South Vietnam's cities stopped." But the news closed with a commentary from NBC's other anchorman, David Brinkley, making it clear that LBJ's credibility gap remained a great canyon. "There are charges the President chose this time, five days before the election, for political reasons," Brinkley said. "It is charged that if ending the bombing is a good idea now, why wasn't it a good idea five months ago? Well, the only answer anyone can give now is, if it stops the killing of Americans and others in Vietnam, then it's the right thing to do, even if it was done for the wrong reason."[21]

It didn't help when the vice president stood in front of the TV cameras and, immediately after saying he hoped the bombing halt would lead to peace, expressed confidence he would win the election. Republicans attacked. House Minority Leader Gerald R. Ford of Michigan did it subtly: "I would not like to believe that the timing of the bombing halt has anything to do with Tuesday's election. We must rely on the President's word that the bombing halt will not result in greater American casualties." Sen. Bourke B. Hickenlooper of Iowa did it brutally: "It's tragic that American lives are being played with this way." Sen. John G. Tower of Texas called the bombing halt "unilateral" and "unconditional," although it was neither. Nixon played it cool, telling a rally in Fort Worth, Texas, "I will not discuss the war in Vietnam for the very reason that any discussion might jeopardize those peace negotiations."[22]

The Secret Service pulled James Rowe out of a Humphrey campaign rally in Peoria to take a phone call from the president. Rowe had been a young New Deal lawyer and Johnson a Texas congressman when they'd first met; now he was a prominent Washington attorney and Humphrey adviser. "I don't want anybody to know that I've called you if I can avoid it," Johnson told Rowe on November 1. There was something the president wanted Humphrey to do, but he told Rowe to present the idea as if it were his own. "You just keep the candidate from mentioning Vietnam until Tuesday night," Johnson said. He blamed Humphrey for angering Thieu. "Now, Nixon picked up that ball right quick and started going into him through your China Lobby friend," Johnson said. "This damn little old woman, Mrs. Chennault, she's been in on it."

Rowe's law partner, Thomas G. Corcoran, was close to Chennault professionally and personally.

> Rowe: You want Tommy to pull her out?
> President Johnson: I don't know. I don't care, now.[23]

Having been requested by the president not to let anyone know they'd spoken or to quote him, Rowe immediately went and informed Humphrey of both the phone call and the identity of the China Lobbyist whose name LBJ had withheld from his vice president.

(Rowe bears great responsibility for the oft-told tale that Johnson himself informed Humphrey about Chennault.[24] Humphrey had another source in William Bundy, confirming Johnson's suspicion that he was an informant for the Democratic campaign. Bundy summarized the intelligence about the Chennault Affair for the Democratic nominee— although he never had a chance to see the actual reports, so closely did Johnson hold them.[25] Writers who wonder why Humphrey didn't go public with the Chennault Affair should bear in mind that there's no evidence on the tapes or in the contemporaneous government records that LBJ ever gave him the option. The president kept the NSA, CIA, and FBI reports and even Chennault's name from his vice president while instructing him specifically not to charge Nixon with knowledge of the partisan sabotage.)[26]

## "Hold On"

Things got worse for Johnson the next day, November 2, the Saturday before the election, when South Vietnam's president made a speech to his national legislature announcing a boycott of the negotiations that the bombing halt had finally made possible. "Thieu Says Saigon Cannot Join Paris Talks under Present Plan," said the front-page headline of the *New York Times*. The objections Thieu raised were smoke screens. He said he couldn't accept bargaining with the NLF as a separate delegation. The United States wasn't asking him to—Thieu's own "our side/ your side" formula took care of that. Saigon's second smoke screen sprang from the first. A separate delegation for the NLF, Thieu said, "would just be another trick toward a coalition government with the Communists in South Vietnam."[1] Johnson had long ago rejected a coalition government with the Communists. But the damage was done. Saigon's public boy-cott of the peace talks made the bombing halt look like a hollow politi-cal trick at the expense of an ally in war.

Nixon played it beautifully. Campaigning in Austin, just a few miles from the LBJ Ranch, the Republican nominee said on November 2, "In view of early reports this morning, prospects for peace are not as bright as they were even a few days ago." As if things didn't look bad enough, Nixon had one of his anonymous minions tell reporters that Johnson had assured all the candidates that South Vietnam would sit down with the NLF in Paris. In fact, LBJ had mentioned in his conference call that the peace talks might not get started, and had a transcript of Nixon acknowledging as much ("With regard to the talks, if they begin, and as I know, you've made it clear that they may not"). But now a "Nixon confidant" and "highly placed adviser" was telling reporters in a memorable turn of phrase, "We had the impression that all the diplo-matic ducks were in a row."[2] Combined with Thieu's refusal, the anony-mous quote made Johnson look deceptive. Instead of getting credit for standing firm until the enemy caved, Johnson was disappearing down his own credibility gap.

At 8:34 p.m. that night, the teleprinter at the LBJ Ranch came alive with the latest FBI report on the South Vietnamese embassy wiretap:

> . . . Mrs. Anna Chennault contacted Vietnamese Ambassador Bui Diem and advised him that she had received a message from her boss (not further identified) which her boss wanted her to give personally to the ambassador. She said the message was that the ambassador is to "hold on, we are gonna win" and that her boss also said, "Hold on, he understands all of it." She repeated that this is the only message. "He said please tell your boss to hold on." She advised that her boss had just called from New Mexico.[3]

Here finally was proof of Republican interference with the peace talks—direct evidence against Chennault, but only indirect evidence against "her boss," who was unfortunately "not further identified." LBJ's national security adviser tried to track down the reference to New Mexico. Nixon wasn't there, but the campaign plane of Republican vice-presidential nominee Agnew had touched down that day at the Al-buquerque airport. "The New Mexico reference may indicate Agnew is acting," Rostow wrote.[4] The dots were nearly connected. Johnson almost had what he needed.

At 9:18 p.m., the president called the highest-ranking Republican of-ficial in the land, Senate Minority Leader Dirksen. "I want to talk to you as a friend and very confidentially because I think that we're skirting on dangerous ground and I thought I ought to give you the facts and you ought to pass them on if you choose," Johnson said. "If you don't, why then I will a little later."

The president spent more time complaining about falsehoods Republicans were spreading about him and the bombing halt than about anything else. He walked Dirksen through the negotiating history, stressing that Saigon had agreed to take part in the peace talks *before* he ordered the bombing halt, then dropped a bombshell.

> President Johnson: And here is the latest information we got. The agent says that she's just—they just talked to the boss in New Mexico.
> Dirksen: Uh-huh.
> President Johnson: And that he says that you must hold out . . . that just hold on until after the election. Now, we know what Thieu is saying to them out there.
> Dirksen: Yeah.
> President Johnson: We're pretty well informed on both ends.
> Dirksen: Yeah.[5]

The president complained about the "ducks in a row" quote and Humphrey and Bundy's bombing halt speeches before returning to the point.

> President Johnson: Some of our folks, including some of the old China Lobby, are going to the Vietnamese embassy and saying, "Please notify the President that if he'll hold out until November the 2nd they could get a better deal."
> Dirksen: Uh-huh.
> President Johnson: Now, I'm reading their hand, Everett. I don't want to get this in the campaign.
> Dirksen: That's right.
> President Johnson: And they oughtn't to be doing this. This is treason.
> Dirksen: I know.[6]

Once again, the president went directly from evidence of sabotage of the Paris peace talks back to that day's attack on him by the Nixon campaign. When he returned to the evidence, he not only threatened to go public, but he exaggerated how much he knew.

> President Johnson: Now, I can identify them, because I know who's doing this. [*Dirksen attempts to interject.*] I don't want to identify it. I

think it would shock America if a principal candidate was playing with a source like this on a matter this important.

Dirksen: Yeah.

President Johnson: I don't want to do that.

Dirksen: Yeah.

President Johnson: But if they're going to put this kind of stuff out, they ought to know that we know what they're doing. I know who they're talking to and I know what they're saying.

Dirksen: Yeah.

President Johnson: And my judgment is that Nixon ought to play it just like he has all along, that I want to see peace come the first day we can, that it's not going to affect the election one way or the other. The conference is not even going to be held until after the election.

Dirksen: Yeah.

President Johnson: They have stopped shelling the cities. [*Dirksen acknowledges throughout.*] They have stopped going across the DMZ. We've had 24 hours of relative peace. Now, if Nixon keeps the South Vietnamese away from the conference, well, that's going to be his responsibility. Up to this point, that's why they're not there. I had them signed on board until this happened.

Dirksen: Yeah. [*pause*] OK.

President Johnson: Well, now, what do you think we ought to do about it?

Dirksen: Well, I better get in touch with him, I think, and tell him about it.

President Johnson: I think you better tell him that his people are saying to these folks that they oughtn't go through with this meeting. Now, if they don't go through with the meeting, I don't think it's going to be me who's hurt, I think it's going to be whoever's elected, and it'd be, my guess, him.

Dirksen: Yeah.

President Johnson: And I think they're making a very serious mistake, and I don't want to—I don't want to say this.

Dirksen: Yeah.

President Johnson: And you're the only one I'm going to say it to.[7]

While the FBI report said Chennault's boss was "not further identified," at times in the conversation the president implied that it was Nixon. At other times in the same call, however, Johnson implied that Nixon didn't know about it and needed to be told.

"Well, I'll try to find them, wherever they are tonight," Dirksen said.[8]

The conversation made the president's priorities clear. He used the leverage the FBI report gave him to pressure the Republicans to stop doing two things that were damaging his image and his historic legacy. He was firm about both: the Republicans must stop publicly saying that he had misled them about the bombing halt and must stop secretly encouraging Saigon to stay home from the Paris talks. The South's boycott and the Nixon campaign's aspersions on the bombing halt negotiations made LBJ look like he was playing politics with peace when he wanted to be seen as the president who held the line on Vietnam. To fight these threats to his reputation, he brandished the ultimate threat to Nixon's—exposure of the Chennault Affair. Humphrey's campaign, however, was not a priority—the only time LBJ mentioned him was to complain about his bombing halt speech.

Dirksen managed to reach Nixon at the Century Plaza Hotel in Los Angeles, but the Republican nominee didn't call the president right away. On November 3, the Sunday before the election, Nixon appeared on NBC's *Meet the Press,* where he made a seemingly generous offer. Nixon volunteered to go to Saigon or Paris after the election to "get these talks off dead center." Nixon had thought of a brilliant way to get credit for solving the problem that Johnson suspected him of creating. The nominee made it sound like he'd be doing the president a favor. "I am simply indicating that I will cooperate in any way President Johnson determines will be helpful," Nixon said. "I am not going to sit out there and wait and let him stew in his juice and then hope to try to do it after January." Together, Nixon said, they would present a "united front."

Journalists decided to stop letting the Nixon adviser who made the "ducks in a row" comment hide behind anonymity. It was Robert H. Finch, a politician skilled enough to get more votes as the Republican nominee for lieutenant governor of California in 1966 than Reagan got for governor. Finch "told two reporters that South Vietnam's refusal to join the Paris talks was evidence that Mr. Johnson had ordered the bombing pause unilaterally and hastily to further the Humphrey candidacy," the *Times* reported. Nixon didn't exactly defend Johnson on *Meet the Press.* "I don't make that charge," Nixon said. "I must say that many of my aides and many of the people supporting my candidacy around the country seem to share that view. They share it, I suppose, because the pause came at a time so late in the campaign, but President Johnson has been very candid with me through these discussions, and I do not make such a charge."[9]

Behind the scenes, Nixon once again called on Sen. George Smathers, the conservative Florida Democrat, to act as his intermediary with

Johnson. Through him, Nixon added another name to the mix. On the phone with Johnson, Smathers said Nixon had told him "that you were getting ready to blast him with the accusation that he had connived with [Sen.] John Tower [R-Texas] and Anna Chennault to bring about the action of the Saigon government in not participating, and that he thought that if you blasted him, he felt like that would be, of course, unsupported by the truth and, secondly, unfair, and, thirdly, unfortunate." Johnson, of course, had not mentioned Tower. The president didn't get distracted by this new variable, noting only that the Texas Republican had unfairly called the bombing halt "unilateral" and "unconditional."[10] While talking with Smathers, however, Johnson did concede a key point about Nixon. "Now, I don't know how much he knows," the president said.[11] That was a step back from what he'd implied to Dirksen the night before, and a step closer to the evidence LBJ had in hand.

Soon after LBJ hung up with Smathers, Nixon called. "I just wanted you to know that I feel very, very strongly about this, and any rumblings around about [*scoffing*] somebody trying to sabotage the Saigon's government's attitude there certainly have no—absolutely no credibility as far as I'm concerned," the Republican nominee said.

"I'm very happy to hear that, Dick, because that is taking place. Now, here's the history of it," Johnson said. Instead of talking about Chennault, however, the president started in on Finch. "The UPI ran a story quoting I guess it was Fink."[12] (LBJ knew how to pronounce Finch's name; he'd pronounced it correctly—like the bird—earlier that day, but for the rest of this conversation, it was Fink. Nixon didn't correct him.) Once again, Johnson read parts of the UPI story aloud, and once again, he summarized the negotiating history of the bombing halt.

President Johnson: Then the traffic goes out that Nixon will do better by you. Now, that goes to Thieu. I don't—I didn't say, as I said to you the other day, I didn't say that it was with your knowledge. I hope it wasn't.

Nixon: [*laughing*] Ah, no.

President Johnson: But—

Nixon: Well, as a matter of fact, I'm not privy to the—what you were doing, of course, with this thing, but—

President Johnson: Well—

Nixon: The whole point is this. I think one thing we have to understand here is that, you know, and I know that within the—there's a hawk-dove complex out there as there is here, and that everybody's been saying, "Well, now, after the election what will happen?" And of course there is some thought that Hanoi would rather deal now than deal later.

President Johnson: Oh, yes.

Nixon: They think Nixon will be tougher, and I understand that. And I think that's one of the reasons you felt you had to go forward with the pause. But my point that I'm making is this, that my God, I would *never* do anything to encourage Hanoi—I mean, Saigon not to come to the table, because basically, that was what you got out of your bombing pause, that, good God, we want them over in Paris. We've got to get them to Paris or you can't have a peace.[13]

The conversation is as revealing for what Nixon didn't say as for what he did. The historian Robert Dallek overstated the case when he wrote, "On November 3, Nixon called Johnson and categorically denied that he was doing anything to disrupt the peace negotiations."[14] Nixon made *no* categorical denial. First, he said that the charge of Republican sabotage had "absolutely no credibility as far as I'm concerned." Lies can be credible if they are believed; truths lack credibility if enough people doubt them.[15] Second, Nixon's laughing "Ah, no," being a sentence fragment, is open to several conflicting interpretations.[16] Finally, when Nixon said he "would never" encourage Saigon to stay away from the peace talks, that was a *conditional* denial, not a categorical one—and it didn't even address the question of whether he already *had* encouraged South Vietnam to boycott the peace talks.[17] These were "non-denial denials," as Bob Woodward and Carl Bernstein would learn to call the ambiguous White House statements about their Watergate stories.[18]

Johnson, for his part, did not ask Nixon if he was involved in the Chennault Affair. He didn't accuse Nixon, either. Instead, the president repeated his complaints about Thieu and "Fink." He did not, however, repeat the threat he'd made to Dirksen the night before; in his last phone call to Nixon before the election, LBJ said nothing about going public with the information he had.

Nixon mollified the president, complimenting Austin, the future home of the Johnson Library, as "a beautiful city," mentioning that he'd told the host of *Meet the Press* that LBJ got "a bad rap" on Vietnam, suggesting the president could negotiate peace in Vietnam during the final two months of his term, and taking a little crack at Humphrey's entourage.

Nixon: Some of Humphrey's people have been gleeful and they said the bombing pause is going to help them and so forth, and our ̣ say it hurts and—

President Johnson: Well, I'll tell you what I say. I say it doesn't help—doesn't affect the election one way or the other—

Nixon: I don't think it does.

President Johnson: —because I've asked all the candidates to please support me, and the other day all three of them said—you led it off—but all three of them said, "We'll back you, Mr. President."

Nixon: Right.

President Johnson: So I say it oughtn't affect the election one way and I don't think it'll change one vote.

Nixon: Well, anyway, we'll have fun. [*laughs*]

President Johnson: Thank you, Dick.

Nixon: Bye.[19]

"When he finally hung up, Mr. Nixon and his friends collapsed with laughter," wrote Godfrey Hodgson, who covered the 1968 campaign for the London *Sunday Times*. "It was partly in relief that their victory had not been taken from them at the eleventh hour."[20]

Although Johnson expressed certainty to Nixon that the nominee himself wasn't undermining the peace talks, he had his doubts. Afterward he told his secretary of state, "Now, I don't know whether he knows, I don't want to question his sincerity, whether he knows what they're doing or not. But it's pretty obvious to me that they've had their effect."[21]

The final Gallup poll of the campaign showed the race too close to call—Nixon: 42 percent, Humphrey: 40 percent, and Wallace: 14 percent.[22]

## Election Eve

On Monday morning, the day before the election, FBI agents observed an unidentified white male arrive by taxi at the South Vietnamese embassy, enter, and, forty-five minutes later, depart. Agents followed the man's taxi, observing him reading "a legal-sized white paper," until approximately noontime, when the cab arrived at the west gate of the White House. Agents watched him enter, then obtained his name from the White House police: Saville Davis, the *Christian Science Monitor*'s Washington bureau chief.[1]

Minutes later, National Security Adviser Rostow was handed a note saying the *Monitor* was "holding out of the paper a sensational dispatch from Saigon (from their Saigon correspondent) the 1st para of which reads: 'Purported political encouragement from the Richard Nixon camp was a significant factor in the last-minute decision of President Thieu's refusal to send a delegation to the Paris peace talks—at least until the American Presidential election is over.'" Davis was waiting upstairs for Rostow to comment.[2]

Rostow immediately phoned the LBJ Ranch, but Johnson was out horseback riding. He left a message asking "the President to get to a telephone as soon as possible for an urgent call." An aide reached the president at the nearby Martin Ranch, and LBJ galloped back to the main house. Johnson didn't tape his phone call to Rostow, but an aide summarized it: "The President told Walt that he couldn't confirm anything. He had his suspicions, but just didn't know. Told Walt not to talk to him, but to have him referred to the State Department."[3]

Then LBJ went out riding again, this time with his daughter Luci Baines Johnson, and his grandson, little Lyn. As they rode together to the Reagan Ranch, off to the right was the Johnson family cemetery.[4] LBJ would live out his final days on this ranch, writing his memoirs, shaping his legacy. And his final legacy on Vietnam, the start of the peace talks that the bombing halt made possible, was in jeopardy. Republicans were attacking him for Saigon's decision to boycott the peace talks—when other Republicans were secretly encouraging it. UPI was quoting House Minority Leader Gerald R. Ford, R-Michigan, saying, "We have botched up Vietnam again. In only three days since the bombing halt, we have our ally, South Vietnam, hurt and angry." And Sen. John Tower of Texas called the bombing halt "hastily contrived" and said it "smacks of sheer politics whether that suspicion is warranted or not."[5] At the Reagan Ranch, LBJ telephoned an aide and asked for a conference call on the *Monitor* story. It would include his two closest hawks, Secretary of State Rusk and Rostow, but this time they'd be joined by the biggest dove in his cabinet as well, Defense Secretary Clark M. Clifford.

A fixture of Democratic politics since the Truman administration, Clifford was a Humphrey man. He had favored a bombing halt even if Hanoi didn't meet all three of Johnson's conditions.[6] Johnson wanted to hear what Clifford thought about going public with the intelligence collected by the NSA, FBI, and CIA.

The president sounded torn when the conference call began at half past noon. "I don't want to be in the position of being a McCarthy," Johnson said. The late Sen. Joseph R. McCarthy, R-Wisconsin, was notorious for making accusations of treason without evidence. "Now, I don't want to have information that ought to be public and not make it so. On the other hand we have a lot of . . . I don't know how much we can do there, and I know we'll be charged with trying to interfere with the election, and I think this is something's going to require the best judgments that we have." The president had just been handed the latest FBI wiretap report. The *Monitor*'s bureau chief had tried to reach Ambassador Diem by phone, but was told he was busy.

> Davis said the dispatch from Saigon contains elements of a major scandal which also involves the [South] Vietnamese ambassador and which will affect presidential candidate Richard Nixon if the *Monitor* publishes it. Time is of the essence inasmuch as Davis has a deadline to meet if he publishes it. He speculated that should the story be published, it will create a great deal of excitement.[7]

President Johnson: Now, what he gets from Saigon is well and good and fine, but if he gets it from us, I want to be sure that (A) we try to do it in such a way that our motives are not questioned and that the public interest requires it, and (2)—and that's the only thing I want to operate under. I'm not interested in the politics of it. The second thing is I want to be sure that what we say is—can be confirmed.

Rusk: Well, Mr. President, I have a very definite view on this, for what it's worth. I do not believe that any president can make any use of interceptions or telephone taps in any way that would involve politics. The moment we cross over that divide, we're in a different kind of society.

President Johnson: Yeah.

Rusk: Now, if this story is coming out of Saigon, I don't myself see how it could have come from American sources in Saigon, because we've been extremely careful not to pass along details of this sort of thing out there. It could have come from South Vietnamese sources. I don't know. Did Saville Davis say from what kind of sources it came?

President Johnson: No, he just says that he informed the ambassador. He wanted to check out a story received from a correspondent in Saigon.

Rusk: Right.

President Johnson: And he planned to come to the embassy and wait for the ambassador to see him. Now, he has also tried to see the White House.

Rusk: Well, I would think that we are—that since we are not involved in any contacts that the Republicans might have had with the South Vietnamese ambassador, that this is a matter on which only the Republicans could comment, and that we stay out of it completely. I really think that it would be very unwise. I mean, we get a lot of information through these special channels that we don't make public. I mean, for example, some of the malfeasances of senators and congressmen and other people that we don't make public, and I think that we must continue to respect the classification of that kind of material. And I think that all we can say is that we're not going to comment on such matters. That's for others to comment on if they have anything to say on it, but to be very sure that we ourselves are not ourselves putting out this story.

President Johnson: Mmm. Clark, do you have any reaction?

Clifford: I couldn't—I could not hear what Dean said.

Rusk: I can't hear whoever that is.

Clifford: I can hear the President very clearly, but all I can hear is Dean's voice, but I can't get his words.

President Johnson: Well, Dean just says he doesn't think that we can confirm or say anything or have any comment in connection with it on the basis of the sensitivity of the information.

Clifford: Well, I would think there'd be a good deal of merit to that. I'd go on to another reason also, and that is I think that some elements of the story are so shocking in their nature that I'm wondering whether it would be good for the country to disclose the story and then possibly have a certain individual elected. It could cast his whole administration under such doubt that I would think it would be inimical to our country's interests.

President Johnson: Well, I have no doubt about that, but what about the story being published and our knowing of it and our being charged with hushing it or something?

Rusk: Oh, I think on that, Mr. President—excuse me.

Clifford: I don't believe that would bother me. I think that the amount of information that we have that we don't think we should publicize—it has to do with the sensitivity of the sources, it has to do with the absence of absolute proof. I don't believe we have the kind of story that we would be justified in putting out.

President Johnson: Fine.[8]

That day the Republican nominee told campaign workers in Los Angeles to emphasize the issue of peace, saying, "when we consider the fact that it was only three days ago that the hopes for peace were tremendously high as a result of the bombing pause, and that now those hopes are quite discouraging because of the developments since then, it is clear that if we are going to avoid what could be a diplomatic disaster, it is going to be necessary to get some new men and a united front in the United States of America."[9] And that night, during an election-eve telethon on NBC, Nixon told viewers, "I have read news dispatches that an Air Force general said that the North Vietnamese are moving thousands of tons of supplies down the Ho Chi Minh Trail and that our bombers are unable to stop them." He didn't give the general's name or any other details. (General Abrams, in fact, used the bombers that no longer targeted North Vietnam to hit the Ho Chi Minh Trail in Laos.)

Minutes later Humphrey interrupted his own broadcast on ABC to blast Nixon's "totally irresponsible, unsubstantiated charge." There was no bombing halt over the Ho Chi Minh Trail, the vice president said, as Nixon knew very well. "The entire Ho Chi Minh Trail is subject to intensive American airpower as it has been in the past and as it is even more so now," said Humphrey. (Humphrey exaggerated; the United States bombed the Ho Chi Minh Trail in Laos, but not at this point in Cambodia.) "To frighten the American people at this time, when delicate negotiations are under way, I think is a rather irresponsible act. What you and I should be doing is asking the government of South Vietnam to attend that peace conference in Paris."[10]

## "I Let You Down"

On Election Day, Americans opened up their newspapers to read an appeal by former president Dwight Eisenhower, issued from his sickbed at Walter Reed Army hospital, urging them not to be swayed by the bombing halt. "Nixon deserves the plaudits of the American people for his extraordinarily responsible conduct of his campaign respecting Vietnam. His outspoken support of the President throughout the campaign in major measures on the war gave the President the freedom to take this action," Eisenhower said. "It would be supreme irony if these statesmanlike positions of Richard Nixon, maintained despite the greatest provocation, should now be turned into instruments of political injury to him."[1] The Harris Poll showed Humphrey edging Nixon, 43 to 40 percent.[2]

The race remained too close to call until the morning after Election Day:

Republican Richard M. Nixon: 31,770,237 votes (43.4 percent), 301 electoral votes from 32 states.

Democrat Hubert H. Humphrey: 31,270,533 votes (42.72 percent), 191 electoral votes from 13 states and the District of Columbia.

Independent George C. Wallace: 9,906,141 votes (13.53 percent), 46 electoral votes from 5 states.[3]

When the results were clear, the vice president called the White House. "Well, I'm sorry I let you down a little," Humphrey said.

"No, you didn't. No, you didn't. It's a lot of other folks, but not you," Johnson said. "It was our own people in the party that created all the problems, all the conditions, and stirred up all the divisiveness, and now they're blaming everybody else."

"Yep."

"But you came out of it in mighty good shape, and I just wish it could have been a few hundred more," Johnson said.

"That's right, well, if we could've done just a little better . . . but we're not going to cry," Humphrey said. "Nothing you can do about it."[4]

## "Time to Blow the Whistle"

After the election, it didn't take long for LBJ to lose patience with the Republicans. On Thursday, he got another FBI wiretap report, this one saying that a "Major Minh expressed the opinion that the move by Saigon was to help presidential candidate Nixon, and that had Saigon gone to the conference table, presidential candidate Humphrey would probably have won."[1]

On Friday, the *Christian Science Monitor* finally ran its big story—which said absolutely nothing about the Nixon campaign encouraging Saigon to stay home from Paris. Worse, the *Monitor* claimed that the *American* side had "made a major concession to Hanoi in the now famous secret peace package deal." The alleged concession was to seat the "NLF as a separate delegation at Paris—meaning that the expanded peace talks would be a four-power conference." There was no mention of the "our side/your side" formula that packaged all participants in the talk into two sides only. The "four-party conference" was spin. "Saigon argues it would probably pave the way for a coalition government and eventual Communist take-over in South Vietnam," the *Monitor* said, although the Johnson administration had opposed a coalition government with the Communists since before the bombing halt talks began. A story that had started as an exposé of the Nixon campaign ended up casting doubt on the Johnson administration's honesty. "American Ambassador Ellsworth F. Bunker explained the package deal to President Thieu and the South Vietnamese government in such a way that this major concession was glossed over."[2] It's impossible to gloss over a concession that was never made.

And Chennault was still at it. Friday's embassy wiretap report included this garbled sentence: "Mrs. Anna Chennault contacted Vietnamese Ambassador Bui Diem and advised that the message on that date from South Vietnamese President Thieu, 'which our boss,' was alright." It sounded like Thieu had used Chennault to transmit the invitation to Nixon that appeared on the front page of Friday's *New York Times*. A Nixon press aide said Saigon had invited the president-elect "to make an on-the-spot assessment of the war and the situation in Vietnam." The president-elect wouldn't make any trip or statement about foreign policy without checking with Johnson first, the aide said.[3] But the FBI report made it sound like he was thinking about it: "Chennault continued that 'they' are still planning things but are not letting people know too much because they want to be careful to avoid embarrassing 'you,' themselves, or the present U.S. government. Therefore, whatever we do must be carefully planned."[4]

Fed up, National Security Adviser Rostow wrote, "First reactions may well be wrong. But with this information I think it's time to blow the whistle on these folks."[5]

Johnson already had a meeting scheduled for Monday with the president-elect at the White House, but he wasn't going to wait through the weekend. He wanted Nixon to join him in delivering an ultimatum to the South Vietnamese government. Toward this end, Johnson first delivered an ultimatum to Nixon by phone Friday night. Not too subtly, LBJ threatened to expose the information US intelligence agencies had gathered on the Chennault Affair.

President Johnson: These people are proceeding on the assumption [*Nixon acknowledges*] that folks close to you tell them to do nothing until January the 20th.

Nixon: You got a—

President Johnson: Now, we think—

Nixon: I know who they're talking about, too. Is it [Sen.] John Tower [R-Texas]?[6]

President Johnson: Well, he's one of several. Mrs. Chennault is very much in there.

Nixon: Well, she's very close to John.[7]

LBJ raised the stakes for Nixon personally in a way he hadn't before the election. "I think they've been talking to [Vice President–elect] Agnew," Johnson said. "I think they think that they've been quoting you indirectly, that the thing they ought to do is to just not show up at any conference and wait until you come into office."

"Right."

"Now, they started that, and that's bad. They're killing Americans every day," Johnson said. "I have that documented."[8]

LBJ acknowledged saying before the election that he didn't think Nixon was responsible personally, but that didn't defuse the threat. If Johnson said in public what he'd just said on the phone—that (1) he thought Nixon's running mate was involved in the Chennault Affair, (2) participants had indirectly been quoting Nixon himself, and (3) the delay in the peace talks was resulting in the loss of American lives—the effect would be politically explosive. Johnson might have a credibility gap, but he also had NSA, CIA, and FBI reports to back him up.

"Let me ask you this," Nixon said. "Is there anything we can do right now?"

The president wanted the president-elect to send "whoever you trust most in Washington" to the South Vietnamese embassy and deliver a three-part message on behalf of both Nixon and Johnson. The first two parts were assurances, the third an ultimatum: (1) The United States would not seek a coalition government for South Vietnam; (2) the United States would not recognize the NLF; and (3) the United States would not support South Vietnam if it didn't take part in the Paris peace talks. LBJ practically dictated the message.

" 'Therefore, Mr. Ambassador, I think you ought to tell the President [of South Vietnam] that I support our President on going to the conference and I think you ought to go and if they try to sell you out, you don't have to agree, but you ought to go because the [Senate Foreign Relations chairman J. William] Fulbrights [D-Arkansas] and the [Senate Majority Leader Michael J.] Mansfields [D-Montana] and even the [Senate Minority Leader] Dirksens will not go along with anybody that won't go to a conference table," Johnson said. "Now that's where they are tonight."

Nixon: Let me ask you this about the ambassador. I met him about five or six months ago.[9] Does he have any influence with that government?

President Johnson: Yes, he is giving them these signals and [*Nixon acknowledges throughout*] he is telling them that he has just talked to New Mexico and he has just talked to the Nixon people and they say hold out, don't do anything, we're going to win and we'll do better by you. Now, that's the story, Dick, and it's a sordid story. I told you that Sunday when I talked to you.

Nixon: Right.

President Johnson: You remember when I talked to [George] Smathers and Dirksen?

Nixon: Right.

President Johnson: Now, I don't want to say that to the country because that's not good.

Nixon: Right.

President Johnson: But they're playing that game. I don't think you're playing it, and I'd get off that hook. I'd just say to them, "You go to that conference [*Nixon acknowledges throughout*] and you protect your country and I'm going to support our President as long as he doesn't agree to a coalition government, as long as he doesn't agree to recognize the NLF, as long he stands on the conditions he does and we're united, and don't depend on me to give you a better deal."

Nixon: We'll do that.[10]

Saigon depended on American support for its very existence. Most of the South Vietnamese government's budget came from American aid.[11] This gave presidents leverage over Saigon that they exercised at crucial junctures. In October 1954, General Nguyen Van Hinh, the South Vietnamese army's chief of staff, threatened to overthrow the government of President Ngo Dinh Diem, but abandoned his plans when "told revolt would mean automatic termination of U.S. aid," according to the Pentagon Papers.[12] There's no point in having a coup if the government you're taking over then ceases to exist. In October 1963, General Duong Van Minh sought assurances from the Kennedy administration that US aid would continue if he overthrew President Diem; he got them and had Diem assassinated a month later.[13] In January 1973, President Nixon would wield the threat of an American aid cutoff to force President Thieu to accept a settlement that would lead to Communist victory following a "decent interval." So a joint statement from Johnson and Nixon, the Democratic president and the Republican president-elect, that South Vietnam would lose American support if it didn't get to the negotiating table constituted a powerful ultimatum—what's now sometimes called "an existential threat."

President Johnson: You won't have ten men in the Senate [*Nixon acknowledges*] support South Vietnam when you come in if these people refuse to go the conference.

Nixon: Absolutely. Well, I'll get on it.[14]

Nixon chose Dirksen, still the highest-ranking Republican officeholder in the land, as his emissary to Ambassador Diem. The senator set up the meeting the following morning. The president wanted the ultimatum to be delivered just right, so he asked Secretary of State Rusk

to brief the Senate minority leader before he got to the South Vietnamese embassy.

Rusk: Does he know about the woman?
President Johnson: Yes.
Rusk: I see. All right.
President Johnson: He knows—
Rusk: Then he'll know what I mean then.
President Johnson: Yes. Oh, yeah, yes, yes. I'd give a pretty strong hint
of it, kind of in indignation, without being unpleasant, but he knows that
there's a good many conversations, and I think Nixon knows it and I
think Nixon has been well aware of it and my judgment is that Nixon
sees the danger of it now. [*Rusk acknowledges.*] But I don't really know.

Rusk: If this thing ever got out, this war is over as far as the American people are concerned.
President Johnson: Yes, yes, I think so.[15]

The idea that exposing the Chennault Affair could end the Vietnam
War may sound like wild exaggeration. But the information in the government's files as of November 1968 was enough to turn the American
voter's world upside down. If LBJ had made it public, Americans would
have learned that:

1. The South Vietnamese government, in whose defense more than
thirty thousand Americans had died and more than a half million
Americans were currently risking their lives, had boycotted the Paris
peace talks for the purpose of swinging the American presidential election to its preferred candidate, Richard Nixon. And it had worked. The
election was close enough, and the impact of South Vietnam's boycott
on the polls obvious enough, to make that clear. The South Vietnamese
could protest that they stayed away from Paris for reasons of policy, not
politics, but the negotiating records show that their publicly stated objections to the talks were just pretexts. And the CIA and NSA reports
confirm that influencing the US presidential election was at least one
of Saigon's motives. The question for Americans would then become
whether they were willing to send their children to fight and die for a
foreign government that used subterfuge to manipulate voters into
electing the presidential candidate it preferred.

2. There was evidence that the next president of the United States
had sabotaged the peace talks to win the election. The FBI wiretap report caught Chennault speaking on behalf of "her boss." That would have
been enough to justify a Justice Department investigation of possible

Logan Act violations. If Chennault had said under oath in November 1968 what she later wrote in her memoir, her testimony would have directly implicated Nixon himself. Americans would have learned that the candidate and his campaign chairman had secretly met with Chennault and Ambassador Diem months before Election Day—and that, according to Chennault, Nixon had secretly designated her as his "sole representative" to the Saigon government in the campaign.[16] That would have identified "her boss." Even if Nixon denied it, his efforts to conceal the fact that the meeting took place left a partial paper trail. If the July 3, 1968, memo about the meeting in New York with Chennault and Ambassador Diem had surfaced, Nixon would have had to explain why he went to such lengths to keep his meeting with Chennault and the South Vietnamese ambassador secret—even from the Secret Service agents whose job it was to guard his life.[17] It would look bad.

Americans had heard candidate Nixon declare in speech after speech that he would not say or do anything to destroy the chance for negotiations to end the war. Confronted with evidence that in the campaign's final days he secretly destroyed the chance for negotiations to even *begin,* Americans would have had reason to conclude that the president-elect was the kind of man to play politics with life-or-death matters of war and peace. His own secretly recorded White House tapes would demonstrate that he was, but not until years after his death. Americans lacked fair warning in 1968, thanks to Johnson's decision to keep CIA, NSA, and FBI reports on the Chennault Affair classified.

## The United Front

The bipartisan Johnson-Nixon ultimatum produced immediate results. Ambassador Diem used the tapped embassy phone to fill in President Thieu, and the resulting FBI report showed that Dirksen had delivered the bipartisan threat just as the president wanted. The two South Vietnamese officials assured one another on the phone that their boycott of the peace talks had nothing to do with American presidential politics.[1] Afterward, Ambassador Diem paid a visit to Bill Bundy and made it clear the message had been received: "congressional and public opinion in U.S. did not understand Saigon's refusal to go to Paris and as consequence negative reaction was building which could create difficulties" if the boycott continued.[2] National Security Adviser Rostow passed the FBI report to Johnson with a triumphant note: "It looks as though with no coalition and no recognition of the NLF as a separate entity—points

Thieu had all along—he is ready to go."[3] South Vietnam's president wasn't happy, but what choice did he have?

Some writers claim South Vietnam would have boycotted the peace talks even without the secret encouragement of the Republicans. "Nixon's pressure on Thieu's government to reach a settlement probably made no difference," Robert Dallek wrote in *Nixon and Kissinger: Partners in Power.* "Even if Nixon had not been discouraging Thieu from joining the Paris talks, Thieu was unlikely to have sent a delegation. He didn't need Nixon to tell him that participation in the discussions would improve Humphrey's chances of winning, and Thieu clearly preferred a more hard-line Republican administration."[4] Historians call this a counterfactual—an attempt to answer a "What if?" question. To be worth anything, a counterfactual must be based on the factual—on what actually did happen. The writers who claim Thieu would have boycotted the peace talks anyway fail to consider the ultimatum that got him to reverse his decision, or the underlying power dynamic between the United States and South Vietnam that made the threat effective. At the same time, they neglect to ask why Nixon went to all the trouble and risk of the Chennault Affair if he could have achieved the exact same result (as they believe he would have) by doing absolutely nothing. The right counterfactual question is, Would Thieu have boycotted the Paris peace talks before Election Day 1968 if he thought that the Republican nominee's true position on the bombing halt was his public one—that he supported the Democratic president completely and that he wanted Saigon to take part in the Paris peace talks—and that therefore there was a united, bipartisan front in the United States that Saigon could defy only at peril of losing American support? Put the question that way, and it's easy to see why Nixon didn't take the risk of allowing Saigon to believe that he meant what he was saying on the campaign trail. The Chennault Affair posed a risk for the Republican nominee, but the start of peace talks before Election Day would have posed a bigger one.

## "Candid and Forthright"

Johnson and Nixon were all smiles and handshakes before the TV cameras assembled on November 11 at the White House to capture their first meeting since the election. "No visiting head of government has been given a warmer reception than the President gave Richard Nixon today," NBC's John Chancellor reported.[1] LBJ had won their secret battle, at least for the time being. After lunch with Lady Bird and

Pat Nixon, the president escorted his successor along the colonnade to the Oval Office for a quick look and then into the Cabinet Room, where Nixon faced the core of LBJ's national security team for over an hour. Secretary of State Rusk gave a date-by-date account of the bombing halt negotiations, with special emphasis on the US government's steadfastness regarding all three of Johnson's conditions. Rusk deemed Minority Leader Dirksen's talk with Ambassador Diem "helpful."

"My position has been to do nothing unless the President and Secretary of State thought it would be helpful," Nixon said.

The president didn't let that stand. "My judgment is that in the month of October the election campaign came at a bad time—delayed us from getting substantive talks," Johnson said. "The first two weeks we were charged by the Democrats. The last two weeks we were charged by the Republicans." No one said the name Chennault out loud, at least according to the meeting notes.[2]

Nixon and Johnson emerged from the White House to present themselves before the cameras again. Nixon's words sounded like platitudes to those lacking the classified subtext. "Our discussion was extremely candid and forthright with regard to the policy decisions and the negotiations and discussions that will go on with regard to Vietnam and other matters. I gave assurance in each instance to the Secretary of State, and, of course, to the President, that they could speak not just for this administration but for the nation, and that meant for the next administration as well," Nixon said.

"It was a very pleasant and cooperative meeting," President Johnson said.[3]

To keep Nixon pleasant and cooperative, LBJ pursued his investigation of the Chennault Affair. The following day he pressed Deputy FBI Director Cartha D. "Deke" DeLoach to get him every telephone number dialed from Republican vice-presidential candidate Agnew's campaign plane during its November 2 stop at the Albuquerque, New Mexico, airport. Chennault had mentioned that "her boss" called from New Mexico to urge the South Vietnamese to "hold on, we are gonna win." LBJ wanted proof.

This put DeLoach in an awkward spot. President-elect Nixon would decide who got to be director of the FBI. DeLoach wanted the position. J. Edgar Hoover, however, wanted to keep it. Digging up dirt on Nixon's running mate could hardly endear DeLoach to the new boss. LBJ sweetened the pot, saying he'd told Nixon that if there had been a vacancy at the top of the FBI, "that I would name you, and I would recommend you, and I thought that he would want to do the same, but that I did not want to humiliate or mortify the other fellow until he was ready." De-Loach had spent his entire FBI career under Hoover, who'd led the bureau since the Roaring Twenties.

President Johnson: Why in the hell doesn't he act?

DeLoach: Well, because he doesn't know how to do anything for himself, because he is a very selfish individual that frankly just feels like he's invincible and . . . [we] can't get along without him, and he wants to be—wants to stay there until he dies. And I think he frankly will stay there.

President Johnson: What is his age?

DeLoach: Seventy-four.[4]

President Johnson: Well, does the new man have to issue an executive order [suspending the FBI's then-mandatory retirement age of seventy for Hoover], too?

DeLoach: Yes, sir, he does. The new man has to ask him to stay on. And he doesn't know how to drive a car. He's never kept book. He doesn't know anything about housework. He doesn't know anything about anything outside the office, because everything is done for him. And I love him and I've always done it. I've worked for him for 27 years. But it's time he's moving on.[5]

LBJ just encouraged him.

President Johnson: What's wrong with his arm?

DeLoach: I don't know, sir. He's been shaking pretty badly [for] some time, and he also has a pretty bad back ailment. He tends to have great difficulty getting in and out of a car and standing up, getting in and out of a chair.[6]

DeLoach assured the president that he'd get the names of everyone called from Agnew's plane if he had to go to Albuquerque himself. He called back the next night with five names. Chennault's was not among them.

DeLoach: Now, there were no toll calls to the South Vietnamese embassy on that date. There were none to the Little Flower or the Dragon Lady, as we call her, from Albuquerque.[7]

## The Man Who Knew Too Little

The next day J. Edgar Hoover trekked to New York to meet with the president-elect. It wasn't easy for an elderly man who had trouble standing and moving to get up to Nixon's transition headquarters on the thirty-ninth floor of New York's Hotel Pierre. A Secret Service agent seated at the elevator made visitors stand and wait between gilt display cases of alligator purses and leopard coats while he called and asked for permission to send them up. The elevator took them only to the thirty-eighth floor; at Secret Service insistence, visitors had to take the back stairs to the thirty-ninth floor. Then they had to wait at a locked door while an agent identified them via closed-circuit TV. (Most Americans could ID Hoover on sight since childhood.) Once allowed entry, there was one final obstacle to surmount: a snarl of numberless, newly installed telephone cables strewn across the floors. Two of the young, waiting Nixon aides, H. R. Haldeman and John D. Ehrlichman, were surprised the director's face was so red. When Hoover first took over what used to be called just the Bureau of Investigation in 1924, Haldeman and Ehrlichman had not yet been born. A future novelist, Ehrlichman cataloged all the visible signs of decay: "His big head rested on beefy, rounded shoulders, apparently without benefit of neck. He was florid and fat-faced, ears flat against his head, eyes protruding. He looked unwell to me."[1]

Face to face with the man who would decide his fate, Hoover told a story—a detailed story, a plausible story, though not quite a true story. Haldeman—privy to many of Nixon's secrets, but not the Chennault Affair—understood the words, but not what they meant to his boss:

> [Hoover] said that LBJ had ordered the FBI to wiretap Nixon during the campaign. In fact, he told Nixon, Johnson had directed the FBI to "bug" Nixon's campaign airplane, and this had been done. Johnson had based his request on national security.
>
> Hoover also said that, at Johnson's orders, the FBI had installed wiretaps on the telephone of Madame Anna Chennault.
>
> This angered Nixon, but he remained still.[2]

Hoover's bluff was masterful. Over the years he'd developed a reputation as the "Man Who Knew Too Much to Fire," but his information about the Chennault Affair was quite limited. President Johnson didn't share the CIA or NSA reports or Alexander Sachs's warnings with the FBI. All Hoover knew for certain from the FBI's wiretap was that Chennault claimed to speak for "her boss" when she urged the South Vietnamese to "hold on." The FBI had collected no other evidence against Nixon himself. Hoover made no accusations against Nixon, no explicit threat that he couldn't back up or carry out. He just told a couple of lies that would frighten the president-elect if Chennault was telling the truth.

The kind of surveillance Hoover was (falsely) talking about could have compromised Nixon's system of cutouts. The candidate had put two between him and the South Vietnamese. Messages went from Nixon to campaign chairman John Mitchell, then from Mitchell to Chennault, and from Chennault to Ambassador Diem. A bug on Nixon's campaign plane (if there had really been one) could have captured some of the candidate's instructions to Mitchell; a tap on Chennault's telephone (if there had really been one) could have captured some of Mitchell's communications with her. In reality, Nixon's use of two cutouts worked. The FBI captured some of Chennault's communications to Ambassador Diem. But the bureau had nothing on Mitchell and Nixon. Nixon, however, didn't know that.

Hoover's story mixed fact with fiction. President Johnson had indeed directed the FBI to place a wiretap on the phone in Chennault's apartment. The bureau didn't follow through on that order, however. It "was widely known that she was involved in Republican political circles," De-Loach wrote to Associate FBI Director Clyde A. Tolson the day after the president issued the order, "and, if it became known that the FBI was surveilling her, this would put us in a most untenable and embarrassing position."[3] Tapping the phone of Nixon's top woman fund-raiser would indeed have been "untenable and embarrassing" for anyone who hoped the president-elect would appoint him FBI director.

As for the notion that LBJ ordered a bug on Nixon's plane and a tap on his phone—Hoover just made that up. There's no evidence that either took place or that Johnson even requested them. For good measure, Hoover cut the legs off his chief rival to head the bureau by telling the president-elect that the FBI official who placed the (nonexistent) bug on the campaign plane was none other than Deputy Director DeLoach.[4]

Hoover had walked into the Hotel Pierre with an uncertain future; he walked out bulletproof. He would remain FBI director until the day he died. Although Nixon often considered firing him, he would never do it. Hoover had given him reason to fear that somewhere in the FBI's files were reports on Nixon's own involvement in the Chennault Affair. There weren't, but (again) Nixon didn't know that. The new president arrived at the White House obsessed with tracking down the paper trail.

## "All the Documents"

In his first month in office, President Nixon gave Haldeman, now White House chief of staff, a long-term assignment regarding the bombing halt:

"There was a lot of phony stuff going on by LBJ, Bob. I want you to make up a full report with all the documents showing just what he did. He let politics enter into a war decision, and I want the whole story on it."

"But that's all behind us," I say.

I make a pitch for my own hoped-for project: to get the real facts from the files on the Kennedy assassination for history's sake. The idea bores Nixon. History, to him, is what has happened to Nixon—and what *might* happen later.[1]

It was an impossible task. Haldeman couldn't get "all the documents." Johnson had taken the most important ones—the NSA intercepts of cables from Ambassador Diem to Saigon, the CIA reports on the bug in President Thieu's office, and the FBI reports on the South Vietnamese embassy and Chennault—with him into retirement at the LBJ Ranch.[2] The former president asked Walt Rostow, who went from the White House to the faculty of the Lyndon B. Johnson School of Public Affairs in Austin, Texas, to hold on to the Chennault file personally for him due to its sensitive nature.[3] The documents Nixon most needed were out of reach.

Haldeman assigned the bombing halt task to a young White House aide. Neither he nor Nixon mentioned the aide's name in their respective memoirs. If they had, it would have connected the dots between the bombing halt and Watergate. The aide was Tom Charles Huston, later notorious as the author of the Huston Plan to expand the use of government break-ins, wiretaps, and mail opening in the name of fighting domestic terrorism. Huston's work on the bombing halt report provides crucial, missing context to the plan that came to bear his name. (The connection was one Nixon would make the first time he ordered his aides to break into Brookings to get a bombing halt file. "Now you remember Huston's plan? Implement it," Nixon said on June 17, 1971. "I want it implemented on a thievery basis. Goddamn it, get in and get those files. Blow the safe and get it.")[4]

Huston focused first on the Chennault Affair. The episode had entered public knowledge in distorted form thanks to Theodore H. White, a journalist often praised (and almost as often blamed) as the father of modern campaign journalism. White created the template for campaign books in *The Making of the President 1960*, a best-seller that fashioned a novelistic narrative out of the Kennedy/Nixon race using behind-the-scenes, insider details like what the nominee ate for breakfast.[5] His storytelling skills were impressive; his reportorial ones, less so. In *The*

*Making of the President 1968,* he provided the outside story of the pivotal moment of the campaign.

> There is no way of getting at the dilemma of both parties except by introducing, at this point, the completely extraneous name of a beautiful Oriental lady, Anna Chan Chennault, the Chinese widow of wartime hero General Claire Chennault. Mrs. Chennault, an American citizen since 1950, comes of a line that begins with Mei-ling Soong (Madame Chiang Kai-shek) and runs through Madame Nhu (the Dragon Lady of South Vietnam)—a line of Oriental ladies of high purpose and authoritarian manners whose pieties and iron righteousness have frequently outrun their brains and acknowledged beauty.[6]

With this analysis, White took the old, sexist stereotype of the pretty airhead and transformed it into a brand new, racist one. The three women were not part of any line, being unrelated (outside of White's head). As America's foremost campaign chronicler told the story, Chennault acted on her own to sabotage the peace talks, "apparently implying, as she went, that she spoke for the Nixon campaign. She had, however, neglected to take the most elementary precautions of an intriguer, and her communications with Asia had been tapped by the American government and brought directly to the perusal of President Johnson."[7] Chennault *was* one of "the most elementary precautions of an intriguer"—a cutout enabling the men behind her to plausibly deny responsibility. White vouched for the Nixon campaign's innocence on the basis of his own powers of observation:

> At the first report of Republican sabotage in Saigon, Nixon's headquarters had begun to investigate the story; had discovered Mrs. Chennault's activities; and was appalled. The fury and dismay at Nixon's headquarters when his aides discovered the report were so intense that they could not have been feigned simply for the benefit of this reporter. Their feeling on Monday morning before the election was, simply, that if they lost the election, Mrs. Chennault might have lost it for them. She had taken their name and authority in vain.[8]

*The Making of the President 1968* didn't weigh the possibility that Nixon kept Chennault's role secret from as many campaign aides as he could; they didn't have to feign fury and dismay, because they didn't really know what was going on.[9] Neither did White.

While White exonerated the Nixon campaign, the government files that Huston examined did not. "Attached is the first of a series of reports for the President on aspects of the Vietnam bombing halt. This paper deals with the Chennault Affair and is highly sensitive," Huston wrote Haldeman on February 25, 1970. "As you will note from reading it, the evidence available in the case does not dispel the notion that we were somehow involved in the Chennault Affair, and while release of this information would be most embarrassing to President Johnson, it would not be helpful to us either."[10]

Huston's inquiry then took a strange turn. At first, it seemed like he'd uncovered the existence of exactly the kind of report Nixon wanted. "After six months of screwing around with the NSC staff, I have done a little digging of my own," he wrote Haldeman on March 13, 1970. In the final days of the Johnson administration, Huston wrote, the Defense Department's Office of International Security Affairs (ISA) had prepared a report "on all events leading up to the bombing halt." Huston claimed the report was at the Brookings Institution, and that former defense secretary Clark Clifford and former assistant secretary of defense for international security affairs Paul C. Warnke had copies. "All these documents are Top Secret and I am amazed that they have been allowed to fall into the hands of such obviously hostile people. A fellow by the name of Les Gelb who was a top aide to Warnke is now at Brookings and apparently is the one responsible for securing these documents," Huston wrote. The story Huston told was full of mystery. "According to my sources, a copy of this report is stashed away in [Defense] Secretary [Melvin R.] Laird's vault. He may not be aware that he has it," Huston wrote. "At one time there was another copy over there, but it has disappeared."[11]

What's most mysterious about Huston's story is the sheer lack of evidence that this bombing halt report even existed. Haldeman eventually asked Huston, more than a year later, for the names of his sources; Huston said he couldn't remember.[12] The claim that ISA produced a report "on all events leading up to the bombing halt" was dubious, since no one in the Pentagon below the level of Defense Secretary Clifford got to see the NSA, CIA, and FBI intelligence on the Chennault Affair, Johnson having kept all copies of the reports under tight control.[13]

It wouldn't have been difficult, however, to mix up the kind of report Huston was talking about with an entirely different one that ISA actually did produce under Clifford, Warnke, and Gelb's leadership. That report covered all the events leading up to the *partial* bombing halt President Johnson ordered in March 1968. Huston referred to it, not entirely inaccurately, when he wrote, "Brookings also has a copy of a five-volume study of the Vietnam War which Secretary McNamara ordered prepared in the summer of 1967 before he left office." Brookings didn't have a copy and it was more than five volumes, but at least the Vietnam War study existed. Nixon didn't pay any attention to it at the time, but he would in 1971, when the *New York Times* got a copy and started publishing excerpts as the "Pentagon Papers." For the time being, he accepted as truth Huston's bad information about a bombing halt study at Brookings. Haldeman observed the president's reaction: "I reported this to Nixon who was irritated. He slammed a pencil on his desk, and said, 'I want that goddamn Gelb material and I don't care how you get it.'"[14]

## The Huston Plan

The same day that Huston warned his superiors about the phantom bombing halt report, March 13, 1970, he got a second memo into the president's hands: "SUBJECT: REVOLUTIONARY VIOLENCE."

An explosion tearing through the walls of a century-old brick townhouse on March 6, 1970, shattered the peace of a quiet Greenwich Village neighborhood and made plain the threat of domestic terrorism. Firefighters at first suspected a gas leak, but when police dug through the rubble, they found lead pipes packed with dynamite. They also found three bodies, one of them a woman "riddled with nails, the shrapnel of homemade antipersonnel bombs," Richard Reeves wrote. Members of the Weather Underground had been using the townhouse as an amateur bomb factory; they'd blown themselves up by accident.[1] On March 12, explosives detonated in three different Manhattan buildings between 1:00 and 2:00 a.m., and police spent the day evacuating buildings in response to another three hundred bomb threats.[2] "Bombings on Rise over the Nation," the *New York Times* reported. "Police Say Most Are Caused by Left-Wing Militants, Both Black and White."[3]

"In the last 48 hours we have had five separate incidents involving bombings," Huston wrote on March 13. "New York bombings have occurred in the offices of three large corporations—a new target of the revolutionaries." Huston painted a vivid picture of a threat to Nixon's personal safety as well as national security. "You should be aware that the most logical target at some point in time for these people is the President and the White House," Huston wrote. "Ask yourself how difficult it would be for a 23-year-old beauty to place her handbag with 5 sticks of dynamite in the ladies room of the residence while going through on a White House tour."[4] The following month, Huston became the White House point man on domestic terror.[5]

Nixon summoned the heads of the CIA, FBI, NSA, and the Defense Intelligence Agency (DIA) to the Oval Office on June 5 and gave them an apocalyptic dressing-down that Huston wrote for him. "We are now confronted with a new and grave crisis in our country—one which we know too little about. Certainly hundreds, perhaps thousands, of Americans—mostly under 30—are determined to destroy our society," Nixon said. The president ordered the four intelligence directors to prepare with Huston a report for him recommending ways to collect hard information on the young revolutionaries.[6] Specifically, Nixon told them to identify "restraints" on effective intelligence collection.[7]

In three weeks all the intelligence chiefs—with one crucial exception—had signed on to a report concluding that restrictions on wiretaps, mail opening, and break-ins were getting in the way of collecting valuable information.[8] The exception was J. Edgar Hoover, whose bureau would have to place the wiretaps, open the mail, and conduct the black bag jobs if Nixon lifted the "restraints." Hoover insisted that his objections be included in the report; Huston added them as footnotes. The footnotes had more impact than the report. On wiretaps and electronic bugging devices: "The FBI does not wish to change its present procedure of selective coverage on major internal security threats as it believes this coverage is adequate at this time."[9] On mail opening: "The FBI is opposed to implementing any covert mail coverage because it is clearly illegal." Moreover, Hoover thought the Post Office would leak to the press "and serious damage would be done to the intelligence community." The bureau, however, had "no objection to legal mail coverage providing it is done on a carefully controlled basis in both criminal and security matters."[10] On break-ins: "The FBI is opposed to surreptitious entry."[11]

Hoover also opposed the creation of a secret interagency domestic intelligence group with members from the CIA, DIA, NSA, FBI, the counterintelligence agencies of the Army, Navy, and Air Force, and "a White House staff representative [who] would coordinate intelligence originating with this committee in the same manner as Dr. Henry Kissinger, assistant to the President, coordinates foreign intelligence on behalf of the President"—that is to say, Tom Charles Huston.[12]

Hoover apparently had no objection to broadening the NSA's coverage of foreign communications to include US citizens using international facilities.[13] He refused, however, to endorse a single recommendation to loosen "restraints" on FBI intelligence gathering.[14]

Huston went ahead and recommended loosening them all. "Everyone knowledgeable in the field, with the exception of Mr. Hoover, concurs that existing [wiretap] coverage is grossly inadequate," Huston wrote in his eponymous plan.[15] He granted that covert mail coverage was illegal, but said the benefits outweighed the risk of exposure.[16] "Surreptitious entry," too, was "clearly illegal. It amounts to burglary. It is also highly risky and could result in great embarrassment if exposed," Huston wrote. But the NSA wanted the FBI to conduct black bag jobs to steal code-breaking material from foreign governments. Huston recommended "selective use" of illegal break-ins against "other urgent and high-priority internal security targets."[17]

Huston assured his superiors that Hoover would accept any decision Nixon made.[18]

President Nixon secretly approved the Huston Plan on July 14. "Even before the paperwork was authorized, the impatient Huston was supplying Haldeman with a ready target: the Brookings Institution," Fred Emery wrote in *Watergate: The Corruption of American Politics and the Fall of Richard Nixon*.[19] Huston wrote Haldeman on July 16:

> If we reach the point that we really want to start playing the game
> tough, you might wish to consider my suggestion of some months ago
> that we consider going into Brookings after the classified material
> which they have stashed over there. There are a number of ways we
> could handle this. There are risks in all of them, of course; but
> there are also risks in allowing the government-in-exile to grow
> increasingly arrogant and powerful as each day goes by.[20]

Haldeman told the new, secret White House coordinator of intelligence collection to inform the intelligence chiefs of the president's decision.[21] "Restraints on the use of surreptitious entry are to be removed," Huston wrote the directors of the NSA, CIA, DIA, and FBI on July 23. Restrictions on mail opening were "to be relaxed to permit use of this technique on selected targets of priority foreign intelligence and internal security interest." Wiretapping was "to be intensified." The directors would sit on a secret interagency committee to evaluate and coordinate domestic intelligence collection and "perform such other duties as the President shall, from time to time, assign." As for himself: "The President has assigned to Tom Charles Huston staff responsibility for domestic intelligence and internal security affairs. He will participate in all activities of the group as the personal representative of the President."[22]

J. Edgar Hoover "went through the ceiling," said Assistant FBI Director William C. Sullivan.[23] Hoover immediately went to John Mitchell. Nixon had appointed his campaign chairman as the US attorney general; technically, that made him the FBI director's boss. This was the first Mitchell had heard of the Huston Plan. The attorney general promised to talk the whole thing over with President Nixon. Hoover went back to his office and gave Mitchell a reason to oppose the plan.[24] The FBI director wrote a memo to Mitchell on July 25 saying he would comply with the president's orders—on one condition:

> Despite my clear-cut and specific opposition to the lifting of the various investigative restraints referred to above and to the creation of a permanent interagency committee on domestic intelligence, the FBI is prepared to implement the instructions of the White House at your direction. Of course, we would continue to seek your specific authorization, where appropriate, to utilize the various sensitive investigative techniques involved in individual cases.[25]

In other words, the attorney general would have to specifically approve individual wiretaps, mail openings, and break-ins. Personally.

On July 27, Huston got a call from the White House chief of staff saying the president was going to reconsider his plan along with Mitchell and Hoover. The White House asked each intelligence agency to return all copies of Huston's memo.[26] The Huston Plan was dead.

"Few noticed that almost exactly one month after Nixon withdrew his approval, a graduate student at the University of Wisconsin was killed by a bomb set off in the math building on campus," the historian Stephen E. Ambrose wrote. "The bomb was placed by the Weathermen, one of the chief targets of the Huston Plan. Who can say if a wiretap on a Weatherman phone might have saved the student's life?"[27] The question assumes that without the Huston Plan the FBI would somehow have been reluctant to tap Weathermen phones—an assumption that proved false. The former assistant FBI director William Sullivan, a strong supporter of the Huston Plan, told the *New York Times* in 1977 that Hoover had ordered the use of "any means necessary" against the Weather Underground in 1970: "Mr. Sullivan said that no specific reference had been made by Mr. Hoover to illegal break-ins, wiretaps or mail openings, but that this was the context in which discussions had taken place and that the statement was 'so clear it needed no interpretation from me.'"[28] Nixon's chief domestic policy adviser, John D. Ehrlichman, recalled Hoover regaling the president, attorney general, and him with stories of "the Bureau's triumphs over Weathermen" and foreign intelligence services during an October 1969 dinner at the director's home. These exploits involved activities later codified in the Huston Plan.

Later, in thinking back to that dinner, I realized that Hoover had every right to believe that both his superiors, Nixon and Mitchell, approved of FBI bugging, taps and bag jobs. He told us about FBI operations against domestic radicals and foreigners, and our reactions were enthusiastic and positive. The Bureau has made much of an order Hoover issued in the late sixties mandating the discontinuance of FBI illegal entries. Maybe so. But he certainly never mentioned that order at dinner in October 1969.[29]

"The irony of the controversy over the Huston Plan," Nixon wrote in his memoirs, "did not become apparent until a 1975 investigation revealed that the investigative techniques it would have involved had not only been carried out long before I approved the plan but continued to be carried out after I had rescinded my approval of it."[30]

By killing the Huston Plan, Hoover didn't bring an end to government break-ins and wiretaps, but he did block the Nixon White House from gaining a larger and secret role in selecting the targets. "I would rather it be the President exercising his judgment than the FBI agent in the field," Nixon wrote.[31] This was a president who exercised his judgment by ordering a break-in at a Washington think tank that wasn't even suspected of terrorism.

And he chose as his secret "personal representative" to the heads of the NSA, CIA, DIA, and FBI someone whose domestic intelligence credentials were on the thin side. Huston's main experience was as a conservative political activist in the Young Americans for Freedom. He founded the local chapter at Indiana University while picking up his undergraduate and law degrees, and rose through the ranks to become national chairman in 1965. The following year Huston endorsed Nixon for president.[32] In 1967–68, he reached his highest position within the nation's intelligence apparatus prior to joining the White House—a stint in the Army working on covert air reconnaissance at the DIA.[33] He also worked on Nixon's 1968 presidential campaign. In January 1969, he got a job on the White House speechwriting and research staff. His first intelligence-related assignment at the White House had political overtones: Nixon wanted evidence of foreign financial support for domestic campus disorders. Huston couldn't find much connection.[34] In October and November he monitored FBI intelligence about massive antiwar demonstrations, and in December he asked Assistant FBI Director Sullivan to prepare a report showing that the Weathermen were to blame for violence during the protests—a conclusion the Justice

Department did not share.[35] Huston wrote an early draft of Nixon's "enemies list," and placed Brookings at the top.[36] He urged Nixon to have the "IRS examine left-wing tax exempt organizations to be sure they were complying with the tax laws," congressional investigators found.[37] On the same day that the White House chief of staff informed him that the president had approved his plan, Haldeman also ordered Huston to use the Internal Revenue Service against the Brookings Institution. At the time, Brookings and the Institute for Foreign Policy Studies were holding weekly seminars that made "New Left Congressional Staffers" more effective, Haldeman's assistant Lawrence M. Higby wrote Huston on July 14, 1970: "With regard to the above you should go after Brookings and the Institute for Policy Studies. You should have the Internal Revenue [Service] make some discreet inquiries *if* it is political."[38]

"Making sensitive political inquiries at the IRS is about as safe a procedure as trusting a whore," Huston replied on July 16. "With the bark on, the truth is we don't have any reliable political friends at IRS whom we can trust and, as I suggested nearly a year ago, we won't be in control of the government and in a position of effective leverage until such time as we have complete and total control of the top three slots at IRS."[39] Huston was a political operative, not an intelligence professional.

Huston revealed the kind of secret police chief he would have made in a memo that's never been published. The subject was the Jewish Defense League (JDL). A pipe bomb exploded on November 25, 1970, outside the New York offices of the Soviet Union's state-run airline, Aeroflot. Anonymous callers taking credit for the blast signed off with the JDL's slogan, "Never again." The JDL's national director, Rabbi Meir Kahane, said his organization had nothing to do with the bombing, "but it applauds those who did bomb the offices." The president of the Anti-Defamation League of B'nai B'rith immediately denounced the bombing as a "mindless act of terrorism."[40] Israeli prime minister Golda Meir condemned it as well.[41] Another bomb exploded on January 8, 1971, outside the Soviet cultural mission in Washington, DC. An anonymous woman called news organizations and warned, "This is a sample of things to come." She, too, signed off, "Never again!"[42] Bombing an embassy is a federal offense. The FBI announced "an extensive investigation."[43]

How would Huston have responded to this new terrorist threat? In part by taking into account the possibility that the JDL's supporters might vote Republican. The man who recommended an expanded, secret, and in some ways illegal federal effort against terrorists of the political Left favored keeping "the federal presence to the minimum" for these new terrorists of the Right. Apologists for the Huston Plan should read its author's January 14, 1971, memo to Haldeman in full:

Before some of our more zealot guardians of "law and order" (particularly as it affects Soviet nationals and their property) launch a Federal pogrom against the JDL, it might be appropriate to consider several relevant factors: (1) the only propaganda advantage we have in the ideological contest between the United States and the Soviet Union is the systematic exploitation of Soviet Jewry by the CPUSSR—an over-kill of JDL could easily amount to booting away this cutting issue; (2) *despite the efforts of our few loyal Jewish friends, the Administration (and indeed the GOP) has not made major inroads into the Jewish voting community and the only inroads we have made (as reflected in Jim Buckley's race in New York City, for example) is with those lower-middle-class Jews of largely Eastern European origin who tend to identify with the JDL)*; (3) while we quite obviously must meet our international responsibility to safeguard Soviet life and property and while we cannot tolerate acts of violence regardless of the political disposition of the perpetrators, we should not resort to a shotgun solution to a problem that requires precise rifle fire—verbal assaults and federal injunctions do not get results, only professional police work at the local level does; and (4) while the "responsible" Jewish organizations quite properly have deplored the violence of the JDL, it will be quite another matter among responsible Jewish citizens if it looks like we are doing the Soviet Union's dirty work by putting the screws to all those who raise forcefully the issue of Soviet persecution of Jews—we could very easily bring down a hornets' nest of criticism if we over-react to the JDL provocations.

In short, we should attempt to identify those individuals responsible for acts of violence, collar them, and make it clear we will not tolerate lawlessness. However, we should keep the federal presence to the minimum, we should be quite precise in recognizing the legitimacy of the Jewish concern about Soviet treatment of Jews, and *we should not be unaware of the political significance of the hard-line attitude emerging in certain Jewish circles.* Moreover, we should above all not lose sight of the international significance of the Soviet Jewry question as a point of leverage in our relations with the Soviet Union. (italics added)[44]

The argument that "only professional police work at the local level" gets results—ironic, coming from the author of the Huston Plan—proved wrong in this case. The Feds got results using one of the techniques called for in the plan. FBI wiretaps played a part in building a case against Kahane that led to his pleading guilty to illegal possession of explosives.[45]

## Nixon Tapes

While the president was down in Key Biscayne, Florida, for Valentine's Day 1971, a handful of Secret Service technicians slipped into the Oval Office and drilled holes into the Wilson desk, where they mounted and concealed five microphones. The sconces holding lamps on either side of the fireplace provided hiding places for two more. The technicians hooked them up to two Sony 800B tape recorders in a locked metal cabinet in a locked room in the White House basement. The Technical Services Division had been reluctant to install the secret taping system; one of its missions was to *stop* anyone from bugging the Oval Office. But the president had ordered it.

He had his reasons, one in particular.[1] "Maybe we need something just to be sure that we can correct the record," he said on February 16, 1971, his first day of secret White House taping.[2] The desire for an incontrovertible record of presidential conversations was one Nixon shared with predecessors who taped. The first one to secretly record White House conversations, Franklin Roosevelt, had his system installed in 1940 after the *New York Times* allegedly misquoted him. (Roosevelt called the misquote "a deliberate lie.")[3] Johnson had used transcripts of a telephone briefing he'd given to the three presidential candidates in 1968 to challenge Nixon on Finch's "ducks in a row" charge. LBJ extolled the value of presidential taping. In 1988, Haldeman recalled that "Johnson had warned Nixon and me about what would happen. 'Everybody in this town,' he said, 'will call somebody else and say, the President wants this and the President wants that.'" The ones who had recently met with the president had extra credibility. "Sometimes the misreporting of fact had a bad intent, sometimes it represented a willful manufacture of false knowledge in order to gain some end," Haldeman wrote.[4] Nixon was already determined to document his White House years better than any predecessor had.[5] NSC staff made near-verbatim transcripts of his and Kissinger's meetings with foreign leaders. White House aides wrote up key Oval Office meetings.

Haldeman personally generated multitudinous records in his role as chief implementer of the presidential will. He kept a detailed diary chronicling the backstage drama starring the P (for President), K (Kissinger), and E (Ehrlichman). Haldeman carried a yellow legal pad at all times to take down Nixon's orders. Not that he followed all of them. "I soon realized that *this* president had to be protected from himself," Haldeman wrote. "Time and again I would receive petty vindictive orders."[6] He'd stall until Nixon reconsidered—or found an aide more willing to carry them out. Haldeman tried to protect Nixon from himself in lesser ways, too. When the president decided to secretly tape, Haldeman insisted on a voice-activated system. He didn't trust Nixon with a switch. The president's desk was equipped with buttons he could push to summon individual aides. He often pushed the wrong one. The voice-activated system installed in the Oval Office (and later Nixon's "hideaway" office in the building next door) saved Nixon trouble and aggravation in the short run, although it would ultimately backfire.

Nixon didn't realize that he was providing historians with the most complete, candid, and raw record of a presidency that has ever existed. The voice-activated recorders plus others that automatically started taping when Nixon used the phone provide an unusually accurate chronicle of a pivotal thirty-month period in Nixon's presidency and American history, something like a time machine for the ears. All told, the system recorded 3,432 hours of the presidency, several times more than the total hours of secret White House recordings of all the other presidents combined. Nixon's tapes provide an intimate, candid, close-up view of the man and his presidency.

## Tricia's Wedding

The front page of the Sunday, June 13, 1971, *New York Times* showed President Nixon, in formal wear, escorting his eldest daughter down the aisle in the first Rose Garden wedding ever. Blond, blue-eyed, ninety-five-pound Tricia Nixon looked as if she'd just stepped off the top of a wedding cake. The bride was "radiantly happy and beautiful on her father's left arm," the *Times* reported.[1]

Inside was a picture of the president dancing with his daughter. In his memoirs, Nixon wrote that it was the one time when "all of us were beautifully, and simply, happy."[2]

"They are so jealous, these women, you know," the president told his chief of staff as the two cooled their heels in the Oval Office waiting for the rain to stop long enough for the ceremony to begin. "They don't want Carruthers around." William H. Carruthers was the president's television adviser; Tricia's wedding was filmed for broadcast. Nevertheless, the bride and First Lady Pat Nixon made a lot of the decisions.

"It's terribly important that someone who knows something about it be getting that done right," Haldeman said. Nixon's chief of staff eyed the First Lady with barely repressed hostility. Behind her back, Haldeman called Pat Nixon "Thelma," her given name, which she hated so much that Dick Nixon didn't learn of it until he applied for their wedding license.[3]

"If I were running this show, I wouldn't have any women running anything," the president said. "I really wouldn't."

"I know," Haldeman said.

"I think they are too unstable to run anything," Nixon said. "Now, we have gone one step too far." He had appointed a woman as vice chairman of the Civil Service Commission. "Now they're bringing her in to swear her in. I mean, isn't that gilding it too much? Or is it?"

"Not as a quick swearing-in ceremony," Haldeman said.

"OK, fine. I just sort of feel sometimes that—"

"I agree, but half the voters are women," Haldeman said.

"You think they care?"

"Yep."

"All right. Do it," Nixon said. "The wedding will help a little with the women, I think."

"It sure as hell will," Haldeman said. "There's a TV series, *Father Knows Best,* or something like that—"

"Yeah!"

"It's been a good series. In one episode of it, one of the kids got married, and they did the wedding as part of the thing. It had almost double the biggest audience that any program in the series had ever had."

CBS had run a one-hour special on Tricia's wedding the night before.

"An hour?" the president asked.

"Yeah."

"What the hell'd they talk about?"

"I haven't any idea," Haldeman said. The network had sold $350,000 worth of ads for a second special to air after the ceremony.

"What'd they advertise?" Nixon asked. "Birth control pills?"

"No."[4]

Across the street from the White House in Lafayette Park members of the Religious Society of Friends held a vigil for peace. "We prayed for nice weather; she has a right to get married," one Quaker told the *Washington Post.*[5]

Nixon was a birthright Quaker. In his memoirs he wrote that his family went to church four times on Sundays and once more on Wednesdays.[6] The president suspected the young men in Lafayette Park of joining the Quakers to use the faith's pacifism to evade the military draft. "Haven't we got some long-haired son of a bitch that could go out there with the press corps and say, 'Gee, I'm just doing a little interview. How long have you been in the Friends meeting?'" he asked Haldeman. "There's a hell of a lot of these people, Bob, that are *new* Quakers."

"Yeah. Making it up."

"I don't believe in the Quakers being a haven for draft evaders. Any Quaker's got a perfect right to keep out of the war, because, you know, he's born that way, but goddamn it, they shouldn't join the Quaker church in order to avoid the war," the president said. "Hire long-haired, dirty-looking bastards."

"We do this kind of thing. Nobody knows we do," Haldeman said.

"Good," Nixon said. "Edgar Hoover, of course, isn't worth shit in this respect." The FBI director hired young men with crew cuts.

The president had another brainstorm: "I think I'd like to see a group of Long Hairs for Nixon. And Beards for Nixon."[7]

## The Pentagon Papers

The glowing coverage of Tricia Nixon's wedding shared the front page of the June 13, 1971, *New York Times* with another story: "Vietnam Archive: Pentagon Study Traces 3 Decades of Growing U.S. Involvement."

A massive study of how the United States went to war in Indochina, conducted by the Pentagon three years ago, demonstrates that four administrations progressively developed a sense of commitment to a non-Communist Vietnam, a readiness to fight the North to protect the South, and an ultimate frustration with this effort to a much greater extent than their public statements acknowledged at the time.

The 3,000-page analysis, to which 4,000 pages of official documents are appended, was commissioned by Secretary of Defense Robert S. McNamara and covers the American involvement in Southeast Asia from World War II to mid-1968—the start of the peace talks in Paris after President Lyndon B. Johnson had set a limit on further military commitments and revealed his intention to retire. Most of the study and many of the appended documents have been obtained by the New York Times and will be described and presented in a series of articles beginning today.[1]

Nixon's first discussion of what the *Times* dubbed the "Pentagon Papers" treated it as an afterthought. After calling his deputy national security adviser to find out the latest casualty figure, he asked, "Nothing else of interest in the world?"

"Yes, sir, very significant, this goddamn *New York Times* exposé of the most highly classified documents of the war," said Gen. Alexander M. Haig.

"I didn't read the story," Nixon said. None of the documents were from his presidency.

"It's brutal on President Johnson," Haig said. The Pentagon Papers revealed deception by the Johnson administration in seeking the Tonkin Gulf Resolution. The administration claimed that August 1964 North Vietnamese PT boat attacks on American destroyers in the gulf were unprovoked acts of Communist aggression, but the Pentagon Papers revealed that the administration had been mounting covert operations against Hanoi for months beforehand.[2] Johnson obtained the Tonkin Gulf Resolution under false pretenses. That didn't stop him from using it as a blank check for all subsequent escalations of the war, including the deployment of American combat troops. "Well, I'm sure it came from Defense, and I'm sure it was stolen at the time of the turnover of the administration," Haig said.

"Who in the Pentagon? I will fire the SOBs," the president said.

"They are all gone now," the general said. "Clifford, Halperin, Gelb." (Haig added a fourth name—Warnke—to his private list of suspects later that day.) Haig was just speculating, but if he had been trying to strike fear into the president's heart, he couldn't have chosen better names. Clifford, Warnke, and Gelb were three of the men who, according to Huston, possessed the legendary bombing halt report. The other name Haig mentioned, former deputy assistant secretary of defense for international security affairs Morton H. Halperin, aroused Nixon's fear of exposure regarding another secret. The president didn't discuss that now, but would turn to it repeatedly in the coming days.

"It's the most incredible thing," the general said. The *Times* ran six full six-column pages of verbatim documents and stories. "All of the White House papers, Rostow papers, communications with ambassadors, JCS studies."

"We have been more careful, haven't we?" the president asked. "We have kept a lot from State, I know, and enough from Defense."

"Your White House papers are in very good shape," Haig said.

"Let's say, apparently this is a fight within the Democratic Party and we are not going to get into it," Nixon said.[3]

Later that day, Haldeman asked Haig if the president had seen the story. "I told him it will keep Vietnam in the headlines," Haig said.

"If it keeps it in the headlines about eight years ago, this is not so bad," Haldeman said. "It may end up to be a great break."

"Could be. If we don't get roused up."

"Does the President understand that?"

"I think so."[4]

National Security Adviser Henry A. Kissinger also saw the Pentagon Papers at first as a political boon.

Kissinger: In public opinion, it, actually, if anything, will help us a little bit, because this is a gold mine of showing how the previous administration got us in there.

President Nixon: I didn't read the thing. Tell—give me your view on that in a word.

Kissinger: It just shows massive mismanagement of how we got there. And it pins it all on Kennedy and Johnson.

President Nixon: [*laughing*] Huh. Yeah![5]

The leak would help answer those who'd begun to call Vietnam "Nixon's War," Kissinger said. "From the point of view of the relations with Hanoi, it hurts a little, because it just shows a further weakening of resolve," he said.

Both Nixon and Kissinger told each other, however, that the leak was treasonable. Kissinger volunteered to talk with Attorney General John Mitchell.[6]

## The Secret Bombing of Cambodia

"How much does Halperin know?" Nixon asked Haldeman the next morning. "For example, does he know about the Menu series?"[1] Operation Menu was the code name for another secret the president didn't want the public to learn.

In the annals of unintended consequences, the secret bombing of Cambodia deserves shame of place. It touched off a series of escalating calamities whose intricate causal relationship would have taxed the comprehension of Rube Goldberg.

"It was the first turning point in my administration's conduct of the Vietnam war," Nixon wrote in his memoirs, which left out or denied the biggest parts of the story. Nixon's motives for bombing were several. He wrote about some of them: (1) The Johnson administration had been bombing the Ho Chi Minh Trail in Laos; the military wanted to bomb the trail in Cambodia, too. Cambodia was one of the places where North Vietnamese troops massed before attacking the South.

(2) A Communist offensive at the start of 1969 in South Vietnam was "a deliberate test, clearly designed to take the measure of me and my administration at the outset," Nixon wrote. "My immediate instinct was to retaliate." (3) Hanoi had violated the DMZ.[2]

Nixon's memoirs omitted other reasons: (1) Intelligence from a defector on the location of Hanoi's mobile military headquarters in Cambodia provided a tempting target for bombers.[3] (2) The Communists had resumed artillery attacks on South Vietnamese civilians, killing forty-five people in Saigon.[4] This is a point Nixon's memoirs sidestep: by sending shells across the DMZ and mounting rocket attacks on Southern cities, Communist forces had violated both of the military conditions LBJ set for the bombing halt. General Abrams, retained by Nixon as US military commander in Vietnam, urged the president to resume air strikes on the North.[5] LBJ had threatened to resume bombing if North Vietnam violated *any* of his conditions, and Abrams recommended the new president make good on that threat, but Nixon decided not to—even after Hanoi violated *two* conditions.

In his memoirs, Nixon implied that the secret bombing of Cambodia in some way served as a substitute for ending the bombing halt: "I said that short of resuming the bombing of North Vietnam, this was the only military action we could take that might succeed in saving American lives and getting the peace negotiations moving."[6] Despite Nixon's conviction that the Communist offensive in early 1969 was Hanoi's way of testing him, he didn't even discuss the possibility that one of the things the North Vietnamese were testing was whether he would make good on his predecessor's ultimatum.[7]

Secretary of State William P. Rogers and Secretary of Defense Melvin Laird opposed the secret bombing of Cambodia. Nixon made it sound as if the two were afraid to take the political heat. "They feared the fury of Congress and the media if I expanded the war into Cambodia," he wrote.[8] Rogers argued that the bombing would damage both the peace talks with Hanoi and relations with Cambodia; Laird saw minimal benefit coupled with a great potential downside of lost public support for the war if the secret got out.[9] One NSC aide, Richard L. Sneider, predicted that B-52 attacks on the Ho Chi Minh Trail would drive the North Vietnamese deeper into Cambodia and thereby increase Communist control of the country.[10]

Nixon gave more than one reason for keeping the air strikes in Cambodia secret. Cambodia's chief of state, Prince Norodom Sihanouk, had carefully preserved his nation's status as a neutral; because of that neutrality, no matter how much the prince objected to the North

Vietnamese presence in Cambodia's border areas, he couldn't endorse American bombing there, Nixon argued. But "as long as we bombed secretly, we knew that Sihanouk would be silent; if the bombing became known publicly, however, he would be forced to protest it publicly," Nixon wrote. The president did not ask the prince.[11] "I did not know about the B-52 bombing in 1969," Sihanouk said in a 1979 interview. "In 1968, I had told [US ambassador to India] Chester Bowles, *en passant*, that the United States could bomb Vietnamese sanctuaries, but the question of a big B-52 campaign was never raised."[12]

Nixon provided additional reasons: The North Vietnamese would have a hard time protesting the bombing, since they didn't admit having troops in Cambodia in the first place. "Another reason for secrecy was the problem of domestic antiwar protest. My administration was only two months old, and I wanted to provoke as little public outcry as possible at the outset," Nixon wrote.[13] Opposition would have come from more than just antiwar protestors. A secret poll commissioned by the Republican National Committee that summer showed only 35 percent support for bombing North Vietnamese forces in Cambodia, with 46 percent opposed.[14]

Reasons to keep the bombing secret swiftly multiplied. The B-52s never did destroy North Vietnam's military headquarters in Cambodia, which changed locations often.[15] While the bombing did disrupt Hanoi's supply lines and claim the lives of many of its soldiers, the North adapted by moving troops deeper into Cambodia.[16] Years later, after the secret was out, Sen. W. Stuart Symington, D-Missouri, asked General Abrams if North Vietnamese expansion into the Cambodian countryside was a predictable result of the bombing and other covert cross-border operations.

> Symington: As an experienced military man, would you not think this pressure made it almost inevitable that they would have to expand their area of control or operations, thus bringing them into increasing conflict with Cambodian authorities?
> Abrams: Yes, I think that is a fair statement.[17]

The effects on Prince Sihanouk's neutralist regime were calamitous. "More and more reports of serious clashes between the Communists and Cambodian villagers and troops reached Phnom Penh," the Cambodian capital, wrote William Shawcross in *Sideshow: Kissinger, Nixon and the Destruction of Cambodia*. "Sihanouk's balance of right against left became more precarious. The bombing was destabilizing him." In March 1970, while the prince was out of the country, the Cambodian

Right moved. Massive demonstrations in Phnom Penh culminated in the sacking of the North Vietnamese and Vietcong embassies.[18] The prince warned the Communists that if they failed to honor Cambodia's neutrality, pro-American forces would oust him in a coup.[19] In Sihanouk's absence, Gen. Lon Nol, Cambodia's premier and defense minister, set a deadline for North Vietnamese and Vietcong forces to withdraw.[20] Cambodian and North Vietnamese forces began shooting at each other before the deadline passed.[21] On March 18, Lon Nol fulfilled Sihanouk's prophecy and overthrew him.[22] The prince, in Russia, learned the news from Soviet premier Alexei Kosygin. Sihanouk immediately began plotting his return to power. At the Moscow airport before boarding an airplane for China, Sihanouk spoke of creating a government in exile.[23] In Beijing, Sihanouk made a radio broadcast calling for a guerrilla uprising against the new regime.[24]

This was no symbolic threat. As a hereditary monarch, Sihanouk commanded fierce, zealous loyalty in the Cambodian countryside. He had ruled as king from 1941 to 1955, stepping down only to become prime minister. In 1960, he once again became head of state and remained so until his 1970 overthrow. Before the coup, Cambodia had easily the most stable non-Communist government in Indochina. Not afterward. The overthrow of the prince struck many Cambodians as "an act of sacrilege," Shawcross wrote.

> Rioting broke out in several provinces; opposition was strongest in the market town of Kompong Cham, Cambodia's second city, 50 miles northeast of Phnom Penh. After Sihanouk's radio broadcast, the town filled with peasants, fishermen and rice farmers from the neighborhood. The townspeople refused the government's orders to remove the Prince's portrait, and they burned down the house of the new governor whom Lon Nol had appointed. . . . The most vivid display of anger against Lon Nol occurred, again in Kompong Cham, when peasants seized his brother Lon Nil, killed him and tore his liver from his stomach. The trophy was taken to a Chinese restaurant, where the owner was ordered to cook and slice it. Morsels were handed to everyone in the streets around.[25]

North Vietnam and the Vietcong pledged their support to Sihanouk.[26] So did Cambodia's tiny, indigenous Communist guerrilla movement.[27] The Vietnamese Communists used Prince Sihanouk's popularity as a recruiting tool to increase the ranks of the Cambodian Reds, known in their native tongue as the Khmer Rouge.[28]

At first blush, a pro-American government in Cambodia might have seemed like a good thing for America. Lon Nol did stop Hanoi's arms smuggling through the port of Sihanoukville, a major supply hub for the Vietcong.[29] But when the North Vietnamese retaliated by invading deeper into Cambodia, Lon Nol's military wasn't strong enough to stop them.[30] By the end of April 1970, Hanoi's forces were within artillery range of Phnom Penh, threatening to overthrow the pro-American government and replace it with one headed by Prince Sihanouk. This time, however, a Sihanouk regime wouldn't be neutral, but pro-Communist.[31]

"It was clear that Lon Nol needed help to survive," Nixon later wrote.[32] On April 30, the president went on television to announce a joint American and South Vietnamese offensive inside Cambodia. Nixon said it wasn't an invasion because once "enemy forces are driven out of these sanctuaries and once their military supplies are destroyed, we will withdraw." (The White House called it an "incursion," an unfamiliar term synonymous with invasion.) The president said nothing about the secret bombing or the role it had played in creating the crisis. He did more than conceal it, saying that "American policy since [1954] has been to scrupulously respect the neutrality of the Cambodian people."[33] The bombing was a break from that policy.

Nixon knew his decision to escalate the war publicly would draw protests.[34] He could not have foreseen, however, how bad things would get or how quickly. Students and faculty at Princeton voted to go on strike; clashes erupted between students and National Guardsmen at the University of Maryland and between protestors and police at Stanford University; a thousand University of Cincinnati students and others mounted a sit-in at one of the city's downtown intersections; two student antiwar groups announced plans for rallies in cities nationwide; the National Student Association called for the president's impeachment—and all that happened on the first day following Nixon's speech.[35] On May 2, protests turned violent. Molotov cocktails hurled from dormitory windows at Southern Illinois University injured three police officers. "At Kent State University in Ohio, a fire of undetermined origin swept through the one-story wooden R.O.T.C. building on the campus last night, and firemen were hampered by students cutting fire hoses and throwing stones," UPI reported.[36] On May 3, student strikes and protests spread.[37] On May 4, Haldeman walked into the Executive Office of the President, a second office Nixon kept in the building next to the White House, and told Nixon that National Guardsmen at Kent State had shot and killed four students. Haldeman captured the president's reaction in his diary.

He's very disturbed. Afraid his decision set it off, and that is the ostensible cause of the demonstrations there. Issued condolence statement, then kept after me all the rest of the day for more facts. Hoping rioters had provoked the shooting, but no real evidence they did, except throwing rocks at National Guard.[38]

Nixon was losing sleep. The night before his televised speech, the president went to bed for one hour. During his televised speech, there was a "horrifying moment when he lost his place on the script, but recovered beautifully," Haldeman wrote. The next day the president "was really beat," the chief of staff noted. "Really needs some good rest."[39] He let the president nap on May 4 before telling him about Kent State.[40] Exhaustion made the president testy. On May 7, Nixon "took me on tour of South grounds to discuss tennis court removal and life in general," Haldeman wrote. A memo from Interior Secretary Wally Hickel urging Nixon to communicate more with the young (and with his own cabinet) had leaked. "So he struck back by ordering the tennis court removed immediately," Haldeman wrote, a move aimed at racket-wielding cabinet members.

The president faced "the first general student strike in the nation's history," the *Washington Post* reported. Gov. Ronald Reagan had closed every state campus in California. More than one hundred thousand demonstrators were converging on Washington, DC. "Feels very concerned about campus revolt and basically helpless to deal with it. It's now clear that many are looking to him for leadership and to calm it down, and there's really no way he can do it," Haldeman wrote. "He's pretty tired, and he knows it. Went to bed early."[41] The next day the president held a televised press conference and announced that the first American troops would withdraw from Cambodia the following week.[42] He had ordered "absolutely no phone calls" afterward—until he realized the press conference was, in Haldeman's word, "masterful." The chief of staff and his crew stayed at the White House until half past midnight fielding calls before going home; then Nixon called Haldeman repeatedly until 2:00 a.m.[43]

Haldeman got a few hours' sleep before his phone rang again at 5:00 a.m. It was Ehrlichman, who said the president, unable to sleep, was at the Lincoln Memorial talking with antiwar demonstrators. "The weirdest day so far," Haldeman wrote. By the time Haldeman caught up to him, Nixon was at the US Capitol. They went out to breakfast at the Mayflower Hotel. "Very weird. P completely beat and just rambling on, but obviously too tired to go to sleep. All worked out fine, he got great press credit for doing the students, and wound down a little."[44]

The story of Nixon's early morning visit to the Lincoln Memorial has often been told, usually without the key bit of context that explains his emotional state. He had brought the invasion on himself. By ordering the secret bombing, his "first turning point" in waging the Vietnam War, Nixon had unintentionally (1) driven the North Vietnamese deeper into Cambodia, thereby (2) touching off clashes between them and rural Cambodians and (3) destabilizing Prince Sihanouk's neutral regime while (4) strengthening Cambodia's right wing and (5) prompting a coup against Sihanouk that installed a rightist, pro-American regime, whose attempts to rid Cambodia of the Vietnamese Communists produced the opposite result, since (6) the North Vietnamese retaliated by going even deeper into Cambodia, where they (7) threatened to overthrow the pro-American regime and replace it with a pro-Communist one. The invasion of Cambodia had other goals besides protecting Phnom Penh—including another attempt to locate and destroy North Vietnamese military headquarters and sanctuaries—but the risk that Hanoi would install a pro-Communist government in Cambodia was what made the invasion an urgent matter for Nixon at the time he launched it.[45]

The secret bombing had backfired catastrophically. Nixon intended to deprive the North Vietnamese of their sanctuaries in a strip of territory on Cambodia's border; instead, less than a year later, they were poised to make the entire country their sanctuary. As a result of his own bad choice, Nixon confronted even worse choices. He could either (1) let the North Vietnamese install a friendly regime in Phnom Penh, thereby increasing the threat to South Vietnam and the remaining American soldiers there, or (2) invade Cambodia with American ground forces to counter the invasion by North Vietnamese ones. When Nixon sent troops into Cambodia, it was to clean up the mess he had made.

And that created another mess at home. The unprecedented wave of protests (both the peaceful ones and the violent), the college closings, the shootings at Kent State and, soon afterward, at Mississippi's Jackson State—all these were unintended consequences of the invasion of Cambodia, itself an unintended consequence of the secret bombing. After the secret leaked, many questioned its morality and its legality; none should question its sheer ineptitude.

Nixon should have seen some of this coming. An NSC aide foresaw that air strikes on the Cambodian border could drive the North

Vietnamese farther into Cambodia.[46] Where else could they go to avoid the bombs? They couldn't evade the B-52s by heading north or south on the Ho Chi Minh Trail (since Nixon was then bombing it) or by heading east into South Vietnam (where Abrams regularly used the B-52s in battle). West, deeper into Cambodia, away from the border area, was the only direction the North Vietnamese could move to avoid the threat of the B-52s. Theirs was a predictable reaction, as General Abrams later acknowledged. The first consequence of the secret bombing, while unintended, should have been obvious.

Nixon's behavior in May 1970 does not seem so strange in the light of his knowledge that he had brought on multiple disasters, foreign and domestic, by his own actions. Although he had to live with that knowledge, he would ultimately stretch the boundaries of the law to conceal it from the nation.

Years later, after the secret bombing became public knowledge, Nixon and Kissinger took great pains to deny its first unintended consequence. Both claimed it had not driven the North Vietnamese deeper into Cambodia. They neglected, however, to get their stories straight. In *No More Vietnams*, Nixon claimed the bombing merely spread Hanoi's forces along the border area.

> Nor did our bombing destabilize Sihanouk's government. No evidence exists to show that our 1969 air strikes pushed the Vietnamese Communist forces deeper into Cambodia. These forces grew at the time of the bombing, both because a steady stream of new troops was coming down the Ho Chi Minh Trail and because the United States and South Vietnamese military sweeps in South Vietnam were pushing more Communist troops into Cambodia. But none of these forces went deeper into Cambodia as a result of the bombing. Communist forces simply dispersed themselves and their supplies more widely along the border with South Vietnam.[47]

Kissinger, on the other hand, claimed the secret bombing forced Hanoi's troops back into Vietnam.

> Nor is it true that the bombing drove the North Vietnamese out of the sanctuaries and thus spread the war deep into Cambodia. To the extent the North Vietnamese forces left the sanctuaries it was to move back into Vietnam, not deeper into Cambodia—until after Sihanouk was unexpectedly overthrown a year later. Then, North Vietnamese forces deliberately started to overrun Cambodian towns and military positions in order to isolate Phnom Penh and topple Sihanouk's successors.[48]

What Nixon and Kissinger denied publicly in print (each in his own, mutually contradictory way), they admitted privately on tape. The president bragged about the secret bombing to Treasury Secretary John B. Connally on May 4, 1972. Nixon even took credit for its code name, Operation Menu. (The air strikes on Cambodia were called Breakfast, Dinner, Dessert, Snack, Supper, and Lunch.)

President Nixon: Before we did Cambodia—this is not known to anybody—I had ordered, and we'd carried out, a series of strikes called the Menu strikes—nobody knows it—on Cambodia, on the sanctuaries, with B-52s. They were called the Menu strikes, well, because [*Kissinger attempts to interject*]—they were called the Breakfast strikes, and then I said, "All right, we're going to"—so I said, "All right, that's what"—that's what I don't imagine the bastards out there called them. I said, "Henry, the hell with that. A menu just isn't breakfast; let's have lunch and dinner, too." So we took Breakfast, Lunch and then we bombed the hell out of those sanctuaries. Nobody ever knew it, and they didn't say a goddamn word.

Kissinger: And actually, that led indirectly—

President Nixon: And that, incidentally, was over the violent objections of Rogers and Laird.

Kissinger: It led to the collapse of Cambodia because it pushed the North Vietnamese deeper into Cambodia, and as a result—

President Nixon: That triggered Cambodia.[49]

In other words, the secret bombing of Cambodia triggered the invasion of Cambodia.

The worst of the secret bombing's unintended consequences was yet to come. Once the Khmer Rouge had Sihanouk on its side, it was able to rally ordinary Cambodians to the cause of restoring the prince to power. The Communist guerrilla insurgency tapped the fervor of the Cambodian countryside's traditional, sometimes fanatical, monarchism. The Khmer Rouge grew in strength and numbers until, in 1975, it overthrew Lon Nol's regime. It then began a murderous reign of terror, horrifying even by the bloody standards of the twentieth century. From 1975 to 1979, the Khmer Rouge orchestrated a genocide that claimed the lives of 1.7 million Cambodian citizens.

During this time, the Khmer Rouge first used Sihanouk as a figurehead, then placed him under house arrest.[50] Sihanouk said in a 1979 interview, "There are only two men responsible for the tragedy in Cambodia today, Mr. Nixon and Dr. Kissinger."[51] In making this claim, Sihanouk ignored his own crucial role in the rise of the Khmer Rouge.

The genocide was not an inevitable consequence of the secret bombing. The Khmer Rouge didn't become a mass, popular movement until Sihanouk allied himself with it. But Sihanouk didn't do that until he was overthrown, and that didn't happen until the secret bombing drove the North Vietnamese deeper into his country, destabilized his regime, and aroused the ire of Cambodia's right wing. A straight line can't be drawn from the secret bombing to the Khmer Rouge's genocide, but there's no reason to believe the latter would have happened without the former. Nixon and Kissinger don't bear all the responsibility, but a crucial part of it is theirs.

In light of the horrific events that sprang, in part, from the secret bombing of Cambodia, it is understandable that Nixon and Kissinger would wish to deny responsibility for the unintended consequences of their actions. Nixon's tapes, however, expose their denials as hollow.

## Leaks

Bits and pieces of information—some accurate, some not—started leaking about the B-52 attacks on the Ho Chi Minh Trail in Cambodia before they even began. Before the first strike, *Newsweek* reported that "Diplomatic sources in Saigon claim Cambodia's Prince Sihanouk is tacitly permitting U.S. air raids on North Vietnamese and Vietcong bases and supply lines in sparsely populated areas along the Vietnam frontier."[1] The March 26, 1969, *New York Times* reported that "high State Department officials" strongly opposed air raids in Cambodia, but didn't mention that they had already begun.[2] Nevertheless, the *Times* reported on May 9, "American B-52 bombers in recent weeks have raided several Vietcong and North Vietnamese supply dumps and base camps in Cambodia for the first time, according to Nixon Administration sources, but Cambodia has not made any protest."[3]

By that point Nixon had ordered the FBI to start using wiretaps on officials the White House suspected of leaking.[4] Hoover somehow came up with the name of Morton Halperin, a thirty-year-old NSC aide recruited by Kissinger during the transition period.[5] The FBI director discussed his reasoning with Kissinger before ordering the tap on Halperin's home phone. The evidence was less than compelling: Halperin knew the reporter (hardly unusual, as one was a government official and the other a journalist). Halperin had once received a copy of a Communist publication, *World Marxist Review: Problems of Peace and Socialism*. (Given the US government's partial reliance on Communist publications for information about Hanoi, Moscow, and Beijing, it would have been more surprising if Halperin read just one.) The FBI director described Halperin as an "arrogant Harvard-type Kennedy man" and "part of the Harvard clique and, of course, of the Kennedy era." (Halperin taught at Harvard at the same time as Henry Kissinger—one of the reasons Kissinger hired him; they were both Republicans; and Halperin worked at the Pentagon during LBJ's presidency, not JFK's.)[6]

But the oddest thing about the wiretap on Halperin was that he just didn't know much about the secret bombing. He hadn't worked on it. He didn't have access to classified documents on it. The only reason he knew it happened at all was that Kissinger had mentioned it in conversation. When Kissinger told him he was suspected of being the source of the leak, Halperin said he didn't even know if the New York Times story was accurate.[7]

The wiretap never turned up any evidence that Halperin had disclosed classified information.[8] Yet the Nixon administration kept the tap on Halperin's home phone for twenty-one months. Even after he resigned from the White House staff in September 1969. Even after he resigned as a consultant to Kissinger in May 1970.[9] And even after he became an adviser to a Democratic presidential candidate, Sen. Edmund S. Muskie of Maine, who had been Humphrey's running mate in 1968.[10] The FBI wiretap on Halperin identified no leakers.

But it did provide the Nixon White House with useful political intelligence. The FBI overheard Halperin talking with his former Pentagon colleague Leslie Gelb about an article that former defense secretary Clark Clifford was writing for Life magazine criticizing Nixon on Vietnam. "He said that Clifford is concerned about 'sharpening up his attack on Nixon,'" the FBI director wrote to the president on December 29, 1969. There was nothing remotely illegal about a former defense secretary criticizing the policies of a president. It posed no threat to national security. Gelb and Halperin didn't even discuss any classified information in the wiretapped conversation. Nevertheless, Hoover sent a letter about Clifford's publication plans to the White House stamped "Top Secret."

"This is the kind of early warning we need more of," Ehrlichman wrote Haldeman. "Your game planners are now in an excellent position to map anticipatory action." The chief of staff agreed.[11]

Life put Clifford's article on the cover of its May 22, 1970, issue: "Clark Clifford on Vietnam: Set a Date and Get Out." It called for an end to all US combat operations in Vietnam by December 31, 1970, and complete withdrawal by December 31, 1971.[12] The former defense secretary drew on the advice of Warnke, Halperin, and Gelb. In other words, the article was the product of the four men Haig would later suspect of leaking the Pentagon Papers.

## The Wrong Men

Since Gelb, Halperin, Warnke, and Clifford fatefully dominated Nixon's thinking in the aftermath of the Pentagon Papers' leak, it's worth sorting out what they did together from what Nixon merely feared they were doing. Some fairly innocuous stuff wound up looking sinister to the president and some of his aides.

When Clifford took over the Pentagon on March 1, 1968, the other three were already working there in International Security Affairs:

— Director of Policy Planning and Arms Control for ISA Leslie Gelb reported to:

— Deputy Assistant Secretary of Defense for ISA Morton Halperin, who reported to:

— Assistant Secretary of Defense for ISA Paul Warnke, who reported to Clark Clifford.

ISA was known as "the State Department within the Defense Department."[1] It advised the secretary of defense on the foreign policy impact of military actions.[2] Since the bombing halt negotiations were all about the foreign policy implications of military actions, Clifford naturally turned to ISA when he took over the Pentagon. Clifford didn't know Warnke before becoming secretary of defense, but the forty-eight-year-old lawyer soon became his top adviser.[3] "His self-deprecating manner and casual style made him easy to work with, but I learned quickly that behind that easygoing style lay an incisive mind that cut fearlessly through the circumlocutions and evasions of others in the government," Clifford wrote.[4]

Halperin and Gelb were already working on the study the *Times* later dubbed the Pentagon Papers.[5] The idea for it came from Clifford's predecessor, Defense Secretary Robert S. McNamara, who by 1967 was wondering how the Vietnam War had gone so wrong. McNamara told ISA to do an encyclopedic, objective study answering a list of questions he had about America's involvement in the war.[6]

Halperin supervised the task force producing the study; Gelb took on the full-time job of managing it.[7] The project had no budget.[8] McNamara told them to keep its existence secret.[9] He later said he feared the document trail would get destroyed or lost.[10] Halperin and Gelb recruited experts from think tanks, universities, and inside the Pentagon.[11]

One with experience in all three and more was Daniel Ellsberg. A former US Marine, Ellsberg had worked for Warnke's predecessor, John T. McNaughton, in 1964–65. He then spent two years in Vietnam working for the State Department on pacification. A severe bout of hepatitis sent him back home in 1967. He was working at the RAND Corporation, the Santa Monica think tank, when Halperin recruited him for the Pentagon Papers.[12] Ellsberg had the right credentials and clearances.

Work on the study continued until the last month of the Johnson administration.[13] During the presidential transition period, Kissinger sought out both Ellsberg and Halperin for help on the next administration's biggest foreign policy challenge. National security policy can be a pretty small world. Kissinger invited Halperin to be guest speaker at the last class on national security policy he taught before becoming Nixon's national security adviser.[14] Gelb had been one of Kissinger's graduate students.[15] Kissinger had asked Ellsberg for advice during a fact-finding trip to Vietnam in 1965.[16] At Kissinger's request, Ellsberg and Halperin worked at Nixon transition headquarters in the Hotel Pierre on a "Vietnam Alternatives" paper that would lay out options for the Nixon administration with the pros and cons of each.[17] This paper would go out to every member of the National Security Council on the first day of the Nixon administration and be the subject of its first meeting.[18] Ellsberg also wrote a long list of questions about all aspects of the war for Kissinger to ask of military, diplomatic, and intelligence officials at the start of the new administration. Ellsberg's questions became the administration's first National Security Study Memorandum, or NSSM-1.[19]

In January 1969, Warnke, Halperin, and Gelb decided to store a copy of the Pentagon Papers at the RAND Corporation.[20] Harry Rowen, the head of the think tank, agreed to keep it in a top secret safe.[21] Warnke, Halperin, and Gelb would control access to the documents.[22] They kept them out of RAND's ordinary system for handling classified documents to keep the study's existence secret.[23] Under their rules, no one could see the Pentagon Papers unless at least two of them approved.[24]

At the start of the Nixon administration, Gelb left the government to become a senior fellow at the Brookings Institution. Halperin stopped working at the Pentagon and joined Kissinger's NSC staff.

In early 1969, Rowen asked permission for Ellsberg to read the complete Pentagon Papers. Halperin and Gelb said no. Rowen tried again, saying Ellsberg was working under contract with the Defense Department on lessons learned from the war, and the Pentagon Papers would help. Eventually, Halperin and Gelb agreed.[25] Ellsberg was still doing government work and had all the required security clearances. At about this time, Kissinger asked Ellsberg to come back to Washington and put together a summary of all the agencies' answers to the tough questions he'd raised about Vietnam in NSSM-1.[26] Ellsberg did that. Before he went home, he made copies of all the agency responses (and his summary of them) to take back with him to RAND.[27]

In the fall of 1969, after the massive clerical task of typing the seven-thousand-page Pentagon Papers study was complete, Halperin and Gelb decided who would get copies. Secretary of Defense Melvin Laird's office approved the list. Halperin and Gelb sent their copy to RAND.[28] Another copy went to the law firm of Clifford and Warnke, who had set up practice together at the end of LBJ's term. Defense Department security officers converted a closet in their law offices into a "security storage area" for classified documents. This wasn't unusual. Former government officials often take copies of top secret documents with them when they retire. Neither partner read the Pentagon Papers, however, until after the *New York Times* started publishing leaked excerpts.[29]

After Halperin left Kissinger's NSC staff in September 1969, he followed in Gelb's footsteps and became a senior fellow at Brookings.[30] "Halperin became part of a small group of people that included Gelb and Warnke, on whom I relied for advice on Vietnam," Clifford wrote. "They were later joined by Tony Lake, an outstanding young Foreign Service Officer who had resigned as Henry Kissinger's aide in protest against the invasion of Cambodia."[31]

All this activity can be placed under the heading "Policy Makers Turn to Experts for Advice." It's "Dog Bites Man" stuff—nothing unusual or noteworthy about it. The professional relationships of Clifford, Warnke, Halperin, Gelb, and Ellsberg are worth mentioning only because they became the subject of intense scrutiny (and fantasy) after one of them, unbeknownst to the others, engineered the biggest leak of classified information the nation had yet seen.

## "Charge Gelb"

By the morning after the *Times* started publishing the Pentagon Papers, Nixon had his targets picked out. "G-E-L-B. At Brookings," he told his chief of staff.

"They knew he had all these files," Haldeman said.

"Why didn't we go get them, then?"

"Well, remember, I talked to you about that a year ago. Tom Huston was all alarmed," Haldeman said. "He argued that what we should do is send some people in on a routine—they have a secure safe over there to hold this stuff in—move some people in on a routine security check, find this stuff in it and confiscate it, and walk out."

"Why didn't we do it, Bob?"

"I don't know," Haldeman said.

"There's another one that's involved in this, is Halperin," Nixon said.

"That's right," Haldeman said. "Halperin and Sam Gelb have been working together." (Gelb's first name is Leslie.)

"Remember, Edgar Hoover was right on Halperin," Nixon said. "Remember, he was the one that put the finger on him." The president worried about current members of Kissinger's staff, too. "Chrissakes, he went over and talked to Brookings people himself. I warned him about it. I said, 'Henry, don't go over there.' You know, I said, 'Those people—that's the Democratic National Committee!' "

"That's right," Haldeman said.

"They are a bunch of bastards," the president said. "They'll lie, cheat, anything—and then squeal when somebody else does."

The facts in the Pentagon Papers hurt the Democrats, Haldeman said, but they also hurt the credibility of the government itself. "To the ordinary guy, all this is a bunch of gobbledygook. But out of the gobbledygook comes a very clear thing, which is: you can't trust the government, you can't believe what they say and you can't rely on their judgment. And that the implicit infallibility of presidents, which has been an accepted thing in America, is badly hurt by this, because it shows that people do things the President wants to do even though it's wrong. And the President can be wrong," Haldeman said.

"Tell you what I want done: Get the story out on Gelb right away for a columnist to use. I want that out," Nixon said. "Charge Brookings. Let's get Brookings involved in this. Get Brookings involved. Another way to do it, rather than having them to do that, is to have a senator make a speech on the Senate floor." Senators and representatives are immune from libel suits for accusations made on the floor of Congress. "That might be better than to have a column," the president said. "Charge Gelb. Use his name. Had the information. He leaked it."[1]

The White House had no evidence that he did.

## LBJ Cracks the Case

"What is your view as to how to handle this?" Nixon asked his secretary of state, William Rogers, later that morning.

"Well, I think on that we should just 'No Comment' it," Rogers said. "I don't think it's too, too massive a work, and it doesn't really relate to us very much."

"Not at all. As a matter of fact, there's nothing in it, as you know, since we came in," Nixon said.

"Well, I wasn't thinking about directly. But, I mean, indirectly it doesn't really relate, either."

"Well, in a sense, though, I suppose its destructiveness is that it casts a very grave doubt on the, frankly, on government people. I mean, that presidents lie and so forth. Both Kennedy and Johnson. You know, and actually, they do," the president said. "I mean, there has to be some. Sometimes you don't tell everything."

Gen. Alexander Haig entered the Oval Office. "I had a call last night from Walt Rostow," Haig said. "And President Johnson and Walt are both very upset about this."

Nixon laughed.

"For obvious reasons," Haig added.

"Wouldn't you be? You realize, though, what it is: it shows that Johnson, in effect, didn't tell the American people the truth before his election," Nixon said. "That's why they may think that we put it out."

"There's some suspicion of that," Haig said.

"Well, Johnson doesn't have that suspicion, does he?" Nixon asked. "Good God, I wouldn't do that."

"No," Haig said, "I called Walt first thing yesterday morning. I said, 'You'd better get the *New York Times,* and you better read this.'" Haig said Rostow called back "late last night and he said, 'Now, I don't want to cast any aspersions about who might have done this, but our strong suspicion is it's Dan Ellsberg.'" Rostow had viewed Haig's list of suspects skeptically. "He said he doesn't think it's Gelb. It may be; he says he doesn't think so." Rostow didn't think it was Halperin either.

"Ellsberg. I've never heard his name before," Nixon said.

"He said whoever did this could not be a good Democrat," Haig said.[1]

This was putting it mildly. Halperin and Gelb were both trying to elect a Democrat president. Exposing the dirty laundry of the two previous Democratic presidents was not the surest way to do that. It would further divide an already divided party. As advisers to the Democratic front-runner, Halperin and Gelb were well positioned to get even better jobs than they'd previously held if he was elected. Not, however, if they engineered the greatest unauthorized disclosure of classified information in history thus far. Doing that would have meant abandoning all hope of ever getting a security clearance again, much less a high government position. Only someone willing to sacrifice his future in government would leak the Pentagon Papers. Neither Halperin nor Gelb was.

## Ellsberg's Decision

Ellsberg's views on the Vietnam War had evolved rapidly over the years. "I saw it first as a problem, next as a stalemate, then as a moral and political disaster, a crime," he wrote.[1]

Nixon and Kissinger inadvertently inspired Ellsberg's decision to leak the Pentagon Papers. On September 30, 1969, Ellsberg opened his front door, picked up the *Los Angeles Times,* and read the top story: "The Army Monday overruled its field commander in Vietnam and dismissed murder charges against eight Green Berets suspected of killing a Vietnamese double agent." The case had been on front pages, magazine covers, and the nightly news for weeks.

> The victim in the case was reported to be Thai Khac Chuyen, 31, a native of North Vietnam, who had been employed by the Special Forces since December 1965. First he worked as an interpreter, then began—according to sources here—working on secret missions in Cambodia connected with allied efforts to keep track of Communist operations and infiltration there. Information reportedly became available that Chuyen had taken part in meetings with Communist intelligence officers. After interrogation—both with lie detectors and under the so-called truth serum sodium pentothal—these charges were allegedly considered confirmed by Special Forces officers. On June 20, Chuyen was reported to have been shot, his body placed in a weighted bag and the bag sunk in the South China Sea.[2]

Although little-remembered today, the Green Beret case introduced a dire euphemism to the American lexicon.

> Local CIA officials reportedly told the Army group to "terminate with extreme prejudice" Chuyen's employment—a phrase said to mean death. Then, according to other reports, the CIA rescinded that direction and urged that Chuyen not be killed. But by then, according to the report, Chuyen was already dead.[3]

In his diary, Haldeman called the case a "real PR problem for the P and administration. Army plans to go ahead with court-martial which will bring out a lot of secret activity, but worse it will give great fodder to the anti-war types, which is just what we don't need as school opens."[4] General Abrams insisted on going forward with the court-martial; so did Secretary of the Army Stanley R. Resor. The president was "justifiably furious" with Defense Secretary Laird for not stopping it, Haldeman wrote, but Kissinger figured out how to make it go away.

> K feels he finally has the Green Beret problem under control. The CIA has been ordered to refuse to let their men testify as witnesses. [CIA Director Richard M.] Helms really dragged his feet, but finally gave in. Now Laird has to get Resor to cancel the trial for lack of case. Will be hard to do, but should have been done months ago, the publicity, especially TV, is really damaging. Laird could have closed it up, and said he was doing so, but didn't, in face of Resor determination to go ahead.[5]

Kissinger's way worked. "K got his Green Beret trial turned off, with Resor dropping the charges because no CIA witnesses," Haldeman wrote on September 29.[6] The president and his men learned a terrible lesson, one they would apply to future problems: they could use the CIA as a brake on the wheels of justice.

Ellsberg had a different sort of epiphany.

> This is the system that I have been working for, the system I have been part of, for a dozen years—fifteen, including the Marine Corps. It's a system that lies automatically, at every level from bottom to top—from sergeant to commander in chief—to conceal murder. That described, as I had come to realize from my reading that month, what that system had been doing in Vietnam, on an infinitely larger scale, continuously for a third of a century.[7]

He'd been reading Warnke, Halperin, and Gelb's copy of the Pentagon Papers at RAND. The study of US involvement in the Vietnam War over the decades confirmed the view that although "we could prolong it year by year, we had no better prospect of winning that struggle than the French had had. Again, zero. That last point, on prospects, had been presented by authoritative advisers to every president from Truman on," Ellsberg wrote. "Each had been told of the likelihood that his chosen approach (and, as some advisers told each of them, any approach) would be stalemated and would at best postpone departure and defeat."

Yet Truman, Eisenhower, Kennedy, and Johnson each had deepened, not ended, American involvement in the war.

At first Ellsberg had felt reassured by Nixon's choice of Kissinger as national security adviser.[8]

> In 1967 and 1968 I had been with him in conferences on Vietnam, where he was expressing a point of view that was well in advance of that of any other mainstream political figure at that point. He argued that our only objective in Vietnam should be to get some sort of assurance of what he called a "decent interval" between our departure and a Communist takeover, so that we could withdraw without the humiliation of an abrupt, naked collapse of our earlier objectives. He didn't spell out how long such an interval might be; most discussions seemed to assume something between six months and two years.

Ellsberg didn't think the war should go on another day, much less for a "decent interval," but Kissinger's objective at least sounded more realistic to him than that of any other mainstream political figure at the time. Nixon's choice of Kissinger as his top foreign policy adviser suggested that the new president was getting out of Vietnam.

But by the summer of 1969, after Halperin had gained insider experience working in Kissinger's NSC, he told Ellsberg that Nixon was staying in the war. To someone who had read the Pentagon Papers, "it was not terribly surprising. It meant simply that a new president was following in the footsteps of his four predecessors," Ellsberg wrote. "Nixon had no readiness at all to see Saigon under a Vietcong flag after a 'decent interval' of two or three years—or ever. Not, at least, while he was in office."

Ellsberg was terribly mistaken. By the time he leaked the Pentagon Papers, Nixon and Kissinger had adopted a "decent interval" exit strategy for Vietnam. As the historian Jeffrey Kimball discovered, Kissinger had written a note in the margin of his massive briefing book for Polo I, the secret visit to Beijing that was a pivotal moment in the diplomatic opening to China: "We want a decent interval. You have our assurance."[9] Nixon and Kissinger would use China's influence as Hanoi's second-biggest supplier of military aid to get North Vietnam to accept a settlement that would put a "decent interval" of a year or two between Nixon's final troop withdrawal and Saigon's final collapse. Kissinger laid out the essentials of a deal the day he met Chinese premier Zhou Enlai: Nixon would withdraw all American ground forces completely from South

Vietnam when Hanoi freed American prisoners of war, but North Vietnamese forces would remain as part of a cease-fire-in-place. During the cease-fire, the North and South would engage in negotiations. "If the agreement breaks down, then it is quite possible that the people in Vietnam will fight it out," Kissinger told Zhou on July 9, 1971. "If the [South Vietnamese] government is as unpopular as you seem to think, then the quicker our forces are withdrawn, the quicker it will be overthrown. And if it is overthrown after we withdraw, we will not intervene." It was an extraordinary statement. Kissinger didn't qualify this assurance. He didn't limit it to intervention by air power or by ground forces. He just said that Nixon would not intervene. "Our position is not to maintain any particular government in South Vietnam. We are prepared to undertake specific obligations restricting the support we can give to the government after a peace settlement and defining the relationship we can maintain with it after a peace settlement," Kissinger said.

"But you have a prerequisite with that, that is, a ceasefire throughout Indochina," Zhou said.

"For some period of time," Kissinger said. "We can put on a time limit, say 18 months or some period."[10] A year or two—that was the length of the "decent interval" Nixon and Kissinger sought. These quotes come from transcripts of the Beijing negotiations by Kissinger's own NSC. Nixon's tapes confirm their intent. "We've got to find some formula that holds the thing together a year or two," Kissinger told Nixon on August 3, 1972.[11]

Nixon and Kissinger's plans were radically different from what Ellsberg thought. Halperin had told him that Nixon planned to keep at least fifty thousand, and perhaps as many as two hundred thousand, American soldiers in Vietnam indefinitely. In fairness to Halperin, at the time he worked on Kissinger's NSC staff in 1969, Nixon was still demanding *mutual* withdrawal, insisting that the Americans would leave South Vietnam when the North's forces did. By May 1971, however, Kissinger was telling Hanoi in secret talks that the United States would agree to complete, unilateral American withdrawal from the South, even though Hanoi's armed forces would remain there.[12]

Ironically, Ellsberg had in his possession a document that could have exposed the fraudulence of Nixon's exit strategy. NSSM-1, the review of Vietnam policy begun on the first full day of the Nixon administration, revealed many disagreements within the US government on the war, but on one point there was unanimity.

The question was whether the South Vietnamese army, once fully "modernized" (trained and equipped by the Americans), would be able to stand up to its North Vietnamese counterpart in the absence of American combat troops. The unanimous answer was no.

Every military, diplomatic, and intelligence agency canvassed for NSSM-1 agreed that South Vietnam would depend on American combat troops for its survival for the indefinite future: "All agencies agree that RVNAF [Republic of Vietnam Armed Forces] could not, either now or even when fully modernized, handle both the VC [Vietcong] and a sizable level of NVA [North Vietnamese Army] forces without U.S. combat support in the form of air, helicopters, artillery, logistics and major ground forces."[13]

The consensus included the Joint Chiefs of Staff, the secretaries of state and defense, the US embassy in Saigon, the CIA, and General Abrams. There were no dissenters. Just a few months after NSSM-1 was completed, however, Nixon announced that he would withdraw *all* American ground forces once his modernization program ("Vietnamization") was complete—even if Hanoi didn't agree to a settlement that included mutual withdrawal.

> We have adopted a plan which we have worked out in cooperation with the South Vietnamese for the complete withdrawal of all U.S. combat ground forces, and their replacement by South Vietnamese forces on an orderly scheduled timetable. This withdrawal will be made from strength and not from weakness. As South Vietnamese forces become stronger, the rate of American withdrawal can become greater.[14]

According to the military, diplomatic, and intelligence officials who took part in NSSM-1, the South Vietnamese would never be able to replace American combat forces completely. If they were right, the strategy Nixon announced couldn't succeed: "Under the new orders, the primary mission of our troops is to enable the South Vietnamese forces to assume the full responsibility for the security of South Vietnam."[15]

Nixon stretched American military withdrawal from Vietnam through all four years of his first term. He said he needed the time for Vietnamization to work. Actually, he needed the time to conceal the reality that Vietnamization would never work. He prolonged the war to prevent South Vietnam from collapsing before Election Day 1972 and taking his chances of a winning a second term down with it. "If we can, in October of '72, go around the country saying we ended the war and the Democrats wanted to turn it over to the Communists, then we're in great shape," Kissinger told Nixon on May 29, 1971. "But on the other hand, if Cambodia, Laos and Vietnam go down the drain in September

'72, then they'll say you went into these, you spoiled so many lives, just to wind up where you could've been in the first year."[16]

In August 1972, after three-and-a-half years of modernizing Saigon's army, Nixon told Kissinger in the privacy of the Oval Office, "I look at the tide of history out there, South Vietnam probably can never even survive anyway. I'm just being perfectly candid."[17] It was an admission he never dared make in public, given the thousands of American lives he sacrificed in the name of giving Vietnamization time to succeed.[18]

It's fascinating to speculate what would have happened if, instead of leaking the Pentagon Papers, Ellsberg had decided to leak NSSM-1 in the spring of 1971. It would have revealed the consensus among Nixon's advisers that Saigon could not survive without major American ground forces—in other words, that Vietnamization could not work as advertised. But Ellsberg believed that Nixon was planning to escalate the war to keep Saigon from falling during his presidency, and he leaked the Pentagon Papers because he thought they showed how Nixon's predecessors did that as well.[19]

## Fear of a Damaging Disclosure

The publication of the Pentagon Papers did arouse Nixon's fear that his own secrets would leak. He didn't know Ellsberg had NSSM-1; in fact, he didn't know Ellsberg had even worked on NSSM-1, since Kissinger hadn't told him before and wasn't about to tell him now. Instead, Nixon worried that someone would reveal the truth about the secret bombing of Cambodia.

Kissinger: The reason you have to be so tough, also, Mr. President, is because if this thing flies on the *New York Times,* they're going to do the same to you next year. They're just going to move file cabinets out during the campaign. I mean, these guys—
President Nixon: Yeah, they'll have the whole story of the Menu series and—
Kissinger: Well, we keep our files separately, Mr. President—
President Nixon: I know. I know.[1]

While individual reports about American air strikes in the Cambodian border area had made it into print, the full story had not. Americans did not then know that the president's first major move in the Vietnam War had yielded disaster abroad and at home—the destabilization of the Sihanouk regime, the coup, the threat of a Communist takeover of

Cambodia, Nixon's order to invade, the wave of protests across America, the violence, Kent State.

None of Nixon's national security rationales for keeping Operation Menu secret applied any longer. In 1971 he couldn't claim he needed to keep it secret because otherwise Cambodia's neutralist regime would protest; Cambodia's government was pro-American and hadn't protested when he intervened with ground troops in the country. During the invasion, Nixon *openly* bombed Communist forces in Cambodia. For the same reasons, he could no longer say the bombing needed to be secret to avoid protests from Hanoi. Nixon could still say he was worried about an American public outcry, but that concern hadn't kept him from ordering the invasion—and fear of unpopularity never was a legitimate reason to keep information classified. Disclosure of the secret bombing of Cambodia was no longer in any way a threat to American national security, but it certainly was a threat to Nixon's political well-being. If the truth got out, voters could hold the president accountable for the consequences of his actions. Legally, that was no reason to keep it secret; politically, it was a compelling one.

Some claim that once the *Times* ran a front-page story on the initial raids in May 1969, the bombing of Cambodia was no longer a secret. In later years, Kissinger sometimes referred to "the so-called secret bombing of Cambodia," or put it in scare quotes ("the 'secret bombing'") or did both at the same time ("the so-called 'secret bombing'").[2] But a smattering of unconfirmed reports do not turn classified information into public knowledge. Official confirmation didn't come until July 1973, when a former Air Force major revealed the bombing to the Senate Armed Services Committee.[3] Before then, President Nixon certainly treated it as a secret. His tapes capture him worrying that it would leak more than two years after it began. When he revealed it to Treasury Secretary Connally in May 1972, the president prefaced his disclosure by saying, "This is not known to anybody."[4]

Crucially for Nixon, no stories had appeared in print drawing the connection between the secret bombing of Cambodia and all of its calamitous consequences. The "whole story of the Menu series," as Nixon put it, remained untold. That meant it could still do him great damage politically.

## Legal Action

Fear of future leaks of his own secrets drove Nixon's response to the Pentagon Papers much more than the unauthorized disclosure of the

Defense Department's history of Vietnam. "You cannot have a massive security breach in government," he told Haldeman on June 15. "Christ, if you do, they're going to steal that stuff from us. You know? That's what I'm thinking of. I'm thinking of our own stuff. You've got to put papers on warning, and others that would go out and do this, that, by God, they're going to be prosecuted."[1]

Nixon spent little time deliberating before launching an unprecedented First Amendment battle with the *Times*. Then again, he didn't realize he was doing that.

"The attorney general has called a couple times about these *New York Times* stories, and he's advised by his people that unless he puts the *Times* on notice he's probably going to waive any right of prosecution against the newspaper," Ehrlichman told Nixon at 7:13 p.m. on June 14, 1971, the second day of the Pentagon Paper series. "And he is calling now to see if you would approve his putting them on notice before their first edition for tomorrow comes out."

"Hell, I wouldn't prosecute the *Times*," Nixon said. "My view is to prosecute the goddamn pricks that gave it to them."

"Yeah, if you can find out who that is."

"Yeah, I know," Nixon said. "Could the *Times* be prosecuted?"

"Apparently so."

"Wait a minute, wait a minute," the president said. "They're going to run another story tomorrow." At the end of Monday's six-page spread, the *Times* had included a preview: "Tomorrow: The President Orders a Ground-Combat Mission." LBJ's decision to send combat forces to Vietnam in 1965 was the pivotal one in "Americanizing" the war.[2] "Why doesn't he just wait until after that one?" Nixon asked.

"He apparently feels under some pressure to either decide to do it, or not do it," Ehrlichman said.

The president chuckled. "Does he have a judgment himself as to whether he wants to or not?"

"Yeah, I think he wants to," Ehrlichman said. "You might want to give him a call and talk with him about it directly, as I'm not very well posted on this whole thing."[3]

Four minutes later, the president asked Attorney General John Mitchell the key question: "Has the government ever done this to a paper before?"

"Oh, yes, advising them of their—"

"Oh."

"Yes, we've done this before," Mitchell said.

"Have we? All right," Nixon said. "As far as the *Times* is concerned, hell, they're our enemies. I think we just ought to do it."[4] The president had decided the matter by 7:22 p.m., nine minutes after he first heard of it.

A telegram from the attorney general to the *Times* stated that publishing "information relating to the national defense of the United States" that "bears a Top Secret classification" violated the 1917 Espionage Act.

> Moreover, further publication of information of this character will cause irreparable injury to the defense interests of the United States.
>
> Accordingly, I respectfully request that you publish no further information of this character and advise me that you have made arrangements for the return of these documents to the Department of Defense.

The *Times* respectfully declined, saying disclosure was in the nation's interest.[5] The Justice Department responded by seeking an injunction blocking the *Times* from publishing any more of the Pentagon Papers. The government had never exercised "prior restraint" to prevent the publication of a newspaper article on national security grounds—a fact unknown to both the president and attorney general when they decided to take the *Times* to court.[6]

"We've got a good judge on it, Murray Gurfein," Mitchell told the president. Gurfein was one of Nixon's Jewish appointees; the Pentagon Papers case was his first.

"I know him well," the president said. "Smart as hell."

"Yeah, and he's new, and he's appreciative, so . . ."

The president chuckled. "Good."[7]

Gurfein placed a temporary restraining order on the *Times* while he decided the case. Even this temporary order was unprecedented.[8]

Before the judge could decide whether to grant the government a permanent injunction, the *Washington Post* got hold of the Pentagon Papers and began publishing its own series on June 18.[9] Mitchell took the *Post* to court that day, but District Court Judge Gerhard A. Gesell wouldn't place a temporary restraining order on the newspaper. Mitchell immediately appealed, and, at 1:20 a.m., the US Court of Appeals reversed Gesell.[10] Now the *Post* was blocked from publishing the Pentagon Papers as well.

Once Judge Gurfein got the opportunity to hear the administration's arguments that the Pentagon Papers would do irreparable harm to national security, he was unconvinced, to put it mildly. The Justice Department provided "no cogent reasons" to think the Pentagon Papers would do more than embarrass the government, Gurfein wrote, and that wasn't a strong enough reason to block publication. "From the time of Blackstone it was a tenet of the Founding Fathers that precensorship was the primary evil to be dealt with in the First Amendment," Gurfein wrote. The judge implied that the decision wasn't a particularly difficult one to make: "Fortunately, upon the facts adduced in this case, there is no sharp clash such as might have appeared between the vital security interest of the nation and the compelling constitutional doctrine against restraint." The *Times* won that round.[11]

Judge Gesell was equally unimpressed with government's case against the *Post*. "There is no proof that there will be a definite break in diplomatic relations, that there will be an armed attack on the United States, that there will be an armed attack on an ally, that there will be a war, that there will be a compromise of military or defense plans, a compromise of intelligence operations, or a compromise of scientific and technological materials," Gesell wrote. He, too, denied the administration an injunction against the newspaper. The case was heading for the Supreme Court.

From the decisions of Judges Gurfein and Gesell, the president drew a bigoted lesson about "all those damn New York Jews" and "the Washington kikes" for his attorney general and other, non-Jewish aides in the Oval Office. "You can never put, John, any person who is a Jew in a civil rights kind of case, or freedom of the press kind of case, and get even a 10 percent chance," the president said on June 22. "Basically, who the hell are these people that stole the papers? It's too bad. I'm sorry. I was hoping one of them would be a Gentile. But, gee, they're all"—he pounded the desk on the last word. "The three Jews. You know? The three suspects. The other fellow. All Jews. I go clear back to, as I said, the whole damn Communist thing." The president ran through a list of Jews named in the Alger Hiss spy case. "They ran off tons of documents and turned them over to the Communists. And boy, if you think things are bloody now, you should have seen how bloody it was then," Nixon said. "'Witch hunt,' 'McCarthyism' and so forth."[12]

Less than a month after Congressman Nixon took to the House floor to celebrate the perjury conviction of Alger Hiss, a backbench Republican senator from Wisconsin named Joseph R. McCarthy climbed on his bandwagon. McCarthy plagiarized Nixon's Hiss speech for a Lincoln Day dinner address he gave in Wheeling, West Virginia, on February 9, 1950, but he added a sensational twist of his own. "I have here in my hand a list of 205 that were known to the secretary of state as being members of the Communist party, and who nevertheless are still working and shaping the policy in the State Department," McCarthy said.[13] The following night in Salt Lake City, McCarthy changed the number, saying he had the names of "57 card-carrying Communists" working at State.[14] McCarthy's meteoric rise had begun, but it bore the seeds of his fall.

"He came to see me in Los Angeles," Nixon recalled for Mitchell in the Oval Office. McCarthy had learned one lesson from the Hiss case: documentation provides credibility. McCarthy's problem was that he lacked the documents. Nixon's specific charges stuck, because the documents known as the Pumpkin Papers backed them up. McCarthy's wild accusations brought discredit on himself and, for a while, on other, better investigators. But Nixon didn't condemn McCarthy for smearing the Roosevelt and Truman administrations as "20 years of treason," or for accusing Gen. George C. Marshall of participating in "a conspiracy on a scale so immense as to dwarf any previous such venture in the history of man," or even for failing to uncover a single Communist spy in the American government despite a whirlwind of accusations.[15]

Nixon faulted McCarthy for leaving himself open to attack by using a specific number that he couldn't back up.[16] "I said, 'Joe, you can't say that. You can't say there's 64 Communists.' I said, 'There are more than that. But don't use a number. Just say there are, and mention the State Department.' Anyway, what I'm getting at is this," the president told his aides. "It's part of the background, the faith, and the rest. We'd probably be that way. 'We are a persecuted minority,' 'concerned about suppression,' 'police state,' et cetera, et cetera, and they always come down that way. Almost always. You just can't find many that don't." It was not especially clear how all these points connected in the president's mind, but his men did pick up on one theme.

"Well, at least the Supreme Court yesterday ruled that the Jews couldn't get into our golf club," Attorney General Mitchell said.

"Is that right?" Nixon asked.

"The Jews are going to come down and harass the Russians this week," Ehrlichman volunteered.

"They're going to free the Soviet Jews?" Haldeman asked.

"That is nice," Nixon said.[17]

The president sets the tone for his administration. Later that summer, the speechwriter Patrick J. Buchanan would refer casually to the "American Jewish community which controls the liberal media" in a memo to the president.[18] He knew what the boss liked.

## The Diem Chapter

At the same time that the president used the legal force of the federal government to block the *Times* from publishing the Pentagon Papers, he wanted to leak some of them himself.

"I'd like to see Teddy [Kennedy] urge that his brother's papers be made public. And then we'll leak those," the president said on June 15, 1971, the very day his Justice Department took the *Times* to court. Sen. Edward M. "Ted" Kennedy, D-Massachusetts, JFK's youngest brother, was a potential presidential candidate in 1972. "It wouldn't look very good, you know. The murder of Diem's in there." The Pentagon Papers covered the Kennedy administration's decision to green-light the coup that overthrew South Vietnamese President Ngo Dinh Diem. The coup climaxed in the assassination of Diem. "It's pretty bad," the president said.[1]

The *Times* had planned to run JFK stories next ("Tomorrow: The Kennedy Administration Raises the Stakes"), but Judge Gurfein's temporary restraining order made that impossible.[2]

"Let me say that I think the Kennedy stuff should get out," Nixon told Haldeman the next morning. "Now, the way it would be getting out is not to put out any documents, just to put out the . . . see, the injunction runs only to the *Times,* Bob. Right?"

"Yeah." The chief of staff didn't remind the president that the non-documents part of the Pentagon Papers—three thousand pages of the seven-thousand-page study—was also classified top secret. He did mention legal ways to make the information public. "Well, if you release all of it to the Hill, then you can get a Hill guy to start talking about that. And if you declassify, you can declassify that."[3]

The president had other ideas. "The stuff on Kennedy I'm going to get leaked," he told Kissinger, Haldeman, and White House Press Secretary Ronald L. Ziegler that afternoon. "Now that it's being leaked, we'll leak out the parts we want." No one pointed out that if they got caught leaking the Pentagon Papers, it would undermine their claim that the leak threatened national security. No one volunteered to do the leaking, either.[4]

The next day Nixon tried to foist the task on the NSC. "Now, goddamn it, Henry, I want to get out the stuff on the murder of Diem. Get one of the little boys over in your office to get it out. I'm going to see it come hell—all right then, I'm going to get it out."

"My guy shouldn't put out classified documents," Kissinger said.

"Get it out. I'm going to put it out," the president said. "I want to see the material. By God, the *Times* is not going to select here."

"Yeah," Haldeman said, "but you don't want to select, either, while you're hanging them for the—"

"That's all right," Nixon said.

"Mr. President, it's in these volumes, and they're going to come out one way or the other in the next few weeks," Kissinger said.

"They aren't going to use that," Nixon said. "They won't use the Diem part. Never."

"Mr. President," Ehrlichman said, "I think we're on a very tough wicket at least until after this lawsuit is in the hopper."

(At this point, the president was thinking of arguing the case before the Supreme Court himself. "I could go down there and really let them have it," he said. Justice Hugo "Black and the rest of them would take out after me like gangbusters, and I'd knock their goddamn brains out.")[5]

When aides seemed reluctant to do something the president demanded, he could always turn to Charles W. Colson, a lawyer whose official title was White House special counsel. Chuck Colson's real role was to be, in the words of an admiring biographer, "the ultimate can-do political operator."[6]

"The beauty of Colson is if you tell him something, he does it," Nixon said.[7]

That was precisely the problem Haldeman had with him.[8] "Unfortunately, Colson encouraged the dark impulses in Nixon's mind, and *acted* on those impulses instead of ignoring them and letting them die," Haldeman later wrote.[9] Nixon once said he saw a lot of himself in Colson.[10] But Colson was a cocky ex-Marine with a Green Beret slogan over the bar in his den ("When you've got 'em by the balls, their hearts and minds will follow") and self-confidence bordering on swagger. Colson had three heroes, according to the journalist J. Anthony Lukas: "Lieutenant General Lewis B. 'Chesty' Puller ('the greatest blood-and-guts Marine who ever walked'), John Wayne, and Richard Nixon." Nixon praised Colson for having "the balls of a brass monkey."[11]

On June 17, after Kissinger proved unwilling to leak the Diem chapter, the president complained to Colson. "He has it but he won't put it out. He's embarrassed," Nixon said.

"Well, there'll be ways that will get out," Colson said. "One way or another, that will get out, Mr. President, I'm sure." Chuckling, he added, "We'll see that it does."[12]

Nixon had no need to leak what had already leaked. On June 21, one of Nixon's most prominent Republican critics on Vietnam, Rep. Paul N. "Pete" McCloskey, who got his own copy of the Pentagon Papers from Ellsberg, said the Kennedy administration "encouraged and authorized" the coup.[13] The *Chicago Sun-Times* ran a story about the coup on June 23, with no assist from the White House.

"There was great writhing in pain in the streets of Boston yesterday over that," Colson told the president that morning.

"Your Boston heroes, the Kennedys, looking like he's [*sic*] got a little blood on his hands this morning," Nixon said.

"He's got some real problems," Colson said.

"I don't mean Teddy," Nixon said. "I meant Jack."

"But I think it gives real problems to Teddy," Colson said.[14]

## "Destroy the *Times*"

The president saw no contradiction between ordering aides to leak parts of the Pentagon Papers and denouncing the *Times* for publishing other parts.

Instructing the White House press secretary on how to attack the *Times,* the president said, "Use the words, 'giving aid and comfort to the enemy.'"[1] Those are words with which the Constitution defines treason.

Nixon devised other lines of attack: "Take the masthead of the *Times*. What does it say? 'All the News That's Fit To Print.' And what they're saying today is, 'Stolen Goods Are Fit To Print.' Put that down. Good one. It's not bad."[2]

He ordered White House aides to boycott the *Times*. "I just want to cool it with those damn people because of their disloyalty to the country," he told Haldeman.[3] He dictated a memo to his chief staff saying, "Until further notice under *no circumstances* is anyone connected with the White House to give any interview to a member of the staff of the *New York Times* without my express permission. I want you to enforce this without, of course, showing them this memorandum."[4]

He also wanted others to level the charge of disloyalty.

"We have to start hollering 'treason' a little bit," Kissinger said.

"You say, 'we.' I really can't do it," the president said.[5]

A congressman, on the other hand . . . "Get Jack Kemp to demagogue," Nixon said the next day, referring to the first-term Republican representative from Buffalo, New York. "Tell him to get out and make, you know, irresponsible charges. That's what they have to do in order to get attention. They say this is treasonable—treasonable—and, you know, don't worry about it."[6]

Nixon didn't argue that publishing the Pentagon Papers was treasonous; he just assumed it: "It does help the enemy. And was intended to."[7]

The public was unconvinced. Even before the Supreme Court decided the issue, Gallup asked, "In your opinion, did the newspapers do the right thing in publishing these articles?" Fifty-eight percent said that publishing was the right thing to do; 30 percent that it was wrong.[8]

A poll for the White House asked the question differently: "Do you think freedom of the press includes the freedom of a paper to print stolen, top secret government documents or not?" Fifteen percent said it did; 74 percent said it didn't.

Other poll results were less favorable for the White House. The chief of staff read them out loud in the Oval Office for the inner circle:

" 'Do you feel the government is trying to suppress information the public should have?' Sixty-two yes, 28 no," Haldeman said. " 'Do you think the government's trying to cover up the wrongdoings of the previous administration?' Forty-seven yes, 40 no."

"It's a bad wicket any time the credibility of government or their motives comes into play," Attorney General Mitchell said, "because they'll vote against you every time."

"Cover-up. It's a cover-up," the president said. "And yet they are against a newspaper publishing secret documents." When top secret documents were described as "stolen," that is.

Haldeman continued: " 'Did the *Times* break the law when it published this secret material or was the publication legal?' Twenty-six [percent said it] broke the law, 48 [said] it was legal."

"See, they don't know what the hell it is," the president said.

" 'Even if it was illegal for the *Times* to publish the secret study,' " Haldeman read, " 'do you think they did or did not do the right thing in bringing these facts about Vietnam to the American people?' Sixty-one [percent said it] did the right thing, 28 [percent said it did] not."

"Good old American morality," Ehrlichman said.

## Illegal Action

The Justice Department had opened a grand jury investigation of the Pentagon Papers leak, and this soon yielded some juicy anecdotes. One of them had a *Times* reporter flashing his White House press badge to convince a copy shop to duplicate a stack of documents marked top secret.[1] Another was about Ellsberg's ex-wife. He'd warned her in advance that he might go to prison, which would mean no more alimony or child support. She reminded him that his obligation to provide it was established by court order. Ellsberg pointed out that he couldn't obey it in prison. He also informed her, after the fact, that he'd told their eldest, fourteen-year-old Robert Ellsberg, what he was doing, and the boy had helped with photocopying the Pentagon Papers. She was not happy.[2]

The former Mrs. Ellsberg's grand jury testimony was well-received in the Oval Office. "That's great," Haldeman said. "That's as good as the Pumpkin Papers."

"You've got to get it out," the president said. "Where are we telling it, in the grand jury?"

"Now, wait a minute, wait a minute," the attorney general said. It's a federal crime for government attorneys to disclose grand jury testimony.[3] "I don't want to go to jail."

The others laughed.

"We got stuff out of the Hiss grand jury," Nixon said. "It was hard, but we did it."

"Of course, if I'm going to jail, I want to go in a hurry," Mitchell said, "so I might get a pardon."

"Ha. You bet," the president said.

"Don't count on it," Ehrlichman said.

They laughed again.[4]

The next morning, the president polished his public line before an audience of top aides: "The President is doing the only thing he can. He has to carry out the law. He would've been derelict in not carrying out the law which the Congress has passed with regard to declassification, and he is meeting his duty, even though politically it would be to his advantage not to carry out the law." Less than a minute later, he added, "You've got to really have a sophisticated assault on the Democrats. Humphrey must be destroyed. Muskie must be destroyed. Teddy Kennedy must be."[5]

## "A Natural Enemy"

On June 28, 1971, Daniel Ellsberg took a taxi to Post Office Square in Boston and arrived to find the largest assemblage of reporters, photographers, and television cameras he'd ever seen waiting for him on the sidewalk. His lawyer had warned them that Ellsberg was about to surrender himself. "Obviously, I didn't think that a single page out of the 7,000 pages in the study would cause a grave danger to the country or I would not have released the papers," Ellsberg told them, "and from what I've read in the paper, the government has not made a showing that the papers contain such a danger."

Having publicly taken responsibility for distributing the Pentagon Papers to the press, Ellsberg walked into the federal office building and became the first American charged under the Espionage Act for revealing classified information to the American people. "The government prosecutor, David Nissen, admitted at the time that after investigation the government had no evidence to substantiate a charge of espionage against Ellsberg," the historian Keith W. Olson wrote in *Watergate: The Presidential Scandal That Shook America*.[1] Instead, Ellsberg was charged with "unauthorized possession of, access to, and control over copies of certain documents and writings related to the national defense" that were classified top secret.

"Unfortunately, they can't do it on stealing, but it's on unauthorized possession, which we can shift in rhetoric to stealing," Haldeman told Nixon on June 29.[2] The pending Supreme Court decision on whether Nixon could block the *Times, Post,* and other papers from publishing the Pentagon Papers threatened to expose another soft spot in the case. If the administration couldn't convince the high court that publication would irreparably harm American national security, it would be that much harder to prove that Ellsberg did. "We've got a sticky wicket, legally, in that if the [Supreme] Court doesn't find that this did any damage, we've got no legal grounds for getting Ellsberg," Haldeman said. "The damn spy law says you have to damage the United States."

"Well, there's one slight difference," Kissinger said. The prosecution in the Ellsberg case didn't have to prove he'd caused *irreparable* damage.

"That's right," Haldeman said. "But they do have to find damage."

"Yeah," Kissinger said. "Damage they have to find."

Ellsberg was also charged with converting government property valued at over one hundred dollars to his own use. The problem with that charge was that Ellsberg hadn't stolen the papers; he photocopied them. He didn't even use a government Xerox machine. Instead, he went to a friend's ad agency and made copies there.[3]

Although polls showed a majority in favor of publishing the secret documents, Colson thought that Nixon's core constituency on the right favored prosecution strongly. "They are not going to want to see us let him off the hook if there's any way we can avoid it," he said.

"He's our enemy," the president said. "We need an enemy."

"Agree completely, and he's a marvelous one," Colson said. "He's a perfect enemy to have."[4]

## Lord High Executioner

The next morning, the president held what he said was probably the most important cabinet meeting of the year. He did all the talking.

His subject was leaking. "We're not going to have any more of this crap," the president said as thunder actually rumbled in the distance. If it happened again, he would hold the top official in the agency from which the story came responsible. "And he goes. Not the underling, but he goes. I want each person in this room to see that this discipline is enforced." Those who could not in good conscience accept the policy of the administration should resign.

Leaks had been a problem for Eisenhower, Kennedy, and Johnson, too. "It's worse now. It's worse now for a reason that is very strange, because I'm considered to be very permissive about it. We have yet to fire one of the sons of bitches who has leaked—and leaked deliberately—and that policy is changing."

Nixon brought only one aide with him: Haldeman. "The reason I have him in the room is that he is going to be the Lord High Executioner. Now, when you hear from him, I don't want anybody—you or any of your subordinates—[to] come whining to me," the president said.

"I can assure you that we are going to crack down and people at the top are going to go. Just like that. Or people at the second level are going to go. But somebody's going to go. And so, look for the scapegoat," the president said. They all had a few loyal lieutenants. "But down beneath you've got a bunch of vipers that are ready to strike," he said. "It isn't going to happen any more. It isn't going to happen without some retribution. Because as you get closer to an election, the tendency for those who are in the bureaucracy, 96 percent of which—that's the count, incidentally, are against us, of the bureaucracy decision-maker types that go on and on and on, because they're left-wing liberal bastards that are here to screw us. Now, that is the fact. Don't kid yourselves. Don't have any illusions."

He closed by recalling Eisenhower's chief of staff during World War II, Walter Bedell Smith. "He drank. He started to cry and said, 'You know, I'm just Ike's prat boy. It's all I've ever been. Because I always do the dirty work for him.' Well, let me say this: Haldeman's my prat boy. He's going to be right down the throats of anybody in this room, wherever it appears that a leak has come out that violates what I have laid down here." Then the president got up and walked out of the Cabinet Room with Haldeman following.[1]

In the Oval Office, Nixon wondered if threatening everyone's job would work. "It may be this will not shake them," he said.

"No, what's going to shake them now is when we start calling them," Haldeman said. "And that's where the tough part's going to be. But we've just got to start doing it."

The president was silent for a few seconds. "Just be mean. Calm," he said. "Scare the living bejeezus out of them."

They had other things to discuss—ambassadorial appointments, White House social affairs, guest lists—but the president soon returned to Topic A. "On this business of the Jew," Nixon said, ". . . I want you to take the hard line that we cannot govern this country—you really can't govern this country—if a man is not prosecuted for stealing documents." The Ellsberg case would take months. It wouldn't be decided until after the 1972 election. "Don't worry what polls show or anything else on his guilt or innocence. We can change it," the president said. "It is tough, Bob. It is tough to live in this town. We're going to fight. And we'll have more on our side than you think. You know, we've got more on our side than you think. People don't trust these Eastern Establishment people. He's Harvard. He's a Jew. You know, and he's an arrogant intellectual."[2]

## Supreme Court Rules

On June 30, 1971, the Supreme Court decided 6-3 against Nixon. The *New York Times, Washington Post,* and other papers were free to publish the Pentagon Papers.

The majority agreed that the administration had failed to justify prior restraint on a free press. All nine justices wrote opinions, a reflection of the case's importance. Justice Thurgood Marshall noted that Congress had twice rejected proposals to give the executive branch power to muzzle newspapers on national security grounds. For the high court to grant what Congress denied would be usurping the power to enact law, he said. Justices Hugo L. Black and William O. Douglas found that the First Amendment prohibited restraints on the press.

Chief Justice Warren E. Burger wrote that it was "the duty of an honorable press" to let the government review all the documents prior to publication. Burger sided with the administration, as did Justices Harry A. Blackmun and John M. Harlan.

The three justices in the middle, Byron R. White, William J. Brennan Jr., and Potter Stewart, said the government could block publication of material that would do irreparable damage to the nation—but the Pentagon Papers posed no such threat.[1]

The lawyer who had to present Nixon's case to the high court, Solicitor General Erwin N. Griswold, ultimately concluded that the majority was right. "I have never seen any trace of a threat to the national security from the publication," Griswold wrote in 1989.

> It quickly becomes apparent to any person who has considerable experience with classified material that there is massive over-classification and that the principal concern of the classifiers is not with national security, but rather with governmental embarrassment of one sort or another. There may be some basis for short-term classification while plans are being made, or negotiations are going on, but apart from details of weapons systems, there is very rarely any real risk to current national security from the publication of facts relating to transactions in the past, even the fairly recent past. This is the lesson of the Pentagon Papers experience, and it may be relevant now.[2]

The Supreme Court decision was bad for Nixon and his case against Ellsberg, but it was far from the worst news he received that day.

## 1969 Documents

National Security Adviser Kissinger broke three pieces of bad news to the president in three minutes on the afternoon of June 30, 1971. The first was the Supreme Court decision.

"Yeah. That's what I expected," the president said.

"It shows what these superannuated fools like Black and Douglas, what they do to the court," Kissinger said. "Because with two more appointments—"

"Yeah, we'd've had it," Nixon said.

The second was that an administration official named Charles M. Cooke had once shown classified documents to Ellsberg. Cooke was a top aide to former under secretary of state Elliot L. Richardson, now secretary of health, education, and welfare.

"How do they know he did it?" Nixon asked.

"I only know what Laird told me," Kissinger said. "He said they had caught him earlier Xeroxing documents and—"

"Well, why didn't they fire him?"

"That's a very good question," Kissinger said. "He's a good friend of Ellsberg's."

Then came the third piece of bad news: "And Senator Mathias has a bundle of documents of Rogers's memos to us, and our replies." Sen.

Charles McCurdy "Mac" Mathias of Maryland was a liberal Republican critic of Nixon on Vietnam. Unlike the Pentagon Papers, the documents Mathias had came from the *Nixon* administration—including some from his own National Security Council.

"What areas? Do you know?" Nixon asked.

"We don't know. We're going to try to get a look at them this afternoon," Kissinger said.

"Who told you?" Nixon asked.

"Laird. You know he has his own investigative branch," Kissinger said. "He gets stuff through his own intelligence agency."

"Now, we don't have any on Cambodia in there, in the NSC, do we?" the president asked.

"(A) It's from '69. (B) Our whole system is different. I don't know what it is," Kissinger said.

"Well, you say it is from '69? What the hell could they have from '69?"

"Oh, proposals for private meetings, ceasefires, nothing," Kissinger said. (Actually, Ellsberg had given Mathias NSSM-1.)

Attorney General Mitchell joined them in the Oval Office.

"Well, let me say that don't you agree, though, that we have to pursue the Ellsberg case now all the more?" the president asked.

"No question about it," Mitchell said.

"I suppose the defense of Ellsberg will be, well, if the documents do not endanger the national security," Nixon said.

"That may be the case," Mitchell said. "We've structured a complaint under the statute, which is a lot clearer, about taking government property, rather than the espionage aspect of it."

"Oh, I see, just taking government property. Technical. But you always use technical things," the president said. "Why not? Just get the son of a bitch into jail." Nixon demanded legal action and illegal action. "Everything, John, that there is on the investigation, get it out. Leak it out. I want to destroy him in the press. Is that clear? It just has to be done," Nixon said. "That's the way we won the Hiss case. I didn't try it in the goddamn courtroom, but I won it before it ever got to court. That's how this has to be done."

"We've got to do this," the attorney general said. "Otherwise he'll become a peacenik martyr."

"Yeah," Kissinger said. "Laird called me and said that Mathias has a batch of documents from '69. Are you familiar with that?"

"Yes, as a matter of fact, Mathias called me about it earlier and—"

"What's he going to do, put 'em out?" the president asked.

"No, no, he's been holding them, and why he never came forward about this Ellsberg, I don't know," Mitchell said. "I chewed him out for that. Ellsberg has been up talking to Mathias—"

"Where'd he get these documents from?" Nixon asked.

"Ellsberg," Mitchell said. "Where would Ellsberg get them, out of RAND?"

"Apparently—allegedly—Laird thinks that he got them from a fellow called Dick Cooke, who was then in Richardson's office," Kissinger said. He didn't mention that Ellsberg might have gotten his hands on them while doing consulting work for the NSC early in 1969. Kissinger still hadn't told Nixon about that. "I know Dick Cooke," Kissinger said, "and I know his views are—"

"He left, liberal?" the president asked.

"Yeah," Kissinger said. "Former army officer, too."

"Well, goddamn it, why didn't they fire him?" Nixon asked.

"Well, up to now, Mr. President," Kissinger said, "the fact that I knew him as a dove didn't mean that I knew him as a traitor."[1]

## "Break In and Take It Out"

Nixon summoned his defense secretary to the Oval Office that evening. "I think we ought to do a little work undercover, and I'd like to ask permission to do that," Laird said. "I mean, we may not need permission, but I've got some damn good stuff on these people that—"

"Good. You've got permission," the president said. He wanted to know more about Cooke.

An Air Force captain who worked in the Pentagon's ISA office, Cooke left in March 1969 to work for Under Secretary Richardson at State, where "he had access to all the national security memorandums," Laird said. "I really think there is a conspiracy that's going on on this whole damn thing."

"I do, too," Nixon said. The president instructed his chief of staff to call Richardson and play a ruse. Tell him that a story about Cooke leaking documents "is going to break in a column," Nixon said. Richardson was to call Cooke in and get all the facts. "Maybe he's not guilty. I think he probably is. Because he's one of these Harvards, isn't he?" Nixon asked. "I checked his record. He's a Harvard, class of '63." (Nixon didn't check very hard. Cooke was an Annapolis graduate, the son of four-star Admiral Charles M. "Savvy" Cooke Jr., who'd commanded the Seventh Fleet. "I've never been to Harvard," Cooke said.)[1]

"Well, we think he gave these [documents] to our friend up with RAND," Laird said.

"Who?" Nixon asked.

"Ellsberg."

The president demanded that the RAND Corporation and the Brookings Institution both be cut off from classified information.

"Brookings has got a lot of stuff now. Don't you want to send a colonel over and pick it up?" Haldeman asked.

"Yes!" Laird said.

"No, no, no, no," the president said.

Brookings has no government contract, Haldeman said.

"The way I want that handled, Bob, is to do it another way. I want—I want Brookings—I want them just to break in," Nixon said. "Break in and take it out. You understand?"

"Yeah," Haldeman said, "but you've got to have somebody to do it."

"Now, don't discuss it here. You've talked enough. I want to break—well, hell, they do that. You're to break into the place, rifle the files and bring them in," the president said.

"I don't have any problems with breaking in," Haldeman said, "it's just in a Defense Department–approved security—"

"Just go in and take it," Nixon said. "Go in. Go in around eight or nine o'clock."

"And make an inspection of the safe," Haldeman said.

"That's right," the president said. "You go in to inspect it, and I mean clean it out."[2]

An hour after the meeting broke up, he called his chief of staff and clarified his meaning: "Break into their files and get that stuff out. Let them scream."[3]

## "Rumors and Reports of a Conspiracy"

The president's fears regarding Clifford, Warnke, Halperin, and Gelb were based, in part, on things he'd been told about them—on information, much of it bad. Hoover had named Halperin as a possible source of a press leak on the secret bombing of Cambodia, although the NSC aide had so little knowledge of the subject that he couldn't tell whether the news story based on that leak was accurate. Huston had claimed that Clifford, Warnke, and Gelb at Brookings had a report on all the events leading up to the bombing halt, although no evidence has ever emerged that the report existed. Nixon's response to the Pentagon Papers leak was, in part, rational.

It was also partly irrational. Years later, in his memoirs, Nixon wrote about the Pentagon Papers that from "the first there had been rumors and reports of a conspiracy."[1] The former president was exaggerating. Haig's suspicions about Clifford, Warnke, Halperin, and Gelb didn't rise to the level of a report or even a rumor. Haig had a hunch; he didn't pretend it was anything more. (To his credit, Haig checked that hunch with someone who had better information and within twenty-four hours obtained the name of the man from whom the *Times* got the Pentagon Papers.) The theory that a conspiracy was involved came from a higher level within the White House.

"The *Times* thing just really convinced me that we're up against, I mean, as Henry said, it's a conspiracy, Bob," the president said on June 15, 1971.

"It's absolutely clear," Haldeman said.[2]

While Nixon made it sound like the idea was Kissinger's, a conversation he had alone with the national security adviser later that day suggests otherwise. Kissinger informed the president that Swedish prime minister Olof Palme was saying the Pentagon Papers proved that the American government had undermined democracy and prepared the way to war by deceit.

President Nixon: Now, isn't that a hell of a damn thing?
Kissinger: Yeah.
President Nixon: "It proves the war—" But also it shows that that's part of the conspiracy, in my opinion.
Kissinger: Oh, yeah.
President Nixon: He wouldn't otherwise pay any attention to it. Somebody got to him. Henry, there is a conspiracy. You understand?
Kissinger: I believe it now. I didn't believe it formerly, but I believe it now.
President Nixon: [*Unclear*] there is. The fellow who leaked the papers, whether it's Gelb or the RAND Corporation guy, he's in conspiracy.[3]

It didn't take a conspiracy to get the prime minister of Sweden to criticize the US government on Vietnam. In 1968, Palme had personally led a march against the war through Stockholm with the North Vietnamese ambassador at his side.[4]

The leading conspiracy theorist in the White House was the president. Nixon's theory centered on three groups: Jews, intellectuals, and Ivy Leaguers. Jews have "an arrogance that says—that's what makes a spy. He puts himself above the law," Nixon said.[5] "Remember that any intellectual is tempted to put himself above the law," he said on another occasion. "That's the rule that I've known all my life. Any intellectual, particularly—watch what schools they're from. If they're from any Eastern schools or Berkeley, those are particularly the potential bad ones."[6] Nixon said the same thing about Jews, intellectuals, and Ivy Leaguers: they were arrogant and placed themselves above the law. It may seem incongruous that Nixon's most important adviser, Henry Kissinger, was a Jewish refugee from Nazi Germany, an internationally renowned foreign policy intellectual, and a man upon whom Harvard bestowed three degrees and a professorship. But just as there are anti-Semites who say that some of their best friends are Jews, Nixon made exceptions for the ones who spent most of their waking hours laboring in his service.[7] "You have a [White House Special Consultant Leonard] Garment and a Kissinger and, frankly, a [speechwriter William L.] Safire and, by God, they're exceptions," he told his chief of staff. "But, Bob, generally speaking, you can't trust the bastards."[8]

Warnke, Halperin, and Gelb were Jews, intellectuals, and Ivy Leaguers—like Kissinger. Unlike Kissinger, they were more interested in defeating Nixon than in reelecting him, so they became subjects of his conspiracy theorizing. (Clifford was Episcopalian, Anglo-Saxon, and a graduate of Washington University in St. Louis, so he didn't capture Nixon's imagination as much.)

Whence came Nixon's fixation on Jews, intellectuals, and the Ivy League? It's impossible to say for sure, but with Nixon, the first place to look is politics. He came of age during the long Democratic reign of Franklin D. Roosevelt. The New Deal brought new kids to town, and the old guard didn't much care for "this upsurge of strange urban types," as the historian Arthur M. Schlesinger Jr. wrote in *The Coming of the New Deal: 1933–1935*. "There were too many Ivy League men, too many intellectuals, too many radicals, too many Jews."[9] In other words, Nixon wasn't the only Republican with a bias against Jews, intellectuals, and the Ivy League.

Nixon owed his rapid rise in national politics to the leading role he played in uncovering a conspiracy involving a spy for the Soviet Union who was connected to some of the most prominent Ivy Leaguers, Jews, and intellectuals of the New Deal era as well as some of its most controversial events—Alger Hiss.

Hiss had a brilliant career: Protégé of future Supreme Court justice Felix Frankfurter, a Jewish intellectual leader on Harvard's faculty who helped found the American Civil Liberties Union. Law clerk for Supreme Court Justice Oliver Wendell Holmes, an intellectual leader and Harvard graduate. Counsel to the Senate Special Committee on Investigation of the Munitions Industry. Director of special political affairs at State. Executive secretary of the Dumbarton Oaks Conference on establishing the United Nations. Assistant to Secretary of State Edward R. Stettinius at the Yalta Conference on postwar Europe. Secretary general of the San Francisco Conference that produced the UN Charter. Hiss's résumé brought together much of what the Far Right loathed and feared; anyone who could show that beneath the liberal surface lurked a Communist would just complete the nightmare.

Whittaker Chambers did just that. A former courier for a Soviet spy ring, Chambers produced microfilm copies of top secret State Department documents and handwritten notes that Hiss had furnished him. Since Chambers hid the film one night in a hollowed-out pumpkin on his Maryland farm, the press called them the Pumpkin Papers.[10] When the *Times* later called its cache of Defense Department documents the Pentagon Papers, it was echoing the key moment in Nixon's political rise. Nixon was just a first-term congressman on the House Un-American Activities Committee when Chambers appeared before it in 1948, but he pursued the leads the witness provided more aggressively than any of his colleagues and reaped the political benefits. The statute of limitations had expired on espionage, but a grand jury indicted Hiss for lying under oath. His first trial ended in deadlock; the second was conclusive. "Hiss Guilty on Both Perjury Counts," the *Times* reported on January 22, 1950. "Betrayal of U.S. Secrets Is Affirmed."[11]

Nixon rose on the House floor four days later to speak on "the broader implications of the case." With great subtlety, he drew an apocalyptic lesson about the Ivy League and the intellectuals it produced. "The tragedy of the case is that the great majority of [Hiss's fellow spies] were American citizens, were graduates of the best colleges and universities in this country, and had yet willingly become members of an organization dedicated to the overthrow of this government," Nixon said. They found "the Communist ideology more attractive than American democracy. This is a serious reflection on our educational system, and it is essential that we remedy the situation if we are to survive as a free people."[12] Nixon insinuated, without quite saying, that the Ivy League made Communism seem more attractive than democracy and thereby threatened America's survival as a free nation.

Likewise, he insinuated that the foreign policies of the Roosevelt and Truman administrations were the product of an enemy within.

The great lesson which should be learned from the Alger Hiss case is that we are not just dealing with espionage agents who get 30 pieces of silver to obtain the blueprint of a new weapon—the Communists do that, too—but this is a far more sinister type of activity, because it permits the enemy to guide and shape our policy; it disarms and dooms our diplomats to defeat in advance before they go to conferences; traitors in the high councils of our own government make sure that the deck is stacked on the Soviet side of the diplomatic table.[13]

Later that year, Nixon ran for the US Senate using campaign posters hailing him as "The Man Who Broke the Hiss Case!!" He called his opponent, the New Deal Democrat and former film star Helen Gahagan Douglas, the Pink Lady, an insinuation no one could miss during a Red scare. California elected him as the Senate's youngest Republican.[14] In 1952, Eisenhower picked Nixon as his running mate, praising his "ability to ferret out any kind of subversive influence wherever it may be found."[15] Nixon rose farther, faster than any politician of his generation. From his first race for the House to his election as vice president, his ascent took just six years. The Hiss case made him.

It also played a part in unmaking him. The case not only reinforced his followers' prejudices, but his own. "Incidentally, I hope to God he's—he's not Jewish, is he?" Nixon asked about Ellsberg on June 17, 1971, when no Jews were in the Oval Office.

"I'm sure he is," Haldeman said, chuckling. (Ellsberg had actually been raised as a Christian Scientist, like Haldeman and Ehrlichman.) "All the spies up to now have been Jewish. Why the hell wouldn't he be?"

"Oh, I know, I know, I know, I know. But it's a bad wicket for us. It's a bad wicket," Nixon said. "Maybe we'll be lucky for once. Look, you can't tell by the name. It might just be German or something like it." The president recalled the Hiss case. "They were all of them Jews. It was a whole Jewish ring," he said. "The only two non-Jews were Chambers and Hiss. Many thought that Hiss was. He could've been a half, but back a ways. But he was not by religion. The only two non-Jews. Every other one was a Jew. And it raised hell with us. But in this case, I hope to God he's not a Jew."

No one spoke for a couple of seconds.

"Well, I suspect he is," Haldeman said.

"I know," Nixon said, chuckling, "except you can't tell by the name."

"Mort Halperin."

"Halperin is, yeah," Nixon said.

"Gelb is."

"Is Gelb a Jew? Hell, well, then, by golly, we've got to—what is Laird doing and what is Rogers doing about cleaning up their own security situations?" Nixon asked.

"Well, what are we doing about cleaning up our own here?" Haldeman asked.

"Well, that's what I mean," Nixon said. "I mean Henry's shop. Exactly. Just don't know when one of them's going to run out and take a lot of papers."

"We are in no position to criticize State or Defense on security leaks or on disloyal personnel," Haldeman said.

"I thought we'd cleared them all out," Nixon said.

"Well, we hope we have," Haldeman said. "But our track record's pretty stinky."[16]

In the aftermath of the Pentagon Papers leak, the president of the United States spoke of Jews in the NSC and the Defense and State Departments as if they were security risks simply because of their religious background.

## Imitation of the Enemy

The president pounded his desk at his first meeting of July 1, 1971, as he told Haldeman and Kissinger, "We're up against an enemy. A conspiracy. They're using any means. We are going to use any means. Is that clear? Did they get the Brookings Institute raided last night? No. Get it done. I want it done. I want the Brookings Institute safe cleaned out."[1]

In his classic essay on conspiracy theorists, "The Paranoid Style in American Politics," the historian Richard Hofstadter wrote, "A fundamental paradox of the paranoid style is the imitation of the enemy."[2] When Nixon conceived of his enemy as Jews, intellectuals, and Ivy Leaguers who arrogantly placed themselves above the law, he gave himself license to do likewise. He placed himself above the law that prohibits the disclosure of grand jury testimony, for one. "This is a conspiracy. It does involve these people, and they are not on very good ground in many cases. Also, we now have the opportunity really to leak out all these nasty stories that'll kill these bastards," he said.[3] Though sworn to preserve the Constitution, he placed himself above the Sixth Amendment guarantee of the right to a fair trial. "Screw the court case," the president said. "I mean, just let's convict the son of a bitch in the press. That's the way it's done!"[4] These orders don't make Nixon a cackling villain out of melodrama, glorying in his own malevolence. Imitation of the enemy is a faulty kind of moral reasoning, a trumped-up claim of self-defense. Nixon did unto others as he feared they would do unto him. His conspiracy theory enabled him to claim he was fighting fire with fire. But it turned him into what he hated.

It's questionable whether what Ellsberg did can accurately be called stealing classified government documents, but that's a perfectly accurate way to describe what Nixon intended to do as he put together an organization to burglarize a think tank, blow its safe open, and obtain a top secret report. Imitation of the enemy, as Hofstadter wrote, produces "secret organizations set up to combat secret organizations."[5] To fight an imaginary conspiracy, the president initiated a real, criminal one.[6]

## Special Investigations Unit

"I need a man, a commander, an officer in charge here in the White House, that I can call when I wake up, like I did last night, at two o'clock in the morning," Nixon said on July 1, 1971.[1] "I really need a son-of-a-bitch like Huston who'll work his butt off and do it dishonorably."[2]

The organization, as yet unnamed, would draw on the work of legitimate investigative agencies for illegitimate ends. "We've got to get another guy who's going to gig J. Edgar Hoover and gig Mel Laird and so forth until we find out who the conspirators are. Then we leak it to the press," the president said.[3] Nixon would use not only the grand jury, but the investigative power of the FBI and the Defense Intelligence Agency to gather information he could use as political ammunition. Attorney General Mitchell "is just too damn good a lawyer, you know, he's a good strong lawyer. It just repels him to do these horrible things. But they've got to be done," Nixon said.[4] "We have to develop now a program, a program for leaking out information. For destroying these people in the papers. That's one side of it—how to get at the conspiracy."

"The other side of it is the declassification," Nixon continued. "And then leaking to, or giving out to our friends, the stories that they would like to have, such as the Cuban confrontation. You get what I mean? Let's have a little fun."[5] Declassification and leaking are two different things. Declassification is the perfectly legal, formal process in which agencies review classified documents and make a determination whether they can be released to the public without jeopardizing national security. If leaking a *still*-classified document were illegal for a current or former government employee—as Nixon claimed it was in prosecuting Ellsberg—then it would be illegal for the president of the United States as well. "I'll go after the conspiracy, and then I'm also going to leak some papers," the president told Haldeman. "I don't know whether you noted this morning, but even the *Times*, to my great surprise, gave a hell of a wallop to the Kennedy thing."[6] On the day after the Supreme Court ruled in their favor, both the *New York Times* and the *Washington*

*Post* ran front-page stories on exactly the part of the Pentagon Papers Nixon wanted leaked. "U.S. Supported Coup against Diem," said the *Post* headline.[7] Nixon now saw for himself that newspapers would publish damaging secrets about JFK. He intended to give them more.

As a general rule, people who believe one conspiracy theory will believe others, and Nixon was no exception: he embraced the notion that FDR knew about the Japanese attack on Pearl Harbor in advance. "Suppose all the elements of the—Roosevelt's involvement—documents of the World War II era came out. You know, how he knew what was happening, and he did it deliberately. I mean, the Pearl Harbor thing was ungodly," the president said on June 14, 1971.[8] This idea soon snowballed into a resolution to leak the foreign policy secrets of the Truman administration. "Can I get my, please, my little comments, my little research on Korea and World War II?" he asked Haldeman on June 17. "Don't ask Henry for World War II, 'cause he's got the Jew complex, too."[9] Next came Kennedy, a target that pushed the others aside. "Now, incidentally, don't go back to World War II first," he told Haldeman on June 24. "The first things I want to go back to are the most relevant things. I want to go to the Cuban Missile Crisis, and I want to go to the Bay of Pigs." He didn't say how they were relevant. Haldeman didn't ask.

About Johnson's secrets, Nixon expressed ambivalence. "The bombing halt story, incidentally, is not in the Ellsberg thing, and I think it's now time we get that out. If it's any good for us," he said. "The only problem there is whether that embarrasses Johnson."

"It does. Badly," Haldeman said. "I think."

Overall, Nixon had high hopes. "Boy, we're going to expose them," he said. "God, Pearl Harbor. I mean, the Democratic Party will be gone without a trace if we do this correctly."[10]

Colson suggested the first recruit to the secret organization, a former CIA agent: "He's a very close friend of Jim Buckley," Colson told the president. James Buckley, brother of the conservative columnist and *National Review* editor William F. Buckley, had won a three-way race as the Conservative Party candidate for the US Senate from New York. Bill Buckley was godfather to two daughters of Colson's ex-CIA agent. "He spent 20 years in the CIA overthrowing governments," Colson said. "Ideologically, he already is convinced this is a big conspiracy."

"What's his name?" Nixon asked.

"His name is Howard Hunt. He's here in Washington now, just got out of the CIA. Fifty. Kind of a tiger," Colson said.[11] Some of Hunt's former colleagues were less impressed. In 1964, Hunt had come up with an idea designed to curry favor with President Johnson. "Hunt proposed to obtain copies of Goldwater's speeches before they were delivered," Evan Thomas wrote in *The Very Best Men*. Chester Cooper, a former CIA analyst who then worked at the White House, "politely declined, saying that he could just send his secretary down to the Republican National Committee and she would be given advance copies without having to steal them," Thomas wrote.[12]

By mid-July, the secret organization had a name: the Special Investigations Unit (SIU). The SIU, unlike the CIA, FBI, or NSA, operated without congressional authorization or oversight. Congress didn't know the SIU existed. Investigators later found its organizational chart. At the top was the president, with a box below for Haldeman and Ehrlichman. (Haldeman wisely kept out of it as much as possible; Ehrlichman drew the short straw and became Nixon's officer in charge.) The SIU reported directly to Ehrlichman. Beneath it on the organizational chart were boxes for Justice (home of the FBI), the Pentagon, the State Department, and the CIA. The legitimate agencies of the government all had to answer to the SIU. It answered to no one but the president and Ehrlichman.[13]

Ehrlichman filled the SIU box with the names of two cochairmen.[14] One was Ehrlichman's thirty-one-year-old deputy on the Domestic Council staff, Egil "Bud" Krogh. Ehrlichman and Krogh were both lawyers, Christian Scientists, and Eagle Scouts.[15] Colleagues considered Krogh such a straight arrow that they nicknamed him "Evil" Krogh. His portfolio under Ehrlichman included the drug problem and crime prevention.[16] "To put Egil Krogh in charge of a secret police operation was equivalent to naming Frank Merriwell chief executioner of a KGB squad," Theodore White wrote, invoking the male equivalent of Nancy Drew.[17] Krogh had long seen a role for himself in internal security. Huston's "skill at analysis and genius at organizing an administration position vis-à-vis militant groups is balanced somewhat by a rather uncompromising, acerbic, and at times paranoid reaction to positions less dogmatic than his own," Krogh wrote Haldeman on February 23, 1970. "We need a central repository for all intelligence matters relating to internal security. My office, it seems to me, should be it."[18] Regarding the whole issue of internal security, Krogh wrote that an "attuned political sensitivity is the most important missing ingredient in our present organization."[19] He would lead the SIU part-time, continuing his work on other domestic issues.

Ehrlichman pulled David R. Young from the NSC staff for the SIU's full-time cochairman. Young was another lawyer, one year older than Krogh.[20] He provided the SIU with the nickname that, years later, the news media adopted. When one of his relatives found out he was working on leaks, she'd said his grandfather would be proud, because he was a plumber. A sign soon appeared on his door: "Mr. Young—Plumber." Years later when the SIU's existence became public knowledge, the media called it "the Plumbers." The nickname is misleading. Plumbers plug leaks, but that was just one of the SIU's purposes; Nixon created the secret organization to provide him with a way to *engineer* illegal leaks.

Krogh's drug war duties had introduced him to the man he would recruit as the fourth member of the team, an ex-FBI agent and indelible character named G. Gordon Liddy.[21] Stories about Liddy are many, memorable, and often feature firearms. He loved telling one from his G-man days about the time he "bailed out of a moving car and outdrew" a fugitive. Later, as an assistant district attorney giving his closing argument in a robbery case, he drew a pistol and fired it into the courtroom ceiling. Gunless, he'd have you know, he could still kill a man using just a pencil, preferably but not necessarily sharpened. Having lost the 1968 Republican primary against liberal Rep. Hamilton Fish of New York, and then refrained from actively campaigning against him on the Conservative Party line, Liddy was rewarded with a job in Nixon's Treasury Department. There he worked on an attempt to stop drug traffic through Mexico, which is how he met Krogh.[22]

Liddy noticed that everyone in the SIU was linked to a member of Nixon's inner circle: Krogh came from Ehrlichman's Domestic Council, Young came from Kissinger's NSC, and Hunt was Colson's recruit. Liddy, as a former FBI agent, was Attorney General Mitchell's man. The only member of the inner circle without a man in the SIU was Haldeman.[23]

Colson, although not a member of the SIU, played an indispensable role. He was responsible for disseminating the information it gathered—either by funneling it to congressional committees that Nixon hoped would hold hearings on the leak of the Pentagon Papers, or by leaking it to reporters.[24]

The creation of the SIU violated both criminal law and the US Constitution. It was illegal because Nixon created the unit for the purpose of committing crimes—for example, to burglarize the Brookings Institution and to obtain grand jury testimony so that he could leak it to the press. It was unconstitutional because those crimes violated the Bill of Rights—specifically, the Fourth Amendment "right of the people to be secure in their persons, houses, papers, and effects, against unreasonable searches and seizures" and the Sixth Amendment right to a fair trial by an impartial jury. This illegal, unconstitutional, secret organization, which the president granted extraordinary police power without congressional authorization or judicial oversight, would investigate Nixon's conspiracy theories, no matter how flimsy.

## "All These Harvard People"

For example, the president sought to use grand jury testimony to destroy Cooke, alleged possessor of a Harvard degree. "Before you say a word about him," Nixon told Haldeman on July 1, 1971, "let me tell you one thing I want you to know about Eastern people. I don't like to go into old history, but in the Hiss case, Bob, the major problem I had was that Hiss came from such a nice family. He was the boy chosen at Johns Hopkins to be the most likely to succeed. His family were just beyond reproach. One of the best, one of the better families in the [Virginia] Hunt Country. And he was graduated from Harvard Law School. Chambers came from a bad family. That argument was made over and over again. I don't want to hear this family shit any more from anybody. The guys from the best family are most likely to develop that arrogance that puts them above the law," Nixon said. "They all are that way. All these Harvard people."

Haldeman cut right to the chase. Cooke said he had shown Ellsberg classified documents in 1970, and Ellsberg had leaked them to the *Washington Star,* but Cooke didn't know Ellsberg was going to do that.

All the documents related to the case of Tran Ngoc Chau, a South Vietnamese lawmaker President Thieu had arrested on the floor of the National Assembly in February 1970. The charge was pro-Communist activity. Specifically, Chau had repeated contacts with a North Vietnamese intelligence official—namely, his brother, Tran Ngoc Hien. Many Americans objected to his arrest. John Paul Vann, pacification chief for the Mekong Delta, testified that Chau had informed him of the contacts. Chau, in fact, passed on information he got from his brother to the US government. Maj. Gen. Edward G. Lansdale, the legendary CIA agent who played a large role in putting together a South Vietnamese government from the remains of its defeated French colonial predecessor in 1954, called Chau loyal, patriotic, and a good friend. According to Cooke, he'd called Ellsberg in to help him go through the government files and make the case for Chau's release. (Cooke and Ellsberg had worked together on the Pentagon Papers and on Nixon's presidential transition, two facts Haldeman didn't mention and may not have known.)[1] "The cables that he showed Ellsberg were later printed by Jimmy Doyle in the *Star,*" Haldeman said.

"Why didn't we catch Ellsberg then?" Nixon asked.

"That's a very interesting point. Rogers at that time was very concerned about it and ran an investigation, found that Cooke had shown the cables to Ellsberg. Ellsberg was at RAND, and there was no security violation in any way, shape or form. He had not given him the cables," Haldeman said. "When the Doyle story appeared in the *Star* with the cables, they started checking on this at State. Cooke volunteered the fact that he had shown the papers to Ellsberg and that in his opinion Ellsberg could very well have been the leak on it, in which he indicated his distrust of Ellsberg." State looked into it with RAND, but by then Ellsberg had already left the think tank. "So State dropped the case because of that," Haldeman said.

The president called this the "biggest line of bullshit I ever heard. Doesn't Elliot know you've got a time bomb there? Oh, I know, I know, they'll say, well, he's moderate, he's nice [*unclear*]. Goddamn it, that isn't the way these sons of bitches work. Fire him. That's enough. Kick the son of a bitch out. That's the way to handle him. What's Elliot want to do?"

"The upshot of the whole thing is, he feels that Cooke did nothing at all that he should not have done. That there is no case against him at all," Haldeman said.

"Ellsberg was working within the bureaucracy to screw us on foreign policy matters," Nixon said.

"But he didn't know that," Haldeman said.

The president was sure he did. "What we're up [against] here is an enemy worse than the Communists. Because they were a few. We're up against people like this Cooke," Nixon said. "This fellow Cooke is part of the conspiracy within this government." Telling himself that Cooke was conspiring against him, Nixon conspired against Cooke. "All evidence that we find with regard to the conspiracy is going to be leaked to columnists and the rest, and we'll kill these sons of bitches. This Cooke, I'm going to get him killed," Nixon said.[2]

In his memoirs, the former president would describe the leak of documents about one South Vietnamese assemblyman's imprisonment in abstract terms that made it sound vast: "We learned that an aide to Elliot Richardson at the State Department had given Ellsberg access to the current Vietnam documents in 1970. Even after the information in them was leaked, presumably by Ellsberg, Richardson had refused to remove the aide."[3] The Chau case was a tiny fraction of "the current Vietnam documents in 1970." Leaking them threatened neither the

South Vietnamese nor the US government with anything more than embarrassment.

At this point, Nixon pursued the wispiest theories. Haldeman said his brother-in-law had overheard someone at an LA Rams game saying, "Next summer we're going to leak some of the papers about the war that we've got set up to go out. We got a man in Kissinger's office who is giving us the material."

"I think there is one," Nixon said. He summoned Kissinger and had Haldeman repeat the story, which the president attributed to "one of our investigations."

Kissinger then retold the story to Gen. Alexander Haig: "Well, Al, the president also mentioned to me that he heard from some investigators, who overheard a conversation saying that somebody on my staff is cooperating with these people."

The president took it from there. "And that two on his staff will resign this summer, leak more documents from the NSC itself and collapse the war," Nixon said. "Al, comb through that staff with a fine tooth comb."[4]

## The Economic Conspiracy Theory

In July 1971, Nixon's conspiracy thinking metastasized; it spread from foreign to domestic policy. His attempts to silence two politically unhelpful voices—one on unemployment, the other on inflation—illustrate with remarkable clarity the role "imitation of the enemy" played in Nixon's self-justifications.

Nixon had received one bit of good news on the day the Supreme Court ruled against him on the Pentagon Papers: the next unemployment announcement would show a sharp drop from 6.2 to 5.6 percent.

"Ho ho ho," the president said when he heard. "Is it all statistical, you think?"

"There was a statistical quirk that was here," said Office of Management and Budget Director George P. Shultz, "and I'm sure that's partly responsible."[1] The statistical quirk came from a seasonal adjustment the Bureau of Labor Statistics (BLS) makes each year to the unemployment rate in June, to compensate for the big influx of students into the market when classes end and the search for summer jobs is on. In June 1971, the BLS did its job survey before school let out for the summer, so it looked like there was a big drop in unemployment, even though there really wasn't.[2]

It was the first good employment news the administration had in months.

"I've talked to Colson already incidentally about goosing up the story on the unemployment thing tomorrow," the president told Haldeman on July 1, 1971. "You probably don't realize what a massive public relations story that can be. It doesn't mean a goddamn thing. There probably hasn't been any shift. Well, there has been a little. A little down."[3]

"Make sure Herb Stein doesn't go out with one of his asshole economic interpretations," Haldeman told Nixon on July 2, the day the jobless figure came out. Stein was vice chairman of the President's Council of Economic Advisers.

"He ain't gonna interpret anything," Nixon said.

The chief of staff read a memo from Stein with mock pomposity: "'Much of the improvement in unemployment is a statistical aberration, rather than a genuine improvement in the labor market.'"

"Oh, Jesus," the president said.

"Here's the best he could come out with. 'It probably would be fair to say that there has really been a small reduction of the unemployment rate the magnitude and timing of which is still difficult to evaluate,'" Haldeman said. "'The drop we have should not be interpreted as a sharp drop in the high unemployment plateau for which we have been looking.'"

"And I know we're not ever going to have it. My whole point is, it's all a goddamn game!" Nixon said. The president didn't think unemployment was too high. "Six percent's about where it ought to be in view of the fact of the makeup of the force," Nixon said.[4]

Secretary of Labor James D. Hodgson told reporters that the drop in unemployment represented "a real improvement" and predicted it would continue to go down over the next year.[5] The headline of the July 2 *Washington Evening Star* read: "Jobless Rate Declines to 5.6%." The second paragraph of the story said, "The Labor Department warned that the dip might have been caused by a statistical quirk."[6] The "might have been" wasn't accurate; the seasonal adjustment *was* the reason the drop was so sharp.

"They threw in their line that maybe it's a statistical fluke, which some damn fool at the Labor Department said," Colson told the president, "but if I can find out who it is, he'll be the first one of the casualties of the Lord High Executioner." Colson chuckled.

"I'd find out, and then he's got to be fired," Nixon said.

"That's right," Colson said. "It's not attributed to anyone. It just says, 'The Bureau of Labor Statistics attributed the sharp decline in the jobless rate to a statistical quirk.'"

"Then it must have been a statistical fluke when it went up," the president said.[7]

In fact, ten months earlier, when a similar statistical hiccup caused the unemployment rate to jump sharply, Bureau of Labor Statistics officials had said so in a news conference. In September 1970, the jobless rate rose from 5.1 to 5.5 percent—the highest in six years. September, of course, was the month when students left their summer jobs and returned to school—the flip side of what was happening in June 1971. In both months, the Bureau of Labor Statistics did its job survey earlier than usual.[8] In September 1970, that made unemployment look worse than it was. Assistant Commissioner of Labor Statistics Harold Goldstein told the press that "there is some overstatement of the [unemployment] rate for September."[9] Needless to say, the president had no objection when the BLS explained that a rise in unemployment was *not* as bad as it looked. The September 1970 jump came at a terrible time for Nixon politically. "This is the last monthly report on the employment situation before the Nov. 3 elections. But officials of the Bureau of Labor Statistics, traditionally insulated from the political arena, were quick to explain that the big increase could be attributed in large part to a quirk in timing," the *Washington Post* reported.[10] Goldstein wasn't some political hack. Reporters depended on him to interpret the unemployment rate because he was a career federal employee and an expert in his field, not a political appointee toeing the White House line. In October 1970, that worked out to President Nixon's benefit. As it had in August 1969, when Goldstein said there was very little evidence that a rise in the jobless rate from 3.4 to 3.6 percent meant the economy was slowing.[11] And in June 1970, when the unemployment rate had risen to 5 percent, its fifth increase in a row. "Harold Goldstein, assistant commissioner of labor statistics, said the current job lag was much milder than during either of the major postwar recessions both in terms of total joblessness and insured unemployment," the *Washington Post* reported.[12]

But it wasn't to President Nixon's advantage when Goldstein said the unemployment rate rose to 6 percent in December 1970—its highest level in nine years—because economic conditions in certain industries were weak.[13] Or when Goldstein described a drop in unemployment of two-tenths of a percent in January 1971—the first drop in seven months—as "marginally significant," adding, "It is not an upthrust in the economy."[14] The president "wanted some action taken immediately to get rid of Goldstein, who he feels is the same guy who screwed us back in the later years of the Eisenhower Administration," Haldeman wrote.[15]

The following month, when unemployment dropped from 6 to 5.8 percent, Goldstein called the results "sort of mixed." Unfortunately, that same day Secretary Hodgson said the decrease meant the economy was moving in the right direction. Asked if he was disagreeing with Hodgson, Goldstein told reporters, "It's not my job to support the secretary's statement or not. My job is to help you understand the figures."[16] Or, as the historian Allen J. Matusow wrote, "Goldstein had seen presidents come and go for 24 years and intended to explain the statistics as he always had, without varnish."[17]

The president's top domestic policy adviser saw two alternatives: "I would suggest either that Mr. Goldstein be transferred to the Billings, Montana, field office of the Department of Labor," Ehrlichman wrote Haldeman on March 6, 1971, "or he be instructed not to make comments to the press under any circumstances about anything ever in the future."[18] Two weeks later the Labor Department announced a decision "made jointly with the White House" to suspend the BLS press briefings on both the unemployment and inflation rates.[19]

The attempt to silence Goldstein failed. Sen. William Proxmire, D-Wisconsin, chairman of the Joint Economic Committee of Congress, announced that he would invite BLS experts to testify every month on the day the unemployment rate was announced.[20]

Nixon mentioned Goldstein by name in his Lord High Executioner speech: "This son of a bitch, Goldstein in the Bureau of Labor Statistics. I know him well. I've known him for 20 years. He's a left-wing radical who hates our guts. He didn't want us to get in. And every time that he has an opportunity, or has had an opportunity—we've piped him down now—to give it to us, whenever the statistics came out, he's done it. So we've stopped having him make comments about this. He works on them. He is an expert. He knows the subject. But we've said the man who will give the political interpretation of this is the Secretary of Labor, which is the way it should be, and not a guy down the line who is dedicated to our defeat."[21]

Haldeman complained to his diary that the BLS had taken a great story and "screwed it up."

> This drove the P right up the wall tonight, and he started hounding
> Colson on the phone every couple of minutes, demanding that we get
> Goldstein fired, etc. Colson overreacted and started bouncing around

in the woodwork, getting action underway and finally got around to calling me. In the meantime, he had Shultz on a special airplane being brought back down for a 7:30 meeting tomorrow morning to get things started, so they can give the P a plan at 8:00, when he says he'll be at his desk. I doubt that he will, but he just might out of orneriness. In any event, Colson and I have agreed that we've got to move on getting Goldstein out and that it's just ridiculous to let this thing keep on dragging on. It's basically a problem of Hodgson's unwillingness to bite the bullet, and we've got to force him to do it. I'm leaving it up to them to handle it in the morning. I'm not planning to go in until a little later. We'll see what happens.[22]

## "Are They All Jews?"

July 3, 1971, 8:00 a.m., the Oval Office. "See, I understand statistical aberrations," Nixon told Colson. "Why didn't they say there were statistical aberrations when it went up?"

They did, but Colson didn't mention that. "Hodgson's fighting to protect him," Colson said. "George Shultz admits that it was *very* badly handled, but thinks we ought to just fix the procedures so it doesn't happen again."

The president was silent for ten seconds.

"Goddamn weak sisters, the whole bunch," Nixon said.

Colson: Well, it seems to me, Mr. President, that the only leverage you have is to tell Shultz and Hodgson this morning that you want that bureau reorganized in such a way that we have control over it, period. And in the process of that, the guys we don't want will quit.[1]

Colson ushered the budget director and labor secretary into the president's office. Secretary Hodgson had done a brilliant job of presenting the unemployment figure, but the BLS made "him look like a goddamn fool," the president said. "I don't want to deny the facts. I don't want to jimmy the facts. I don't want to jigger the facts. But I want them to screw us . . . whenever we're wrong, but I want them to do it even-handed. And they're not doing it that way. They are not doing it that way. Every release has been loaded against us. And deliberately." He demanded a plan.

Shultz: Well, I think the only kind of organization that would be sensible under these circumstances is a reorganization that separates Goldstein from the employment and unemployment figures and gets him into something else entirely.

Colson: I don't think the president would ever have any confidence in any other arrangement.[2]

The president said he wanted someone honest. "I just want a son of a bitch who isn't going to lie for anybody, not for him or for us," he said. "You fellows have got to realize we are getting political interpretation of these statistics by people within the Bureau of Labor Statistics and always against us. And so on. That's what I want to stop. That's all. The political interpretation."

Colson urged them to act quickly, "because the closer you get to 1972 the more this would look—"

"Political. That's right," Nixon said.

"Well, let us set a deadline—by the end of the summer," Shultz said.

"Well, why don't we say the first of September? Labor Day. That's a good thing. Labor Day, the Bureau of Labor Statistics is to be reorganized," the president said. "Or August. I would prefer the latter."[3]

After Hodgson and Shultz left, the president vented his exasperation. "I really believe that they think these sons of bitches are honest," he said.

"Yeah, they do. They did. They don't now," Colson said. He'd called them in at 7:00 a.m. and showed them the statements one of his aides surreptitiously tape-recorded the night before while calling the bureau and pretending to be a reporter from *Time* magazine. "And when they saw what the BLS people were actually saying, they just caved in. They know now," Colson said.

"You get the names?" the president asked.

Colson's aide couldn't reach Goldstein, but he got other BLS officials.

"And they all talked?"

"Every one of them. Every one! And every one of them said, 'Don't listen to anybody in this business except Goldstein,'" Colson said.

President Nixon: Well, listen, are they all Jews over there?

Colson: Every one of them. Well, a couple of exceptions. Oh, Jesus.

President Nixon: See my point?

Colson: Gordowsky [*President Nixon acknowledges*] and Levine and you just go right down the damn list. You know goddamn well they're out, I mean, they're out to kill us.[4]

Shultz's chief statistician at OMB thought the bureau needed reorganizing.

"Julius Shiskin," Colson said. "He's Jewish also, but he's—"

"Well, goddamn it, there's some damn good Jewish [employees]," the president said.[5] (In two years, Nixon would put Shiskin in charge of the BLS.)

## "They're All Over"

On July 3, 1971, the White House chief of staff arrived at work later, as planned.

"Beautiful day," the president said.

"It is the most beautiful day I have ever seen in Washington," Haldeman said.

"Lovely."

They discussed a speech the president would deliver that night at the National Archives to kick off a multiyear celebration of the American Revolution's bicentennial. On display was the original Declaration of Independence, which Nixon would quote in his opening line: "We are, in this room, in the presence of some immortal phrases: All men are created equal . . ."[1]

The president turned to more timely matters. "Well, I found a very interesting thing this morning," he said. "Colson discovered something. He's a clever bastard. He had his office call the Bureau of Labor Statistics."

"Posing as a *Time* reporter," Haldeman said.

"And they all said it was Gold-stine, Gold-steen," Nixon said, mispronouncing a name he'd had a lot of practice saying.

President Nixon: I said, "What kind of people were they?" I said, "Were they all Jews?" He said, "Yes." Everyone who answered was a Jew. Now, point: [White House Personnel Director Frederic] Malek is not Jewish.

Haldeman: No.

President Nixon: All right. I want a look at any sensitive areas around where Jews are involved, Bob. See, the Jews are all through the government, and we have got to get in those areas. We've got to get a man in charge who is not Jewish to control the Jewish . . . do you understand?

Haldeman: I sure do.

President Nixon: The government is full of Jews.

Haldeman: I sure do.

President Nixon: Second, most Jews are disloyal.[2]

Nixon offered some exceptions to this generalization, all of whom happened to be on his White House staff. "But, Bob, generally speaking, you can't trust the bastards. They turn on you," Nixon said.

"Sure, and their whole orientation is against this administration anyway, or against you," Haldeman said.

"No, but they have this arrogant attitude, too," Nixon said.

"And they're smart," Haldeman said. "They have the ability to do what they want to do, which is to hurt us. Which is a problem."

Nixon found it interesting that Kissinger didn't have many Jews on the NSC staff. Maybe one, a "horrible bastard who's probably all right," the president said. "I don't tend to judge a person by his looks. That's wrong. It's terribly wrong."

"None of his aides have ever been Jewish," Haldeman said. "Even Tony Lake, who turned on us." Lake had resigned over the invasion of Cambodia.

President Nixon: Was Tony Lake homosexual?
Haldeman: I don't think so. I wondered about that.
President Nixon: He looked it.
Haldeman: I know it.
President Nixon: OK.[3]

Malek was to look throughout the administration and find out if there was a "Jewish staff in anyplace—and they're all over, Bob—and see what we can do about them," the president said. "I really feel that I want the Jews checked."[4]

First, the White House chief of staff had an aide double-check that *Malek* wasn't Jewish.[5]

## "Somebody Sits on High"

Before the sun set on July 3, 1971, the president, who had started the day saying he didn't want to jimmy the jobless rate, was floating ideas on how to do exactly that. "Certainly, the best way to adjust that would be on a gradual basis. From our standpoint," Nixon told Colson. "So you go down one-tenth one [month], two-tenths another, one-tenth another, two-tenths another. The worst way from our standpoint is to drop it like this and then have a lot of doubts raised about it and then start to raise it gradually until you get up to 5.8 or [5.]9 or to whatever they think it is. You see my point?"

"Mm-hmm."

"In other words, a big drop in any month is not in our interests," the president said. "Small increments is very much in our interest." Nixon was, once again, imitating the enemy—without first making sure that the enemy was doing what he thought, or was an enemy at all. "They fiddle with these figures," he said. "Somebody sits on high and determines how you're going to have the numbers come out."[1] At least that's what the president told himself as he maneuvered to become that somebody.

## Counting Ivy Leaguers

The president's top aides started updating him on conspiracy theories regarding foreign and domestic policy at the same time. Robert C. Mardian, assistant attorney general in charge of the Internal Security Division, had followed up on a lecture Nixon gave him about there being too many Ivy Leaguers in the Justice Department. "He went back to check and see how it stacks up. And it's really pretty good. It's predominantly non–Ivy League as defined as Harvard, Yale, Columbia, Cornell, Penn," Ehrlichman reported on July 20, 1971. "Total: 84 percent not Ivy League, 16 percent Ivy League."

"That's fine," the president said.

Mardian broke the numbers down to look specifically at US attorneys appointed during the Nixon administration. "Of our appointees, heavily non–Ivy League by four-to-one, five-to-one. So he's got the message. On our conspiracy," Ehrlichman said.

"How does it presently stand?" Nixon asked. "Did you find anything? How did Cooke come out?"

"Cooke spent 14 hours with Ellsberg," Ehrlichman said.

"He couldn't have talked 14 hours about Chau," the president said.

"No. That's the point, you see. There just wasn't that much material," Ehrlichman said. "Senator Mathias would not give up the National Security Council papers." They still didn't know what Nixon White House documents Ellsberg had given the senator.

Nixon suggested having Secretary of State Rogers ask him to turn them over. "If the son of a bitch doesn't do it, then we demand it," the president said.

OMB Director George Shultz joined them to discuss reorganizing all the major statistical agencies of the federal government, including the BLS. "That will also be an occasion when Goldstein's duties can be shifted without any great strains. And he would be moved into something else, probably a statistician-as-such-type job. That's the way he would be gotten out of the employment statistics analysis business, just be removed from that area," Shultz said. "I think one thing we have to be very careful about is that we don't get labeled as fixing the numbers."

"Particularly at a time when the numbers may begin to get better," Nixon said.

The president expressed displeasure with the chairman of the Federal Reserve. Arthur F. Burns was a Nixon appointee and political ally for more than a decade. He was also a Jewish immigrant from Austria-Hungary, a pipe-smoking intellectual, and a former professor at Columbia University. Once Nixon made him chairman of the Fed, Burns was independent enough to talk and act like "the archetype of the conservative economist," as the *Wall Street Journal* put it.[1] With unemployment rising and the economy in recession, Nixon wanted lower interest rates and monetary expansion.[2] Burns worried that the policies Nixon favored would fuel inflation, and said so in public. "Differing sharply with President Nixon, Arthur F. Burns again called for stronger government action to curb inflation," the *Journal* reported on July 1, 1971.[3]

"I've told [Treasury Secretary John B.] Connally to find the easiest money man he can find in the country and one that will do exactly what Connally wants and one that'll speak up to Burns, and Connally is searching the goddamned hills of Texas, California, Ohio," Nixon told Shultz and Ehrlichman. "We'll get a populist spender on that board one way or another. But that's what we have—if you know of somebody that's that crazy, let me know, too."

Shultz chuckled.[4]

## Counting Jews

During the next conspiracy round-up in the Oval Office on July 24, 1971, Ehrlichman informed the president that Robert Mardian was furnishing him with raw data from the grand jury investigation of the Pentagon Papers leak. He passed on one tidbit that to this day remains closed by statute.

"That sort of thing, leak it right out," Nixon said. "That sort of thing can kill the bastards. But, John, if you wait, they'll cover it up."

"I understand," Ehrlichman said.

"Does Mardian understand?" Nixon asked.

"I haven't let Mardian get into that at all," Ehrlichman said. He just had the assistant attorney general hand the information over to him. "We're going to put that out here through Colson and Hunt," Ehrlichman said.

Haldeman gently reminded Nixon that having a Justice Department lawyer leak grand jury information would be problematic (it being against the law).

"My point is, leaking is a game," the president said. "I'm going to leak this out. I'm going to leak the Ellsberg thing out." He told them to leak a story on Gelb as well. "One other thing I want to know. Colson made an interesting study of the BLS crew." He found out that sixteen were registered Democrats, only one a Republican. The president wanted another number. "Bob, how many were Jews?" Nixon asked.[1]

Haldeman had someone working on that.

"There's a Jewish cabal, you know, running through this, working with people like Burns and the rest," the president said. "And they all—they all only talk to Jews."[2] This was a historic moment. While conspiracy theories about the Fed are as innumerable as grains of sand (plug the words "Fed Jewish Conspiracy" into a search engine and see for yourself), this was the first—and to date the only—such theory articulated by someone who actually exercised the power to appoint members to the Federal Reserve Board.

To add even greater irony to the moment, Burns had privately assured Nixon that he would goose the economy for 1972. The reason the Federal Reserve is independent is to keep politicians from making decisions about interest rates that boost their short-term electoral prospects at the expense of the long-term health of the economy. Yet on March 19, 1971, when the president and the chairman were alone in the Oval Office, Nixon asked for and received assurances that the Fed would help him out on unemployment when it mattered most politically.

President Nixon: Arthur, the main thing is next year, now that unemployment has got to—let's don't let it get any higher, but I hope we can—

Burns: That's what I have my eye on.

President Nixon: Yeah. But I think we've really got to think of goosing it.

Burns: Yes.

President Nixon: Shall we say late summer and fall this year in order to affect next year?

Burns: Exactly.[3]

If Burns was conspiring with anyone, it was with Nixon, to reelect a president of their party. But on the morning that Nixon conjured a "Jewish cabal" out of thin air, the Federal Reserve chairman had aroused his patron's ire with a front-page *New York Times* headline: "Burns Says Inflation Curb Is Making Scant Progress."[4]

"Now, what do you want to do with Arthur Burns? Raise his salary?" the president asked Haldeman and Ehrlichman that afternoon. "Arthur loves to get his name in the paper." Nixon would get the Fed chairman's name in the paper in his own way. "Could you get one story leaked through Colson's apparatus on Arthur?" he asked. Part of the story was that the president's economic advisers had recommended expanding the membership of the Federal Reserve Board. Another part was that the Fed might have to be brought under control. Nixon started writing the story out loud: "The independence of the Fed . . ."

". . . has been put seriously into question by the economic results in the last year," Ehrlichman said.

Both parts were made up. The president said he got the idea from Treasury Secretary Connally. "He thinks it might sort of worry Arthur a little," Nixon said.[5] The third part (equally fictitious) would shame him.

Exclusive 7-28

By Norman Kempster

Washington (UPI)—President Nixon is considering a proposal to double the size of the Federal Reserve Board, it was learned today. The suggestion, if put before Congress, could touch off a controversy rivaling President Franklin D. Roosevelt's attempt to "pack" the Supreme Court.

Administration officials also disclosed that Nixon rejected a request from Arthur F. Burns—Chairman of the Reserve Board—for a 20,000 a year pay raise. Burns currently makes 42,500.

Burns, however, denied he had "lobbied for an increase in salary."[6]

"Did you ever get the number of Jews that were in BLS?" the president asked Ehrlichman at their first meeting of July 28, 1971.

"I got their biographies yesterday. I'm having them analyzed," Ehrlichman said.[7]

Haldeman, who wasn't present, already had a number. "What is the status of your analysis of the BLS, specifically of the 21 key people?" he asked Personnel Director Frederic Malek on July 26. "What is their demographic breakdown?"[8]

Malek replied the next day with a breakdown of thirty-five BLS employees by party registration: twenty-five Democrats, one Republican, four independents, five unregistered. "In addition, 13 out of the 35 fit the other demographic criterion that was discussed," Malek wrote.[9]

Turning to another conspiracy theory, Ehrlichman said, "Instead of going after Brookings, we're going to go after Gelb personally." He had arranged with the Justice Department to "have our guy who sits right in there and sees the raw data as it comes in every day and he'll feed us the stuff that's available," Ehrlichman said. "There's a ton of raw data like that over there. Just a ton of it."

The president was pleased with the Burns story. "The salary increase thing is the most potent one. That's the kind of thing everybody can understand," Nixon said. "And I'll never forget Arthur sitting in here telling us a year ago there shouldn't be a salary increase and that the Cabinet officers should give it back."

Ehrlichman laughed and said, "Yep. Oh, absolutely."[10]

Later that afternoon, Haldeman said, "The Arthur Burns ploy worked with a bang."

"Yeah. We've denied it all over the place now. That's good," the president said.

"Arthur squealed to Shultz last night," Haldeman said. "And then he talked to Alan Greenspan today. He said, 'This is—this is awful.'" Greenspan was one of Nixon's economic advisers in 1968. "Greenspan said, 'Well, I understand that there's real concern in the administration by the political people about the great political harm that you're doing the president by running around making all these negative remarks.' And Arthur babbled on and on about, the last thing he would ever do in the world is any political harm to the president and that he's not doing it for that," Haldeman said. "So I told him to tell Greenspan to tell [Burns] that what he could do is make a damn positive, constructive speech on the economy and what a great job the president's doing. And that would clear the thing."[11]

Assistant Commissioner of Labor Statistics Goldstein didn't have that option. The reorganization plan hatched in the Oval Office to take Goldstein out of unemployment analysis went forward later that summer. "Harold Goldstein will be moved to a routine, non-sensitive post in another part of BLS," Malek wrote Haldeman on September 8, 1971. "He has been told of this and will move quietly when the reorganization is announced. A sensitive and loyal Republican is also being recruited for the employment analysis function being vacated by Goldstein."[12]

## Above the Law

As the president pursued imaginary conspiracies through July 1971, a partially subterranean warren of offices on the first floor of the Executive Office Building (EOB) next to the White House was retrofitted as a high-security area and equipped with a special alarm system, a combination safe, and "scrambler" telephones.[1] EOB Room 16 was the SIU's headquarters. An August 26, 1971, status report from Cochairman David Young to Ehrlichman shows how closely the unit's agenda reflected the president's theorizing.

> The plan then was to slowly develop a very negative picture around
> the whole Pentagon Study affair (preparation to publication) and then

to identify Ellsberg's associates and supporters on the new left with this negative image. The end result would be to show (1) how they were intent on undermining the policy of the government they were supposedly serving, and (2) how they have sought to put themselves above the law.

Putting themselves above the law was the accusation Nixon leveled against Jews, intellectuals, and Ivy Leaguers in general and three in particular.

> In fact, it appears that those in Justice and Defense most familiar with this whole enterprise believe that substantial evidence is being developed for the criminal prosecution of individuals other than Ellsberg; namely, Gelb, Halperin, Warnke and RAND executives.[2]

If it ever appeared that way, looks deceived; the vast, multiagency investigation coordinated by the SIU never did develop the evidence needed to prosecute Warnke, Halperin, or Gelb.

Hunt and Liddy did, however, come up with a bold plan to break into Brookings. According to Liddy, they were told that either Halperin or Ellsberg "or both of them were believed to be using Brookings for storage of substantial additional amounts of classified documents at least as sensitive, if not more so, than the Pentagon Papers. Further, the Brookings security vault might have evidence shedding light on the identity of Ellsberg's criminal associates in the purloining of top secret defense files [and] whether Paul Warnke and Leslie Gelb were among them," Liddy wrote.[3] In his 1980 memoir, *Will,* Liddy revealed their spectacular proposal to penetrate Brookings using Cuban CIA assets of Hunt's acquaintance.

> We devised a plan that entailed buying a used but late-model fire engine of the kind used by the District of Columbia fire department and marking it appropriately; uniforms for a squad of Cubans and their training so their performance would be believable. Thereafter, Brookings would be firebombed by use of a delay mechanism timed to go off at night so as not to endanger lives needlessly. The Cubans in the authentic-looking fire engine would "respond" minutes after the timer went off, enter, get anybody in there out, hit the vault, and get themselves out in the confusion of other fire apparatus arriving, calmly loading "rescued" material into a van. . . .
>
> Hunt submitted the plan for approval, but this time the decision was swift. "No." Too expensive. The White House wouldn't spring for a fire engine.[4]

## "Pretty Much Carte Blanche"

The president personally got FBI Director Hoover to unwittingly furnish leakable material to the SIU. "He asked that I forward to you all information acquired to date, including individual reports of interviews," Hoover wrote Krogh on August 3, 1971.[1]

The CIA's charter prohibits it from conducting domestic intelligence activities, but the White House impressed it into the service of the SIU. "I want to alert you that an old acquaintance, Howard Hunt, has been asked by the President to do some special consultant work on security problems," Ehrlichman told Lt. Gen. Robert E. Cushman, deputy CIA director, on July 7, 1971. "He may be contacting you sometime in the future for some assistance." Ehrlichman wanted him to know that Hunt was working for the president. "You should consider he has pretty much carte blanche."[2]

The SIU used it.

The CIA does psychological profiles of foreign leaders. Young requested that agency psychiatrists profile Ellsberg.[3] Howard J. Osborn, the CIA's director of security, noted that Ellsberg was an American citizen and said he would need the personal approval of Director Helms.[4] Under White House pressure, Helms reluctantly gave it.[5] On August 11, Osborn sent a draft psychological profile of Ellsberg to the SIU with a note: "I know that you appreciate that however this is used, the agency should not become involved."[6] The agency already was.

The profile wasn't what the SIU was looking for. "There is nothing to suggest in the material reviewed that Subject suffers from a serious mental disorder in the sense of being psychotic and out of contact with reality. . . . An extremely intelligent and talented individual, Subject apparently early made his brilliance evident. . . . There is no suggestion that Subject saw anything treasonous in his act. Rather, he seemed to be responding to what he deemed a higher order of patriotism."[7] Leaking that certainly wouldn't destroy Ellsberg.

Young and Krogh wanted the CIA to take another crack at it, this time fortified with additional information from the FBI and what they referred to in an August 11, 1971, memo to Ehrlichman as a "covert operation." It had several aims.

Although the government never turned up evidence to charge Ellsberg with actual espionage, the SIU took seriously the notion that Ellsberg had turned over classified information not only to the American people, but to a foreign government. In his memoirs, Nixon wrote that "we received a report that the Soviet Embassy in Washington had received a set of the Pentagon Papers before they had been published in the *New York Times*."[8] He didn't mention that the story was never confirmed. (He also significantly altered it; according to the unconfirmed report, the embassy got the papers four days *after* the *Times* started publishing them, not before.) The White House didn't even ask the FBI to investigate.[9] Nixon's inner circle thought so little of the tale that they gave it to Victor Lasky, a journalist with standards low enough for Haldeman to refer to him as "a leaker of last resort. If nobody else'll print it, Lasky will."[10] Ellsberg's indictment didn't even mention the story, although it would have given Nixon a reason to charge him with treason, if only it had been true.[11]

"I was confident," Krogh would write decades later, "that we all agreed that Ellsberg was very likely at the center of a Soviet-sponsored conspiracy to diminish U.S. influence in the critical theater of Vietnam. It was an easy conclusion to reach, somehow made all the easier by the complete lack of corroborating evidence."[12]

Liddy looked for links between the leaker and Soviet intelligence: "who was Daniel Ellsberg? Romantic rebel of the left and lone wolf? Or part of a spy ring that had deliberately betrayed top secret information in unprecedented quantity to the Soviet Union?" Liddy came up with his own Oxbridge twist on Nixon's suspicions of Ivy League intellectuals. "Ellsberg had, according to FBI reports, a long psychiatric history and had studied in England at Cambridge University, the place that had proved so fruitful in the recruiting of Soviet spies from among the British intelligentsia," Liddy wrote. This is the overseas equivalent of suspecting people of spying because they have degrees from Harvard. Ellsberg's "long psychiatric history" was short and uneventful; for two years starting in 1968, he'd seen a psychoanalyst in Los Angeles, Dr. Lewis Fielding. Hunt and Liddy wanted a look in Dr. Fielding's patient records. They agreed that Ellsberg might have told his psychoanalyst whether he had coconspirators in leaking classified documents. "I thought a bag job in order," Liddy wrote.[13] Hunt mentioned that the CIA did that sort of thing overseas. He offered to draw on the Cuban American CIA assets he knew in Florida from his Bay of Pigs days.[14]

Krogh and Young asked Ehrlichman's authorization on August 11.

> In this connection, we would recommend that a covert operation be undertaken to examine all the medical files still held by Ellsberg's psychoanalyst covering the two-year period in which he was undergoing analysis.[15]
>
> Approve _____ Disapprove _____

Ehrlichman wrote his initial next to "Approve," adding "if done under your assurance that it is not traceable."[16]

On August 25, Hunt got a camera hidden in a tobacco pouch and alias documents (false ID) from the CIA and flew with Liddy out to California to case Fielding's office. They took pictures inside and out. At Hunt's request, a CIA employee met Hunt at Dulles Airport, picked up the exposed film, took it back to the CIA's lab for developing, and furnished the SIU with prints. Hunt said it looked like "a perfect situation here for a clandestine surreptitious entry." He requisitioned a disguise and alias documents from the CIA for Liddy.[17]

Over Labor Day weekend, Hunt and Liddy flew to Chicago, where they bought cameras and walkie-talkies. The two continued to Los Angeles, where they met up with three of Hunt's CIA assets: Bernard Barker, Eugenio Martinez, and Felipe de Diego. There they purchased a crowbar, glass cutter, and other tools of the trade. Hunt took one walkie-talkie and staked out Fielding's home. Liddy stood watch outside the office building as Barker, Martinez, and de Diego broke a window on the first floor to get in, then broke through the door to Fielding's office. "I drew the Browning knife from the case attached to my belt and unfolded the blade," Liddy wrote. "Only if there were no other recourse would I have used the knife, but use it I would, if I'd had to; I had given my men word that I would protect them."[18] Luckily, no one on whom Liddy "had to" use a knife wandered into the area or arrived to investigate the crime in progress.

There are two different versions of the outcome of the Fielding break-in: the SIU's and the doctor's. According to the SIU and Barker, Martinez, and de Diego, they got nothing. They couldn't even find Ellsberg's file.[19]

Dr. Fielding, however, testified that Ellsberg's file had been removed from his filing cabinet.

Back in EOB Room 16, Hunt and Liddy passed around Polaroids.[20] The idea was to make it look like a drug-related break-in gone bad. "I was stunned and appalled by what I saw," Krogh wrote. "I couldn't understand what was unclear about the word 'covert' in 'covert operation.'"[21]

Hunt tried to show the photos to Colson. "Howard, get that stuff out of here. Do not tell me anything like this. I don't want to be involved," Colson said as he walked into his office and closed the door.[22]

## "One Little Operation"

Ehrlichman glided right past the Fielding break-in when next he briefed the president. He spent more time on the latest rabbit hole the SIU had gone down chasing Nixon's conspiracy theory. "It's taken this long to pull everything together because the Ellsberg case took this funny bounce," Ehrlichman said on September 8, 1971, "where it became pretty clear as we get farther and farther into it that Ellsberg's guilty of what he's charged with, which is stealing the documents and copying them, but that he probably didn't give them to the *New York Times*."

"Who the hell did?" the president asked.

"Well, we think that Gelb did," Ehrlichman said. "Now that's speculation at this point." (It would remain so.)

"Does Gelb know we're looking into him?"

"I don't think so," Ehrlichman said. "We tried a few—we had one little operation that aborted out in Los Angeles, which, I think it's better that you don't know about, uh—"

"OK," Nixon said.

"—but, uh, we've got some dirty tricks underway that may pay off." (Ehrlichman's later claims to have informed the president in advance of the California operation and received his approval ring false in the light of this conversation.)[1]

"We're running into a little problem," Ehrlichman said. Some of the secrets Nixon wanted to leak about his Democratic predecessors were embarrassing to the CIA as well, and its director was not handing them over. "I've got to talk to Helms about getting some documents which the CIA have on Bay of Pigs and things like that, which they would rather not see [get] out."

"Never get 'em," Nixon said. The failed 1961 invasion of Cuba by CIA-trained Cuban expatriates was a disaster for all involved. Helms was the CIA's chief of operations at the time. "They're very sensitive about it," Nixon said.[2]

## The CIA Bluff

Ehrlichman couldn't get the CIA to give up the documents Nixon wanted to leak on three subjects: the Bay of Pigs, the Cuban Missile Crisis, and the 1963 overthrow of South Vietnamese president Diem. All of these crises occurred during the Kennedy administration.

Nixon decided he needed to talk directly to Helms. Ehrlichman furnished him with talking points designed to mislead the CIA director about White House intentions: "The President wants to see all of the documents requested. He recognizes that many are sensitive and could damage the agency if used by the wrong people (even, Helms suggests, some White House staff). The President will be discreet."

Nixon was to couch the request in terms of declassification, not leaks, and promise to protect information whose disclosure would damage CIA operations. But he was to avoid promising that no CIA documents would be declassified "or released." The talking points invoked the proper standard for declassification: "Career or personal embarrassment of present or past employees is not a reason to keep documents secret."[1] Nixon applied this general rule to the secrets of his Democratic predecessors and the CIA, but not to his own.

"You're probably wondering what the hell it's all about," the president said to Helms on October 8, 1971, in the Oval Office. "Why are we interested in all these things? I mean, muckraking, politics, et cetera, et cetera." He dropped a broad hint that he needed the Cuban Missile Crisis documents for possible upcoming negotiations with the Soviet Union. "It has to do with events that will be quite clear within a few weeks. That is, I just want to be sure that I am totally aware of everything we have ever dealt with [regarding] the Russians in the past," Nixon said. "I just want to be prepared. That's what that's all about."

"Sure," Helms said.

"I don't think that poses much of a problem," the president said. "Now, when you get to the dirty tricks department, which is the department we're really concerned about, as I understand. I well understand it. I know what happened in Iran. And I also know what happened in Guatemala." (The CIA engineered the overthrow of Iranian prime minister Mohammad Mossadegh in 1953 and Guatemalan president Jacobo Árbenz Guzmán in 1954, when Nixon was Eisenhower's vice president.)

"Sure," Helms said.

"And I totally approved of both. And I also know what happened in the planning of the Bay of Pigs. Remember, I said I totally approved of it," Nixon said. "I remember talking to Kennedy the day—it was right in this room. The only time I was in it. The *only* time I was in it, actually, in the eight years I was out of office. Kennedy got up and raved and ranted about the people. I would've, too. He said people had misled him and so forth. And the problem was not the CIA. The problem wasn't your plan. It was not carried out. I mean, you had a goddamn good plan." The president said he just wanted to know the facts.

The Pentagon Papers had "whetted the appetite of every goddamn scandal-monger in town" for everything else, Nixon said. "We've done a lot of things. You know about the Menu strikes. You know about the things that we've tried. Our trouble is, in this field, we've tried things and we haven't succeeded. But that's part of it. That is, we should never have lost the Chilean election. Once we got to the point that we did, why, we should have done something more effective than we did." When Socialist Salvador Allende won the 1970 presidential election in Chile, Nixon directed the CIA to prevent him from taking office. The agency's attempt to foment a military coup failed at the time. (A second coup attempt in 1973 would succeed and usher in the bloody dictatorial regime of Augusto Pinochet.)

The CIA director sounded perfectly amenable. "I regard myself, you know, really as working entirely for you," Helms said, "and anything I've got is yours, any time you want it, any time of the day or night."

"Well, that's really the case. That's really the case. But I want you to know that I'm not asking for this for the purpose of spreading it out," the president said. "But on the other hand, we have to be well aware of the fact that stuff does kick around." The meeting ended cordially.[2]

But the CIA didn't turn over the documents Nixon wanted.[3] The following year, after the Watergate break-in, the president would attempt to use the agency's reluctance to air its dirty linen regarding the Bay of Pigs as leverage to engineer a cover-up.

## The Smoking Gun

Four decades of investigations great and small have produced no proof that President Nixon knew about the Watergate break-in before it occurred. The question retains a fascination that sometimes overpowers critical judgment. Jeb Stuart Magruder, deputy director of Nixon's 1972 reelection campaign, made headlines in 2003 on the thirtieth anniversary of the Senate Watergate hearings by claiming to have overheard Nixon approve the break-in during a phone call between the president and Campaign Chairman John Mitchell on March 30, 1972. Reporters naturally wanted to know why Magruder hadn't mentioned this three decades earlier. His answer, "Nobody ever asked me that," should have set off alarms.[1] Magruder had testified on the subject under oath on live national television during his June 14, 1973, appearance before the Senate Watergate Committee. "Throughout the hearing, Magruder said repeatedly that to his knowledge President Nixon was not aware of the bugging plans or the cover-up," the *Washington Post* reported.[2] The White House, which logs the president's calls, didn't record any with Mitchell on March 30, 1972, nor does the conversation Magruder described in 2003 appear on Nixon's tapes. Magruder's story about Nixon approving the Watergate break-in received great attention in the media; the holes in it, much less.

Why the yearning for proof that Nixon ordered the break-in and bugging at Watergate? For some, it would resolve the seeming mystery of why the president orchestrated the Watergate cover-up. After all, the most commonly drawn lesson of Watergate is, "It's not the crime, it's the cover-up." The knowledge that Nixon lost the presidency because he ordered the cover-up becomes, for some, the assumption that he wouldn't have lost it if he hadn't ordered it. Howard Baker, the ranking Republican on the Senate Watergate Committee, who famously asked what the president knew and when he knew it, put it this way:

> Richard Nixon made one fatal political mistake. He made it in the very beginning. It's pretty clear, I think, from the record evidence, that President Nixon did not know of that break-in before it occurred. And had Richard Nixon gathered up those people on the south lawn of the White House and had summoned up the TV cameras and fired them, he would've been a moral giant. And it wouldn't have affected the outcome of that election one bit in my judgment. But he didn't do that. He decided instead to try to contain it. And that was his fatal error. Containing it almost always is a disaster. And that has become the single most important lesson that, I think, Watergate teaches us. Whatever it is, get it out of the way.[3]

Baker tells a neat story with an appealing moral. But the choice Nixon had to make wasn't the easy one Baker imagined. If there were a path that allowed Nixon to be both a moral giant and a landslide winner, he would have taken it.

Unfortunately for Baker's theory, the two men who had the most foreknowledge of the break-in—the ones who planned it—were E. Howard Hunt and G. Gordon Liddy, and they were both members of the SIU. If Nixon had allowed the FBI to fully investigate their crimes, they would have led back to his own. The felonies that Nixon created the SIU to help him commit—breaking into the Brookings Institution, leaking grand jury testimony—were impeachable offenses. Indeed, the very creation of the SIU as an illegal, unconstitutional secret police organization was an impeachable offense. Nixon couldn't afford to let the FBI get answers to simple, basic questions. How did Hunt and Liddy meet? Was Watergate their first break-in? Orchestrating a cover-up did ultimately cost Nixon the presidency, but he would have lost it sooner if he had just let investigators do their jobs. The notion that Nixon could simply have cut loose the guilty parties in the Watergate break-in and walked away scot-free himself is mistaken. If only to protect himself, he had to protect Hunt and Liddy from any investigation of their illegal SIU activities.

The president was in the Bahamas on June 17, 1972, when Washington, DC, police arrested five burglars in the Democrats' Watergate headquarters, so his initial reaction to the news is not on tape. By the time of Nixon's second recorded conversation about Watergate on June 20, 1972 (the first one having been erased multiple times, leaving the notorious "18½-minute gap"), the president was well aware of Hunt's involvement—and thus of his own legal jeopardy.[4] By June 21, he'd learned of Liddy's role.[5] At that point, a cover-up was a political necessity for the president.

Not that it was simple. Hoover's death one month before the break-in allowed Nixon to put in his own man, L. Patrick Gray, as acting FBI director, but command wasn't control. "On the investigation, you know, the Democratic break-in thing, we're back in a problem area, because the FBI is not under control, because Gray doesn't exactly know how to control them," Haldeman told Nixon on June 23. The problem of the day involved the money trail: the FBI had found a check signed by a Nixon fund-raiser in the bank account of one of the burglars. It would reveal that contributions to Nixon's reelection campaign had financed the Watergate break-in.[6]

Mitchell had an idea. The news media played up the CIA connections of the five Watergate burglars. NBC had reported the night before that four of the burglars had been involved in the agency's anti-Castro efforts. (Hunt had drawn on the same pool of CIA assets he had used for the burglary at the office of Ellsberg's psychiatrist; two burglars had taken part in both break-ins.) Nixon had used the CIA to stop the investigation of the Green Beret case in 1969. The month before Watergate, Nixon had put in Lt. Gen. Vernon A. Walters, his military attaché in Paris, as deputy CIA director. Mitchell suggested that "the way to handle this now is for us to have Walters call Pat Gray and just say, 'Stay the hell out of this. This is—there's some business here we don't want you going any further on.' That's not an unusual development," Haldeman said. "And that would take care of it."

"What's the matter with Pat Gray? You mean he doesn't want to?" Nixon asked.

"Pat does want to. He doesn't know how to, and he doesn't have any basis for doing it. Given this, he will then have the basis," Haldeman said.[7]

That afternoon, Nixon suggested Haldeman tell the CIA, "The President's belief is that this is going to open the whole Bay of Pigs thing up again."[8] The agency had been worried about the remaining secrets of that fiasco leaking in 1971; now the president would take advantage of that concern to stop the Watergate investigation from revealing one of his own secrets—the SIU.[9]

Haldeman and Ehrlichman met with CIA Director Helms and Deputy Director Walters that day. Helms gripped his chair, according to Haldeman, and shouted, "The Bay of Pigs had nothing to do with this. I have no concern about the Bay of Pigs."[10] But the CIA complied with the president's wishes. Afterward, Walters later testified, Helms said to him, "You must remind Mr. Gray of the agreement between the FBI and the CIA that if they run into or appear to be about to expose one another's assets they will notify one another, and you must remind him of this." Five days later in a June 28 memo to Walters, Helms wrote that "we still adhere to the request that they [the FBI] confine themselves to the personalities already arrested or directly under suspicion and that they desist from expanding this investigation into other areas which may well, eventually, run afoul of our operations."[11] The cover-up, personally authorized by the president, was working—for the time being.[12]

Watergate also understandably renewed Nixon's determination to get his hands on FBI records that would prove LBJ bugged his 1968 campaign plane. They would have provided Nixon with an everyone-does-it defense. "But the evidence had mysteriously disappeared," Haldeman wrote.[13] It hadn't; the evidence never existed. There were no FBI reports on what Nixon had said in his plane during the last two weeks of the '68 campaign, because there was no bug.

Although the Washington Post published groundbreaking articles by Bob Woodward and Carl Bernstein on Watergate in the months after the break-in, the cover-up held through the 1972 election. A grand jury indicted Hunt and Liddy along with the five Watergate burglars on September 15, but only for their role in that break-in, not for any crimes committed by the SIU.[14] The Democrats tried to make a campaign issue out of it, but failed. Seventy-six percent of voters told the pollster Louis Harris they'd followed the story, but 62 percent dismissed it as "mostly politics," and 66 percent didn't think "President Nixon was involved in or had knowledge of the Watergate affair."[15] Nixon won the biggest Republican landslide in history, capturing 60.7 percent of the popular vote and 521 electoral votes from forty-nine states. His Democratic opponent, Sen. George S. McGovern of South Dakota, got 37.5 percent and the 17 electoral votes of Massachusetts.[16]

After the election, a Democratic Congress prepared to investigate Watergate. White House Counsel John W. Dean III came up with an idea to head off congressional hearings, Haldeman wrote: "if we can prove in any way by hard evidence that our plane was bugged in '68, he thinks that we could use that as a basis to say we're going to force Congress to go back and investigate '68 as well as '72 and thus turn them off."[17] The chief of staff brought the idea up with the president on January 8, 1973. "But the question is whether we have any hard evidence on it," Haldeman said. "The only input we have on it is J. Edgar Hoover, who's dead, I presume."

"I'd play that right up to the hilt. What does it do to the Bureau? It's a nasty story, but it's just too damn bad. They should not have bugged the candidate's plane," Nixon said. "You don't really have to have hard evidence, Bob. We're not going to take this to court. All you have to do is to have it out, just put it out on authority, and the press will write the goddamn story."[18] The president decided to have Mitchell get confirmation from the FBI official Hoover claimed had done the bugging, Deke DeLoach.[19]

The White House quickly learned that this threat wouldn't work on LBJ, as Haldeman noted in his diary on January 12:

> I talked to Mitchell on the phone on this subject and he said DeLoach had told him that he was up to date on the thing because he had a call from Texas. A *Star* reporter was making an inquiry in the last week or so, and LBJ got very hot and called Deke, and said to him that if the Nixon people are going to play with this, that he would release *(deleted material—national security),* saying that our side was asking that certain things be done. By our side, I assume he means the Nixon campaign organization. DeLoach took this as a direct threat from Johnson.[20]

It's not difficult to guess what Johnson threatened to release: information from NSA, CIA, and FBI reports on the Chennault Affair. Ten days later, on January 22, Johnson died of a heart attack at age sixty-four.

Nixon didn't let it go. He ordered Acting FBI Director Gray to give a lie detector test to everyone in the bureau to find out what role they played in bugging his plane.[21] When he heard that according to DeLoach the bugging had not taken place, Nixon rendered a one-word judgment: "Bullshit."[22]

## "I Don't Kiss and Tell"

The president got a close-up, personal reminder of the Chennault Affair on March 6, 1973, during a one-on-one meeting in the Oval Office with the Washington lawyer Thomas Corcoran. An old New Dealer nicknamed "Tommy the Cork" by FDR himself, and "White House Tommy" by those who noted his habit of starting phone conversations by revealing where he was calling from, Corcoran, like many other Democrats, had moved to the right during the Cold War.[1] He supported Nixon on foreign policy and other matters, such as the president's wish to be succeeded in the Oval Office by his favorite Democrat, John B. Connally, who headed Democrats for Nixon in 1972.

"You know, I have a protégé," Corcoran said out of the blue. "Her name's Anna Chennault."

"Yeah, sure," Nixon said. In 1952, Corcoran had set the stage for Gen. Claire and Anna Chennault to greet Republican presidential candidate Eisenhower when his campaign plane landed at the New Orleans airport. Corcoran blamed the Truman administration's "abandonment of China" for the Chennaults' switch from Democrats to Republicans.[2]

"She is one of the best and loyalest friends you've ever had."

"I know. I know."

"Mr. President, I have never written a book. I don't kiss and tell."

"Yeah."

"I am amazed at some of the people in your administration that break under pressure and talk too much."

"Yeah, yeah."

"But I happen to know what was going on in '68, when Anna kept her mouth shut, when [Nixon campaign communications manager] Herb Klein asked her to.[3] And through all the pounding, you remember?" Corcoran asked.

"Oh, yeah, because of that?" The president didn't elaborate on what "that" was.

"Yeah," Corcoran said. "I know about it, because I happened by accident to be [*unclear*] and she came to me crying. Now, how did I get to know Anna? You don't remember, I was Chennault's—"

"I know," Nixon said. Corcoran was one of the owners of Gen. Chennault's airline and co-ran it after his death.

Anna Chennault "wrote you a letter not so long ago and she wonders whether you ever got it," Corcoran said.

(Nixon's secretary, Rose Mary Woods, told the president on January 8, 1973, that Chennault "has had a letter asking that she be appointed—and I didn't bother you with it—and I don't know whether it should see daylight—she sent it down to my desk saying she'd be appointed your special ambassador to the Far East, because nobody else understands the Far, you know, the Oriental mind." Woods suggested giving it to the personnel director. "And then he'll just brush it off," Nixon said. "It'll never reach the light of day.")[4]

Corcoran told the president that "she's asked you if she may have an interview with you alone by herself." Apparently he'd brought another letter from Chennault. "That's her own writing. She is worth her weight in gold," Corcoran said.

"All right, all right. Good," the president said.

"Thank you very much, sir," Corcoran said.[5]

Anna Chennault got to see Nixon at the White House one more time before his resignation—along with several hundred other people attending a March 17, 1973, evening at the White House featuring the country music star Merle Haggard. There's no record of her meeting with the president alone then or at any other time for the rest of his presidency.

## Dean Testifies

At times the Chennault Affair threatened to come to the surface during the Watergate investigations, but it never quite did. Corcoran's meeting with the president was one such time; another, vastly more public one was during the testimony of the Senate Watergate Committee's star witness on June 25, 1973. John Dean, Nixon's former White House counsel, had turned state's evidence and was now furnishing information about the administration officials with whom he had previously worked on the cover-up. The three commercial television networks broadcast all six hours of Dean's appearance live. The thirty-four-year-old lawyer was a genuine White House insider who dropped bombshell after bombshell to investigators, but there were limits to his knowledge. Dean knew that Hoover had told Nixon that his campaign plane was bugged in 1968, but not why. Dean had turned over a copy of the Huston Plan to investigators—but didn't know that Nixon had ordered it implemented to break into the Brookings Institution. Dean knew of a different plan to break into Brookings than the one Hunt and Liddy devised—but didn't know what documents it was intended to obtain.

Dean recalled that Jack Caulfield, a former New York police detective turned White House gumshoe, had come running into his office in late June or early July 1971. "You've got to help me. This guy Colson is crazy! He wants me to firebomb a goddamn building, and I can't do it," Caulfield said. "Colson's been pestering me for weeks to get this guy Halperin's Vietnam papers out of the Brookings Institution." Caulfield and another former New York police officer, Anthony J. Ulasewicz, did private-eye work on the public payroll for Nixon—tailing Sen. Ted Kennedy, investigating the Quakers protesting Vietnam in Lafayette Park, looking into a story involving the Speaker of the House, alcohol, and a nightclub called the Zebra Room. "Well, Tony cased the place," bribed a guard to get in, and found out the papers were in a big safe, Caulfield said. "The security on that vault is tough." He'd told Colson it was impossible. "Chuck says, 'I don't want to hear excuses! Start a fire if you need to! That'll take care of the alarms. You can go in behind the firemen.'"

This put Dean in a bind. He now had advance knowledge of a planned burglary-with-arson. He called Ehrlichman, who was with the president at the "Western White House" in San Clemente, California, and asked to fly out and see him the next day. As he told the story in the chief domestic policy adviser's West Coast office, Dean was impressed with Ehrlichman's calm. No questions, no expression of surprise, just an occasional eyebrow twitch. When Dean finished, Ehrlichman said he'd take care of it and made a phone call to Colson, apparently calling the whole thing off.[1]

Dean's testimony about the aborted break-in was unintentionally, unavoidably comic: "What prompted Mr. Caulfield to come to me was that he thought the matter was most unwise and his instructions from Mr. Colson were insane." The blend of formal diction and casual criminality ("Mr. Colson had . . . instructed him to burglarize"), bathos ("his instructions from Mr. Colson were insane"), and sly understatement ("he thought the matter was most unwise") uncannily evoked the style of Damon Runyon, the bard of Brooklyn's Prohibition-era mobsters best remembered today for the short stories that inspired the Broadway musical *Guys and Dolls*. The firebombing of Brookings seemed like a comic subplot to the story of Watergate—and a not particularly important one. None of the networks mentioned Brookings in their news programs; most newspaper reporting ignored it as well.

Attention focused naturally on the break-ins that did occur—at Watergate and the office of Ellsberg's psychiatrist. The Fielding break-in had come to light at Ellsberg's trial in May 1973 and, along with the revelation that the government had failed to disclose that its wiretap on Halperin had picked up Ellsberg as well, prompted the judge to throw out the case against the Pentagon Papers leaker. Investigators now had two break-ins on which to focus, along with the related activities of the SIU, known far and wide as "the Plumbers." During Ehrlichman's July 24, 1973, appearance before the Senate Watergate Committee, chief counsel Samuel Dash spent little time questioning him about the aborted plan to break into Brookings.

> Dash: Do you know who authorized it?
> Ehrlichman: No, I don't.
> Dash: Did you ever look into who authorized it?
> Ehrlichman: No, I didn't.[2]

Ehrlichman had heard the president authorize it personally in the Oval Office. To conceal that fact, Ehrlichman committed perjury. And he got away with it. While Nixon remained in office, investigators didn't trace Watergate back to its origin. To that extent, the cover-up worked.

## The *X* Envelope

On day two of Dean's testimony before the Senate Watergate Committee, June 26, 1973, Walt Rostow handed an envelope marked with the letter *X* and the words "Eyes Only" to the head of the LBJ Library with the instruction that it not be opened for fifty years. LBJ's former national security adviser provided minimal explanation.

> Sealed in the attached envelope is a file President Johnson asked me to hold personally because of its sensitive nature. In case of his death, the material was to be consigned to the LBJ Library under conditions I judged to be appropriate.
> The file concerns the activities of Mrs. Chennault and others before and immediately after the election of 1968. At the time President Johnson decided to handle the matter strictly as a question of national security; and, in retrospect, he felt that decision was correct.

Rostow thought 2023 might be too soon. If the head of the library then believed "the material it contains should not be opened for research, I would wish him empowered to re-close the file for another 50 years," Rostow wrote.[1]

Dean's opening statement had touched on the Chennault Affair briefly and vaguely. He testified about an attempt to substantiate the claim that LBJ bugged Nixon's plane: "The surveillance that DeLoach reported to Mitchell was related to Mrs. Anna Chennault and a foreign embassy. Also the telephone toll records from the vice presidential candidate Agnew's airplane when he had stopped in Albuquerque, New Mexico, had been checked by the FBI."[2] Sealed in the file Rostow directed to remain closed for half a century were the FBI records of that surveillance, along with the corresponding NSA and CIA intelligence reports and related White House memos.

Rostow also included his own "personal reflections" on the Chennault Affair and Watergate.

> I am inclined to believe the Republican operation in 1968 relates in two ways to the Watergate affair of 1972.
>
> First, the election of 1968 proved to be close and there was some reason for those involved on the Republican side to believe their enterprise with the South Vietnamese and Thieu's recalcitrance may have sufficiently blunted the impact on US politics of the total bombing halt and agreement to negotiate to constitute the margin of victory.
>
> Second, they got away with it. Despite considerable press commentary after the election, the matter was never investigated fully.
>
> Thus, as the same men faced the election of 1972, there was nothing in their previous experience with an operation of doubtful propriety (or, even, legality) to warn them off; and there were memories of how close an election could get and the possible utility of pressing to the limit—or beyond.[3]

Rostow's reflections, dated May 14, 1973, are remarkable. He sensed a connection between the Chennault Affair and Watergate. But if he considered the possibility that the root of Watergate lay in the president's urgent desire to obtain exactly the kind of documents that Rostow was then sealing away, he didn't mention it. Rostow's choice of words makes it sound as though he was distressed that "they got away with it" and that "the matter was never investigated fully." But no one could fully investigate the Chennault Affair *without* the documents in the *X* envelope. Sealing them away ensured that it would *not* be fully investigated, that "they" would continue to get away with it.

If there ever was a moment when the country wanted to get to the bottom of Watergate, it was while millions of Americans were riveted to their television sets watching the hearings unfold in real time. Rostow thought the roots of Watergate lay in the Chennault Affair. He had the evidence that could expose those roots, yet he chose that precise moment to ensure that it didn't see the light of day. It was a decision he made unilaterally, not just for himself or for historians, but for the entire nation. He left us no explanation.

## The White House Tapes

Reluctantly, under oath, in response to a direct question on live national television, Alexander P. Butterfield told the Senate Watergate Committee on July 16, 1973, that President Nixon secretly recorded White House conversations. From the moment Haldeman's assistant revealed the existence of the White House tapes, it was clear that there was an objective way to answer some of the most pressing questions about the Watergate cover-up.[1] (Americans found out that week that Presidents Kennedy and Johnson secretly taped as well.) The Watergate special prosecutor subpoenaed them as potential criminal evidence. The president fought all the way to the Supreme Court to keep the recordings in his possession and control, but his claim of "executive privilege" didn't persuade a single member. The court ruled 8-0 on July 24, 1974, that the president had to turn over the tapes.

That month, the House Judiciary Committee approved three articles of impeachment against President Nixon, only one of which even began to skim the surface of the SIU's illegality.

> He has, acting personally and through his subordinates and agents, in violation or disregard of the constitutional rights of citizens, authorized and permitted to be maintained a secret investigative unit within the office of the President, financed in part with money derived from campaign contributions, which unlawfully utilized the resources of the Central Intelligence Agency, engaged in covert and unlawful activities, and attempted to prejudice the constitutional right of an accused to a fair trial.[2]

Investigation of the SIU had by then produced three convictions for criminal conspiracy. A jury convicted Ehrlichman and Liddy of conspiring to violate the civil rights of Ellsberg's psychiatrist in connection with the burglary of his office.[3] Krogh pled guilty to the same charge.[4] Prosecutors granted Hunt and Young immunity.[5] (A grand jury had named the president as an unindicted coconspirator in the Watergate cover-up.)[6] None of them were charged with criminal conspiracy to break into Brookings; Liddy didn't reveal the SIU's role in that plot until the publication of his 1980 memoir, *Will,* and the tapes revealing Nixon's part didn't emerge until 1996.[7] Even with convictions, guilty pleas, and prison sentences for former administration officials, the cover-up was still working in important ways.

On August 5, the White House released a transcript of what soon became known as the "smoking gun" tape. The June 23, 1971, conversation captured the president's decision to thwart the FBI investigation of Watergate on the false pretense that it threatened to expose CIA activities. In legal terms, the tape proved that the president had taken part in a criminal conspiracy to obstruct justice; in simple terms, that Nixon was a liar and a crook. He announced his resignation on August 8, 1974. The next day, before the helicopter carried him away from the White House, he bade farewell to his staff. One thing he said stands out above all else: "always remember, others may hate you, but those who hate you don't win unless you hate them, and then you destroy yourself." To many, this sounds like Nixon had a moment of insight into his own character and downfall.

At most, however, he was criticizing himself for stooping to the level of those who hated him—for "imitation of the enemy," his ever-handy enabler. The flaw that brought Nixon down was his ability to convince himself, without evidence, that enemies were conspiring against him, and to use that to justify his conspiring against them. Federal Reserve Chairman Arthur Burns wasn't conspiring against him; he was just prescribing conservative economic policies. Assistant Commissioner of Labor Statistics Harold Goldstein wasn't conspiring against him; he was just analyzing unemployment figures without regard to whether it helped or hurt Nixon politically. Paul Warnke, Morton Halperin, and Leslie Gelb were working together to elect a Democrat in 1972, but they weren't engaged in a criminal conspiracy against the Republican incumbent. This president fought imagined evils with real ones, slandering Burns, forcing out Goldstein, and hijacking the investigative power of the federal government to gather information for the express purpose of destroying Warnke, Halperin, and Gelb. His hate did destroy him, but it required no outside provocation.

Nixon's presidency was over, but not his battle to keep the American people from hearing the rest of his tapes. When President Gerald R. Ford announced a blanket pardon of his predecessor on September 8, 1974, he eliminated the chance of the tapes being subpoenaed as evidence against Nixon. Before the year was out, the ex-president reached an agreement with the Ford White House that would have destroyed all the tapes upon his death. Congress asserted the government's control over the recordings to preserve and ultimately release them.[8] Nixon launched a legal battle to keep the tapes from the public that continued until his death on April 22, 1994. Just three months later, on July 22, 1994, Walt Rostow decided to open the X envelope, reversing his previous decision to keep its contents sealed for fifty years.[9]

In 1996, the historian Stanley Kutler's valiant legal battle to get the government to open Nixon's tapes to the public finally bore fruit with the release of 201 hours of conversations related to the late president's abuses of power. Christopher Matthews soon revealed that one of those tapes proved that Nixon personally ordered the Brookings break-in.[10] In 1997, Kutler published a book of transcripts, *Abuse of Power*, showing that Nixon demanded the burglary multiple times.[11]

I made the connection between Nixon's break-in order and the Chennault Affair in a September 24, 2007, essay, suggesting that Nixon acted out of an understandable fear that if the think tank had a report on the events leading up to the bombing halt, it would include evidence of his own role in Republican sabotage of the peace talks.[12] Since then, other writers have adopted this view.[13]

It certainly makes more sense than the explanations Nixon gave during and after his presidency. *RN: The Memoirs of Richard Nixon* offered up plea bargains with history. The ex-president owned up to lesser offenses while evading more substantial charges. Nixon knew that one day readers would be able to compare his book with his tapes. *RN* furnished a rationale for the Brookings break-in without ever admitting that the author ordered it, or that it was one of the reasons he created the SIU.

From the first there had been rumors and reports of a conspiracy. The earliest report, later discounted, centered on a friend of Ellsberg, a former Defense Department employee who was then a Fellow at the Brookings Institution. I remembered him from the early days of the administration when I had asked Haldeman to get me a copy of the Pentagon file on the events leading up to Johnson's announcement of the bombing halt at the end of the 1968 campaign. I wanted to know what had actually happened; I also wanted the information as potential leverage against those in Johnson's administration who were now trying to undercut my war policy. I was told that a copy of the bombing halt material and other secret documents had been taken from the Pentagon to Brookings by the same man. I wanted the documents back, but I was told that one copy of the bombing halt report had already "disappeared"; I was sure that if word got out that we wanted it, the copy at Brookings might disappear as well.

In the aftershock of the Pentagon Papers leak and all the uncertainty and renewed criticism of the war it produced, my interest in the bombing halt file was rekindled. When I was told that it was still at Brookings, I was furious and frustrated. In the midst of a war and with our secrets being spilled through printing presses all over the world, top secret government reports were out of reach in the hands of a private think tank largely staffed with antiwar Democrats. It seemed absurd. I could not accept that we had lost so much control over the workings of the government we had been elected to run—I saw absolutely no reason for that report to be at Brookings, and I said I wanted it back right now—even if it meant having to get it surreptitiously.[14]

Nixon leaves out the most important parts: his attempt to abuse the Huston Plan for political ends, Huston's role in convincing the White House that this mysterious disappearing bombing halt report existed in the first place, Nixon's repeated demands for a break-in, and the fateful step the president took in creating a secret police unit to break into Brookings.

The former president's explanation of his motives just doesn't hold up under scrutiny. Nixon could only maintain the pretense that he "saw absolutely no reason for that report to be at Brookings" by leaving out Leslie Gelb's name, since an obvious reason for him to have it was that, according to Tom Huston, he oversaw its writing.[15] Leaving out names was also how Nixon could get his readers to take seriously the notion that he thought he could use the report as "potential leverage against those in Johnson's administration who were now trying to undercut my war policy." His critics were Clifford, Warnke, Halperin, and Gelb—the very people under whose supervision the (alleged) report was written. Why would they include damaging information about themselves in it? For comparison, look at the Pentagon Papers, which actually were written under their direction. The forty-seven volumes contain not one critical word about Warnke, Halperin, or Gelb. They do contain a single critical sentence about Clifford, but it was uttered by North Vietnamese foreign minister Nguyen Duy Trinh, so it almost counts as praise in America.[16] Nixon had no reason to think these men would stuff a bombing halt report with blackmail material on themselves.[17]

The explanation Nixon gave on tape—"to blackmail" Lyndon Johnson—is even weaker.[18] It raises three questions: (1) What blackmail material would a bombing halt report contain on LBJ? (2) What would Nixon blackmail Johnson to do? (3) Would the benefit of obtaining the alleged bombing halt report offset the risk of committing a felony?

1. While many people outside the government suspected LBJ of calling the bombing halt to elect Humphrey, Nixon knew better—from both LBJ's 1968 briefings and Kissinger's reading of the classified documents. Johnson not only stuck with his three demands until Hanoi met them (admittedly at a politically inconvenient time for the Republican nominee), he'd actually helped the opposition party campaign against his own vice president.

2. Johnson, unlike some of his former subordinates, wasn't a critic of Nixon on the war. At the time Nixon said he wanted to blackmail LBJ, all he wanted the former president to do was take a public stand against leaks.[19]

President Nixon: He should speak up. Don't you think so?

Kissinger: Well . . .

President Nixon: Not for his interest, but for ours.

Kissinger: I'm not so sure. Frankly, I think they're also eager to . . . well, it would certainly get a tremendous brawl started between Johnson and the press.

President Nixon: That's right, and it'd get off of us. You see what I mean?

Kissinger: Well, it would get it off us on the immediate problem, but it would also drag the whole issue down to the level of "was Johnson guilty or not?"

President Nixon: That's a hell of a lot better than having whether I was guilty or not, Henry.[20]

3. Understandable as Nixon's desire to deflect the heat from himself to his predecessor may be, it hardly seems worth the risk of committing an impeachable offense. This wasn't the kind of chance Nixon generally took. As noted earlier, Brookings is the only break-in Nixon ordered on tape. In fact, it's the only political break-in anyone can prove he ordered, period. It just doesn't make sense.

Unless Nixon was attempting to remove all the evidence of his involvement in the Chennault Affair from the hands of some of his most prominent Democratic critics. Huston had told him (wrongly) that they had a classified report "on all events leading up to the bombing halt." That made the report a threat to Nixon's political survival—if he was guilty of violating the Logan Act to win the 1968 election. In that case, breaking into Brookings was less of a risk than leaving the evidence that he'd sabotaged the Paris peace talks to win the previous election in the hands of men who wanted to defeat him in the next one. Johnson had decided, for his own reasons, to keep the intelligence reports on the Chennault Affair secret in 1968; that was no guarantee that Clifford, Warnke, Halperin, and Gelb would keep them secret in 1972.

Warnke did, in fact, try to use the Chennault Affair in the 1972 presidential campaign. On August 16, 1972, he held a press conference charging that Nixon had blown a chance for peace. "There would have been a good chance of bringing the war to a political end" in late 1968 and early 1969, when Hanoi signaled a willingness to reduce hostilities, Warnke said. President Johnson couldn't follow up on that signal because the South Vietnamese "were dragging their feet" regarding negotiations "at the strong hint of someone connected with the Nixon campaign," Warnke said. He identified that someone as Chennault, saying she told the South Vietnamese they would "get a better deal if they waited until President Nixon was in office." The story was buried on page 25 of the *New York Times* (which at least ran it, unlike other newspapers).[21] Warnke had no documents to substantiate the charge, and the story quickly died. (If he'd had the report "on all events leading up to the bombing halt" that Huston claimed, things might have worked out differently.)

It's remarkable how little Nixon said about the Chennault Affair, a scandal that cast doubt on the legitimacy of his entire presidency. During his administration, Nixon made no statement on the subject, nor did anyone ask him about it during a press conference, interview, or public appearance.[22] He didn't confirm or deny involvement on his White House tapes—or on Johnson's, apart from the ambiguous "non-denial denials" he gave the president two days before the 1968 election. In his many postpresidential books, he didn't mention Chennault at all.

David Frost briefly forced Nixon to address the subject during his famous 1977 TV interviews.

Frost: . . . there have been a lot of reports that Madame Chennault was in touch with President Thieu via the Vietnamese Embassy and urging him to take a firm line, because he would get better . . . better terms, better support from you than from a Democratic president, and so on. Did you ever hear about that?

Nixon: I, of course, I'm hearing about it from you today, and I have read the reports. Just let me make this one point very clear, however. As far as I was concerned, as I told President Johnson on the phone when he informed me on October the thirty-first that he was going forward with the bombing halt, and when he said, in answer to my direct question, that he had solid commitments that they would negotiate seriously, that they would respect the DMZ and that they would quit or reduce their shelling of the cities, the major cities of South Vietnam, he said, I said, under the circumstances, I would support the talks. Let me, and I would do nothing to undercut them. I did nothing to undercut them. Ah, as far as Madame Chennault or any number of other people, like whoever may have felt, if they did, that the talks should not go forward or that the South Vietnamese should not go along. I did not authorize them, and I had no knowledge of any contact with the South Vietnamese at that point, urging them not to do so. Because I couldn't have done that in conscience.[23]

This was another "non-denial denial." By narrowing the time frame to LBJ's October 31, 1968, conference call with the three candidates, Nixon avoided the question of whether he did anything to sabotage the negotiations before that date.[24] By then, he wouldn't have *had* to do anything, if his campaign chairman John Mitchell was already secretly encouraging the South Vietnamese, through Chennault, to boycott the talks.

The Chennault Affair returned to the headlines a few more times before Nixon's death, notably after Chennault published her memoir in 1980 revealing the New York City meeting with Nixon, Mitchell, her, and Ambassador Diem, and again when Diem confirmed it in his 1987 memoir. No public denial issued from the former president on either occasion.

Nixon's defense was sporadic and ambiguous, but he and his apologists mounted an aggressive, consistent offense, accusing Johnson of using both the bombing halt and the federal government's investigative power for political ends.[25] Kissinger took up this tactic of compensatory accusation in 2003's *Ending the Vietnam War:*

Nixon may thereupon have sent a message to Thieu through intermediaries though Nixon never admitted this. It would have been highly inappropriate if true. But neither did the Johnson administration cover itself in glory in that respect. For in his memoirs, former Soviet

Ambassador Anatoly Dobrynin has reported that, at the same time, Secretary of State Dean Rusk was urging the Soviet Union to speed up the negotiations in order to elect Hubert Humphrey, who was likely to offer better terms than his opponents.[26]

Anyone who searches through Dobrynin's memoirs, *In Confidence,* for the story Kissinger tells about Rusk trying to elect Humphrey will be disappointed; it's not there.[27]

*It Didn't Start with Watergate* by Victor Lasky, the Nixon White House's columnist "of last resort," accused LBJ of "illegal wiretapping and surveillance" on Chennault.[28] Lasky offered no evidence to back up the claim of illegality. William Safire, Nixon's former speechwriter, claimed the wiretap on Chennault's phone was illegal because the attorney general never authorized it.[29] (The FBI didn't ask him to, having decided on its own not to place the tap.) Safire also wrote that Richard Allen, a Nixon campaign foreign policy adviser, "had been a target of a clumsy CIA probe," another unsubstantiated charge.[30]

Mainstream writers (with some laudable exceptions) have often repeated partisan spin about the bombing halt as if it were settled history.[31] Walter LaFeber exemplified the problem in 2005's *The Deadly Bet:* "Nixon's charges, indirect as they were, appeared to be true: Johnson had been caught trying unfairly to put a last-minute charge into his vice president's campaign."[32] LaFeber offered no evidence to substantiate the charge, nor did he display any awareness that the historian Catherine Forslund had already shown why it was false: LBJ simply stuck with his three conditions until Hanoi accepted them. "The Americans had no control over the timing of Hanoi's response and thus no way to manipulate the peace talks," Forslund wrote in 2002's *Anna Chennault.*[33]

Echoing another unsubstantiated partisan charge, LaFeber wrote that LBJ learned of the Chennault Affair "from illegal wiretaps set by U.S. intelligence officials," but provided no evidence to justify the claim of lawbreaking. (Besides, LBJ learned of Republican interference from Alexander Sachs, NSA intercepts of South Vietnamese cables, and the CIA bug in Thieu's office, not from any wiretap; Johnson ordered FBI wiretaps *after* he learned of the Chennault Affair.) LaFeber also referred to "FBI and CIA wiretaps, some of which were doubtfully legal," again with no supporting evidence (or any explanation of what upgraded the taps from "illegal" to "doubtfully legal"). At least the FBI wiretap existed; LaFeber didn't furnish any evidence of a tap by the CIA, nor do his sources, nor do the reports in the *X* envelope. LaFeber cited other writers who claimed there was something, somehow, illegal about the FBI wiretap, but they didn't substantiate the charge either.[34] In the 1970s, a Senate select committee headed by Frank Church, D-Idaho, did an extensive investigation into allegations of abuses by US intelligence agencies. The Church Committee didn't find any violation of the law in connection with the Chennault Affair.[35] No court did, either.

There is no excuse for writers to repeat politically motivated myths as if they were facts. Phony charges have a real effect. They reinforce the standard partisan defense of Nixon in Watergate: everyone does it; he just got caught.

Except he didn't. He got away with more than we realized—with more than *he* realized. The Chennault Affair worked. By using two cutouts (Mitchell and Chennault) between him and the South Vietnamese government, Nixon did manage to evade direct detection. No FBI bug picked up his campaign plane talk in the final weeks before the election; the bureau didn't even place the tap on Chennault's home phone that President Johnson requested. Neither the NSA nor the CIA picked up any direct evidence against Nixon either. The NSA, CIA, and FBI reports on the Chennault Affair never made it into the hands of Warnke, Halperin, and Gelb. (Clifford saw them, but didn't get to keep any.) There was no top secret bombing halt report prepared under Clifford, Warnke, Halperin, and Gelb at Brookings or anywhere else. Nixon didn't need it or the Huston Plan or the SIU. He was chasing shadows. If only he had known. To save himself, he destroyed himself.

His self-destruction was not complete, despite appearances. The cover-up held, at least regarding the Chennault Affair. Americans still split the difference regarding Nixon, seeing him as both a domestic political trickster and a statesman in foreign policy. Things could have turned out differently. If the nation had learned in 1973 that the president had ordered the Brookings break-in himself. If Congress had investigated that order as thoroughly as it did the Watergate break-in. If investigators had looked into Nixon's stated reason for ordering the burglary—to "blackmail" Johnson—and found it wanting. If they had investigated Republican interference with the bombing halt negotiations. If Chennault had testified under oath—as she later wrote in her memoirs—that candidate Nixon had secretly made her his "sole representative" to the Saigon government before the 1968 election. If Americans had seen the FBI wiretap report of her conveying her "message from her boss" to Saigon to "hold on" three days before the election. If only *we* had known. Nixon wasn't a rogue with a redemptive streak of patriotism. He played politics with peace to win the 1968 election.

He did the same to win reelection in 1972 at the cost of thousands of American lives.

# ACKNOWLEDGMENTS

The University of Virginia's Miller Center, under the farsighted leadership of Gov. Gerald L. Baliles, has been my intellectual home for more than a decade. By giving me the opportunity to devote several months to writing this manuscript, the Center helped me fulfill a dream, and for that I am deeply grateful.

Marc J. Selverstone, Chair of the Presidential Recordings Program (PRP), brought a wealth of expert knowledge in Cold War history, a discerning eye, and vast reservoirs of patience to reading numerous drafts, suggesting changes, and debating fine points of Vietnam historiography with an obsessive first-time author. Marc's many hours of work and helpful comments improved this manuscript in ways too numerous to count. With his work I am truly impressed; for his support I am truly grateful. Keri Matthews, Assistant Editor for the PRP, is a marvel of efficiency who daily rescues me and others from the perils of our own relative disorganization. Marc and Keri did invaluable work reviewing and revising the transcripts published in conjunction with *Chasing Shadows* and caught numerous errors that had eluded me. Thank you both for doing so much, so quickly, and so well.

The PRP has brought together scholars of extraordinary talent over the years, all of whom have in ways great and small contributed to my understanding of history and/or saved me from making some howling errors: David Coleman, W. Taylor Fain, Patrick J. Garrity, Kent Germany, Max Holland, Erin R. Mahan, Ernest R. May, Guian A. McKee, Timothy J. Naftali, Marc Selverstone, Dave Shreve, and Philip D. Zelikow. The interns who have done impressive scholarly work for the PRP are too numerous to mention and too valuable to ignore. And thank you, Pat Dunn and Lorraine Settimo, for your patience and wisdom.

Mark H. Saunders, Director of the University of Virginia Press, along with Marc Selverstone, had the vision to see that *Chasing Shadows* would be greatly enhanced if readers could go straight from the text to the tapes and transcripts and listen to history as it actually happened. Even better and rarer, they and their colleagues had the dedication to make that vision a reality.

Richard Holway, History and Social Sciences Editor at the University of Virginia Press, provided just the right guidance at just the right moment. Managing Editor Ellen Satrom brought grace and patience to shepherding the final draft to publication. Copy Editor Susan Murray made me look better than I deserve. Marketing and Publicity Manager Emily Grandstaff made more people notice.

The Richard M. Nixon Presidential Library, formerly the Nixon Presidential Materials Project, has provided me with invaluable assistance over the decades. Dedicated, knowledgeable, hardworking civil servants have labored behind the scenes to bring the records of the Nixon administration to light with little public recognition for their magnificent efforts—and sometimes not a little condemnation. Their work is all the more heroic for being unsung. My experience with the Lyndon B. Johnson Library is more limited, but all of it has been good. The staff of the LBJ Library could serve as a model of courtesy and helpfulness for the public and private sectors.

Thomas A. Schwartz of Vanderbilt University read *Chasing Shadows* in manuscript and provided incisive, extremely well-informed, challenging, yet gracious, generous, and thoughtful comments that spurred me to improve the book. Evan Thomas generously shared his insights into Cold War Washington, E. Howard Hunt, and the CIA. Doug Macdonald of Colgate University brought his great, probing mind and keen analytical skills to bear on the Chennault Affair during some valuable, in-depth exchanges that helped me clarify my views; his forthcoming book on the entire 1968 election period is certain to illuminate the shadows of this pivotal year in American history.

Writers are strengthened by every good book they read. I must single out two historians whose work has influenced me profoundly: Taylor Branch and Garry Wills. The complete list of authors from whom I've learned would fill another book. You've all enriched my life.

Michael J. Hayes has given me his priceless guidance, wisdom, and (above all) friendship through the decades. Dessy Levinson has provided me with valuable critical advice, personal and professional support, and true friendship.

The strengths of this book reflect those of the persons mentioned above and countless others who have helped me through the years; the flaws are my own.

# NOTES

1. "The President's Address to the Nation Announcing Steps to Limit the War in Vietnam and Reporting His Decision Not to Seek Reelection," 31 March 1968, *Public Papers of the Presidents of the United States: Lyndon B. Johnson, 1968* (Washington, DC: GPO, 1970), www.presidency.ucsb.edu/ws/?pid=28772 (hereafter *PPPUS: Johnson, 1968*).

2. The popular vote in 1968 was 31,770,237 for Republican Nixon (43.4 percent), 31,270,533 for Democrat Humphrey (42.72 percent), and 9,906,141 for independent candidate George C. Wallace (13.53 percent). The remaining candidates received 239,908 votes (0.35 percent) (see Theodore H. White, *The Making of the President 1968* [New York: HarperCollins, 1969], Kindle edition, chap. 12, "The Election: Passage in the Night," 462). In 1960, it was 34,221,463 for Democrat Kennedy (49.72 percent) and 34,108,582 for Nixon (49.55 percent). Other candidates got 502,773 votes (0.73 percent) (see Theodore H. White, *The Making of the President 1960* [New York: HarperCollins, 1961], Kindle edition, chap. 14, "To Wake as President," 350).

3. Conversation 525-001, 17 June 1971, 5:15–6:10 p.m., Oval Office. All Nixon White House tapes come from the collections of the Nixon Presidential Library.

4. Conversation 519-001, 14 June 1971, 8:49–10:04 a.m., Oval Office.

5. Nixon revealed the "highly unusual channel" from Kissinger to his presidential campaign in his 1978 memoir (Richard M. Nixon, *RN: The Memoirs of Richard Nixon* [New York: Touchstone, 1978], 323–26).

6. Conversation 525-001, 17 June 1971, 5:15–6:10 p.m., Oval Office.

7. "As William Bundy, the Assistant Secretary of State in charge of the negotiations, has written, I had no access to information on the negotiations," Kissinger wrote in 2003 (Henry Kissinger, *Ending the Vietnam War: A History of America's Involvement in and Extrication from the Vietnam War* [New York: Simon and Schuster, 2003], 585n2). Kissinger cites William Bundy, *A Tangled Web: The Making of Foreign Policy in the Nixon Presidency* (New York: Hill and Wang, 1998), 39–40, to back him up. Unfortunately, Bundy wrote something different from what Kissinger claimed. "Even if one or more members of a disciplined delegation was ready to confide in a former colleague, there was simply no useful 'inside information' at that point," Bundy wrote. In other words, Bundy's argument was not that Kissinger lacked access to inside information on the negotiations during his 18–22 September 1968 visit to Paris, but that there wasn't any useful inside information for him to access.

Bundy was mistaken. Right before Kissinger arrived in Paris, President Johnson personally briefed the lead American negotiator, Ambassador W. Averell Harriman, on the administration's negotiating position on the bombing halt (see three Memoranda of Conversations from 17 September 1968, in *Foreign Relations of the United States [FRUS], 1964–1968: Vietnam, September 1968–January 1969,* ed. Kent Sieg [Washington, DC: GPO, 2003], 7: Document 19, Document 20, and Document 21 [hereafter *FRUS 1964–1968, 7*]). The president personally spelled out three demands, saying that he could stop the bombing of the North only as long as the Communists (1) respected the demilitarized zone dividing Vietnam, (2) entered peace talks that included representatives of the South Vietnamese government as well as Americans, and (3) stopped shelling the civilian populations of Southern cities (Memorandum for the Record by Walt W. Rostow, ca. 17 September 1968, "Memos to the President re Bombing Halt 9/30–10/22/1968" folder, National Security File, Country File, Vietnam, Box 137, Lyndon B. Johnson Library [hereafter LBJL], http://gateway.proquest.com/openurl?url _ver=Z39.88-2004&res_dat=xri:dnsa&rft_dat=xri:dnsa:article:CVI02165). This was part of a renewed diplomatic initiative by Johnson that included enlisting the influence of the Soviet Union, the largest supplier of military aid to Hanoi. On 16 September 1968, the day before LBJ briefed Harriman, National Security Adviser Rostow handed Soviet Ambassador Anatoly Dobrynin a memorandum that spelled out Johnson's three demands as well: "the simple fact is that the President could not maintain a cessation of the bombing of North Vietnam unless it were very promptly evident to him, to the American people, and to our allies, that such an action was, indeed, a step toward peace. A cessation of bombing which would be followed by abuses of the DMZ, Viet Cong and North Vietnamese attacks on cities or such populated areas as provincial capitals, or a refusal of the authorities in Hanoi to enter promptly into serious political discussions which included the elected government of the Republic of Vietnam, could simply not be sustained" ("Memorandum from the Government of the United States to the Government of the Soviet Union," 16 September 1968, *Foreign Relations of the United States [FRUS], 1964–1968: Soviet Union,* ed. David C. Humphrey and Charles S. Sampson [Washington, DC: GPO, 2001], 14: Document 299). Johnson's true negotiating position on the bombing halt was, of course, precisely the kind of information that was most valuable to candidate Nixon. If the president wasn't willing to back down from any of his three demands—and he wasn't—that made a bombing halt much less likely before Election Day, and that information was very relevant to Nixon's prospects for winning the race. So Bundy's assertion that there "was simply no useful 'inside information' at that point" for Kissinger to get his hands on just doesn't hold up under scrutiny.

Nixon defended Kissinger from the charge that he had provided the campaign classified information before anyone had the chance to level it. "Kissinger was completely circumspect in the advice he gave us during the campaign. If he was privy to the details of negotiations, he did not reveal them to us," Nixon wrote. A campaign memo, however, shows that Kissinger did not have to reveal details of the negotiations to imply that the advice he was giving Nixon was based on inside information: "The following is the report from the top diplomatic source who is secretly with us and has access to the Paris talks and other information: Our source feels that there is a better than even chance that Johnson will order a bombing halt at approximately mid-October. This will be tied in with a big flurry of diplomatic activity in Paris which will have no meaning but will be made to look important." When Nixon quoted this report in his memoir, he omitted the reference to Kissinger's access to the bombing halt negotiations. Nixon made it clear that Kissinger's surreptitious campaign role impressed him: "One factor that had most convinced me of Kissinger's credibility was the length to which he went to protect his secrecy." He also acknowledged that Kissinger's status as an informant played a role in his decision to make him national security adviser: "During the last days of the campaign, when Kissinger was providing us with information about the bombing halt, I became more aware of both his knowledge and his influence" (Nixon, *RN*, 323–26, 340; see also Haldeman to Nixon, "Confidential—Eyes Only," 27 September 1968, "WHSF 1–11" folder, Box 1, Nixon Presidential Returned Materials Collection: White House Special Files, Richard M. Nixon Library [hereafter RMNL], http://nixon.archives.gov/virtuallibrary/documents/whsfreturned/WHSF_Box_01/WHSF1-11.pdf).

Richard V. Allen, Nixon's foreign policy adviser in the campaign, said: "Henry Kissinger, on his own, volunteered information to us through a spy, a former student, that he had in the Paris peace talks, who would call him and debrief, and Kissinger called me from pay phones and we spoke in German. The fact that my German is better than his did not at all hinder my communication with Henry and he offloaded mostly every night what had happened that day in Paris" (see Transcript, Richard V. Allen, Oral History Interview, 28 May 2002, by Stephen F. Knott, Russell L. Riley, and James Sterling Young, Miller Center, http://millercenter.org/president/reagan/oralhistory/richard-allen).

8. G. Gordon Liddy writes of breaking "into many an empty house or apartment to search for clues" as an FBI agent (*Will: The Autobiography of G. Gordon Liddy* [New York: St. Martin's Paperbacks, 1980], 108).

### The Chennault Affair

1. David Wise, "The Twilight of a President," *New York Times,* 3 November 1968, www.nytimes.com.

2. Conversation WH6405-10-3519, 27 May 1964, 10:55 a.m., *Lyndon B. Johnson: 6: Toward the Great Society, April 14, 1964–May 31, 1964,* ed. Guian A. McKee (New York: Norton, 2007), 872.

3. Conversation WH6406-05-3681, 11 June 1964, 12:26 p.m., *Lyndon B. Johnson: 7: Mississippi Burning and the Passage of the Civil Rights Act, June 1, 1964–July 4, 1964,* ed. Guian A. McKee (New York: Norton, 2011), 240.

4. Conversation WH6810-10-13612-13613, 30 October 1968, 10:25 a.m., President's Little Office. Robert "KC" Johnson expertly analyzed this conversation and others in "Did Nixon Commit Treason in 1968? What the New LBJ Tapes Reveal," *History News Network,* http://hnn.us/article/60446.

5. Richard Rhodes, *The Making of the Atomic Bomb* (New York: Simon and Schuster, 1995), 306–14.

6. "Alexander Sachs, Economist, Dead," *New York Times,* 24 June 1973, www.nytimes.com.

7. Eugene Rostow to Walt Rostow, Document 44a, 29 October 1968, Reference File: Anna Chennault, South Vietnam and US Politics, LBJL.

8. Eugene Rostow to Walt Rostow, Document 45a, 29 October 1968, Reference File: Anna Chennault, South Vietnam and US Politics, LBJL. President Eisenhower had settled the Korean War in 1953 on terms short of the victory Republican campaign rhetoric demanded during the 1952 election campaign.

9. "Notes of Meeting," 29 October 1968, 2:30 a.m., *FRUS 1964–1968,* 7: Document 140.

10. South Korea furnished troops for the Vietnam War, and most US air strikes on North Vietnam were launched from bases in Thailand.

11. Conversation WH6810-10-13612-13613, 30 October 1968, 10:25 a.m., President's Little Office.

12. For all the declassified NSA and CIA reports, see Reference File: Anna Chennault, South Vietnam and US Politics, LBJL.

13. Conversation WH6810-10-13612-13613, 30 October 1968, 10:25 a.m., President's Little Office.

14. Associated Press, "Louisiana Divorce Disclosed of 'Flying Tiger' Chennault," *Washington Post,* 18 December 1946, www.proquest.com.

15. The Associated Press misreported her age as twenty-four in one story (see Associated Press, "Gen. Chennault Marries Chinese Reporter; Former Flying Tiger Chief to Stay in China," *New York Times,* 22 December 1947, www.proquest.com). In another, the wire service noted, "Her age was not given" (see Associated Press, "Gen. Chennault of Flying Tigers Weds Chinese News Girl," *Chicago Tribune,* 22 December 1947, www.proquest.com).

16. Anna Chennault, *The Education of Anna* (New York: Times Books, 1980), 138–39.

17. Ibid., 133–34, 138.

18. David R. Legge, "Cafritz Axiom Revisited," *Washington Post,* 9 October 1972, www.proquest.com; Judith Viorst, "The Three Faces of Anna Chennault," *Washingtonian,* September 1969, Reference File: Anna Chennault, South Vietnam and US Politics, LBJL.

19. Viorst, "The Three Faces of Anna Chennault."

20. Ibid.; Bui Diem, *In the Jaws of History,* with David Chanoff (Boston: Houghton Mifflin, 1987), 236.

21. "Women's Group Set for Nixon," *Washington Post,* 2 October 1968, www.proquest.com.

22. Russell Warren Howe and Sarah Hays Trott, *The Power Peddlers: How Lobbyists Mold America's Foreign Policy* (Garden City, NY: Doubleday, 1977), 45.

23. Conversation WH6810-10-13612-13613, 30 October 1968, 10:25 a.m., President's Little Office.

24. Memo quoted in William Safire, *Before the Fall: An Inside View of the Pre-Watergate White House* (New York: Ballantine, 1975), 73, 111–12. Safire published the memo years before Chennault and Diem wrote their memoirs, which revealed and confirmed that the meeting of Nixon, Mitchell, Chennault, and Diem had in fact occurred.

25. According to Diem, he informed Assistant Secretary for East Asian and Pacific Affairs William P. Bundy in advance of the meeting. Bundy later wrote that he had "no recollection of such a conversation, but would surely have told

him that such a meeting (in itself) would not be objectionable or improper."
Regardless of whether Bundy was forewarned, information about the meeting
did not reach LBJ (Diem, *In the Jaws of History,* 237; Bundy, *A Tangled Web,* 37).

26. Chennault and Diem differ on details. Chennault, for example, says the
meeting took place on a snowy Sunday; Diem gives it the specific date of July 12,
1968, a Friday. Chennault says the two of them took a shuttle flight from Washington; Diem says he met her in the lobby of the building where the meeting
with Nixon and Mitchell was to take place. Chennault sets the meeting in Nixon's
New York apartment; Diem, at Nixon campaign headquarters (Chennault, *The
Education of Anna,* 175; Diem, *In the Jaws of History,* 237).

27. Chennault, *The Education of Anna,* 175–76. Diem's account doesn't refer to
Chennault as Nixon's "sole representative" or "only contact" with the Saigon
government, but confirms that the candidate designated her as a conduit from
his campaign to the South Vietnamese ambassador: "Finally, Nixon thanked me
for my visit and added that his staff would be in touch with me through John
Mitchell and Anna Chennault" (Diem, *In the Jaws of History,* 237).

28. Conversation WH6810-10-13612-13613, 30 October 1968, 10:25 a.m.,
President's Little Office.

29. According to one CIA report on the bug in Thieu's office: "Concerning
the enforcement of the bombing halt, this will help candidate Humphrey and
this is the purpose of it; but the situation which would occur as the result of a
bombing halt, without the agreement of [South] Vietnamese government, rather
than being a disadvantage [*sic*] to candidate Humphrey, would be to the advantage of candidate Nixon. Accordingly, he [South Vietnamese president Thieu]
said that the possibility of President Johnson enforcing a bombing halt without
Vietnam's agreement appears to be weak." Also: "Thieu has said that Johnson
and Humphrey will be replaced and then Nixon could change the U.S. position"
(CIA to Walt Rostow, 26 October 1968, "President Thieu's Views Regarding the
Issues Involved in Agreeing to a Bombing Halt," Reference File: Anna Chennault, South Vietnam and US Politics, LBJL).

30. Conversation WH6810-10-13612-13613, 30 October 1968, 10:25 a.m.,
President's Little Office.

31. "Notes of the Meeting of the President with His Foreign Policy Advisers
at Lunch," 24 July 1968, *Foreign Relations of the United States, 1964–1968:
Vietnam, January–August 1968,* ed. Kent Sieg (Washington, DC: GPO, 2002), 6:
Document 308 (hereafter *FRUS 1964–1968,* 6.)

32. Although President Nixon made the phrase "peace with honor" and its
variant, "an honorable peace," into cornerstones of his Vietnam rhetoric,
President Johnson used the same language frequently to characterize America's
goal in Vietnam and throughout the world (see "Remarks to the First Graduat-
ing Class at the Foreign Service Institute's Vietnam Training Center," 21 March
1968, *PPPUS: Johnson, 1968,* www.presidency.ucsb.edu/ws/?pid=28748; "Remarks
upon Dedicating the Hall of Heroes and Presenting the Medal of Honor to a
Member of Each of the Nation's Military Services," 14 May 1968, ibid., www
.presidency.ucsb.edu/ws/?pid=28856; and "Remarks in Independence, Mo., at a
Ceremony in Connection with the Establishment of the Harry S. Truman Center

for the Advancement of Peace," 20 January 1966, *Public Papers of the Presidents of the United States: Johnson, 1966* [Washington, DC: GPO, 1967], www.presidency.ucsb.edu/ws/?pid=27593). For his reference to "honorable peace" on the night he withdrew from the presidential race, see "The President's Address to the Nation Announcing Steps to Limit the War in Vietnam and Reporting His Decision Not to Seek Reelection," 31 March 1968, *PPPUS: Johnson, 1968*, www.presidency.ucsb.edu/ws/?pid=28772.

33. "The President's Address to the Nation Announcing Steps to Limit the War in Vietnam and Reporting His Decision Not to Seek Reelection," 31 March 1968, *PPPUS: Johnson, 1968*, www.presidency.ucsb.edu/ws/?pid=28772.

34. Conversation 248-016, 14 April 1971, 4:20–5:10 p.m., Executive Office Building.

35. Chalmers M. Roberts, "McCarthy Offers 8-Point Plan on How to End Vietnam War," *Washington Post*, 21 March 1968, www.proquest.com.

36. Robert J. Donovan, "Kennedy Declares Antiwar Campaign," *Los Angeles Times*, 17 March 1968, www.proquest.com.

37. See Ted Van Dyk, *Heroes, Hacks, and Fools: Memoirs from the Political Inside* (Seattle: University of Washington Press, 2007), 74.

38. See reference to mid-July 1968 poll number in George Gallup, "Nixon Leads Both Democratic Rivals in First Test since GOP Convention," *Washington Post*, 21 August 1968, www.proquest.com.

39. Howard Seelye, "Voters Explain Switch to Wallace," *Los Angeles Times*, 10 December 1967, www.proquest.com.

40. Conversation 469-013, 18 March 1971, 6:25–7:32 p.m., Oval Office.

41. "President Johnson's Notes on Meeting in Cabinet Room with Richard Nixon. Joined Later by Secretary Rusk, Tom Johnson, and Walt Rostow," 26 July 1968, *FRUS 1964–1968*, 6: Document 310. Oddly, these notes include only two of LBJ's three conditions, mentioning the DMZ and the cities, but not the presence of Saigon at the negotiating table. South Vietnamese participation in the talks was, however, already one of LBJ's demands (Clark Clifford and Richard Holbrooke, *Counsel to the President: A Memoir* [New York: Random House, 1991], 549). Humphrey quotes about LBJ's threat to denounce him: Van Dyk, *Heroes, Hacks, and Fools*, 74; biographical information about Rusk and Rostow: David Halberstam, *The Best and the Brightest* (New York: Ballantine, 1972), 156–58, 312–16. Nixon can be heard praising Rusk on his own White House tapes (Conversation 469-013, 18 March 1971, 6:25–7:32 p.m., Oval Office). "This Rusk is smart. He handles himself well," Nixon said in Conversation 006-086, 1 July 1971, 6:30–6:37 p.m., White House Telephone.

42. Robert Semple Jr., "President Gives Briefings to Nixon and Wallace," *New York Times*, 27 July 1968, www.nytimes.com.

43. "Text of Nixon Statement to G.O.P. Platform Panel on the War," 2 August 1968, *New York Times*, www.proquest.com.

44. Ibid.

45. Ibid.

46. Conversation WH6808-01-13304, 8 August 1968, 4:09 p.m., Lewis Ranch.

47. Conversation WH6808-01-13302, 8 August 1968, 2:01 p.m., LBJ Ranch.

48. Conversation WH6808-01-13304, 8 August 1968, 4:09 p.m., Lewis Ranch.

49. "Transcripts of Acceptance Speeches by Nixon and Agnew to the G.O.P. Convention," *New York Times,* 9 August 1968, www.proquest.com.

50. David Brinkley, "Republican Ticket/Johnson Invitation/Hubert H. Humphrey/Piano," *NBC Evening News,* aired 9 August 1968, http://tvnews.vanderbilt.edu.

51. Carl Solberg, *Hubert Humphrey: A Biography* (New York: Norton, 1984), 349–50.

52. "Notes of a Meeting," 8 May 1968, *FRUS 1964–1968,* 6: Document 227.

53. "Notes on Briefing of Former Vice President Nixon and Governor Agnew," 10 August 1968, *FRUS 1964–1968,* 6: Document 327.

54. E. W. Kenworthy, "Senator Proposes Plank Urging 4-Way Talks to Form New Regime," *New York Times,* 18 August 1968, www.proquest.com.

55. Conversation WH6808-01-13306, 18 August 1968, 5:01 p.m., LBJ Ranch.

56. Conversation WH6808-01-13309-13310, 20 August 1968, 11:22 p.m., Oval Office.

57. White House Daily Diary for 20 August 1968. For Johnson's version of Humphrey's commitment, see Conversation WH6808-01-13313, 13314, 13315, 26 August 1968, 8:04 a.m., LBJ Ranch.

58. Richard Harwood, "Humphrey: Takes Harder Vietnam Line," *Washington Post,* 26 August 1968, www.proquest.com.

59. John W. Finney, "Defeat for Doves Reflects Deep Division in the Party," *New York Times,* 29 August 1968, www.proquest.com.

60. "Transcripts of Humphrey and Muskie Acceptance Speeches at Chicago Convention," *New York Times,* 30 August 1968, www.proquest.com.

61. Russell Freeburg, "Hubert Hints Shift on Viet," *Chicago Tribune,* 30 August 1968, www.proquest.com.

62. George Gallup, "Nixon Leads HHH 43 to 31 Percent; Wallace Given 19," *Washington Post,* 15 September 1968, www.proquest.com.

### Johnson v. Humphrey

1. R. W. Apple Jr., "Humphrey Concedes That G.I.'s Are Staying but Clings to Hope," *New York Times,* www.proquest.com; "Remarks in New Orleans before the 50th Annual National Convention of the American Legion," 10 September 1968, *PPPUS: Johnson, 1968,* www.presidency.ucsb.edu/ws/?pid=29107.

2. E. W. Kenworthy, "Nixon Says Humphrey Harms Efforts of U.S. in Paris," *New York Times,* 26 September 1968, www.nytimes.com.

3. George Gallup, "Nixon Holds Wide Lead, Wallace at New High," *Washington Post,* 29 September 1968, www.proquest.com.

4. "Transcript of Speech by the Vice President on Foreign Policy," *New York Times,* 1 October 1968, www.proquest.com.

5. Conversation WH6809-04-13432-13433, 30 September 1968, 6:45 p.m., Oval Office.

6. Ibid.

7. Ibid.

8. Hubert H. Humphrey, *The Education of a Public Man: My Life and Politics,* ed. Norman Sherman (Garden City, NY: Doubleday, 1976), 403.

9. Conversation WH6809-04-13435, 30 September 1968, 7:30 p.m., Oval Office.

10. R. W. Apple Jr., "Humphrey Vows Halt in Bombing if Hanoi Reacts; A 'Risk for Peace'; Aides Hopeful Doves Will View Speech as Rift with Johnson," *New York Times,* 1 October 1968, www.proquest.com.

11. Conversation WH6810-01-13501, 1 October 1968, 10:21 a.m., Mansion.

12. Conversation WH6810-01-13506, 1 October 1968, 11:22 a.m., Mansion.

13. E. W. Kenworthy, "Nixon Asks Clarification Lest Foe Be Misled," *New York Times,* 2 October 1968, www.nytimes.com.

14. R. W. Apple Jr., "Humphrey Stands on Vietnam Talk; Says It 'Speaks for Itself'—Declines to Elaborate," *New York Times,* 2 October 1968, www.nytimes .com.

15. Hedrick Smith, "Harriman Denies Nixon Charge That Humphrey Harmed Talks," *New York Times,* 3 October 1968, http://www.nytimes.com.

16. Conversation WH6810-02-13512-13513, 3 October 1968, 10:15 a.m., Mansion.

## Nixon v. Nixon

1. E. W. Kenworthy, "Nixon Suggests He Could Achieve Peace in Vietnam; Indicates He Might Be Able to Agree to a Settlement Johnson Cannot Accept," *New York Times,* 8 October 1968, www.nytimes.com.

2. Conversation WH6810-02-13516, 7 October 1968, 10:02 a.m., Oval Office.

3. Conversation WH6810-03-13523, 7 October 1968, 5:11 p.m., President's Little Office.

4. Ibid.

5. "Memorandum from the Under Secretary of State (Katzenbach) to President Johnson," undated, *FRUS 1964–1968,* 7: Document 55.

6. "Telegram from the Embassy in France to the Department of State," 11 October 1968, *FRUS 1964–1968,* 7: Document 58; Luu Van Loi and Nguyen Anh Vu, *Le Duc Tho—Kissinger Negotiations in Paris* (Hanoi: Gioi, 1996), 45–46.

7. "Telegram from the Embassy in France to the Department of State," 12 October 1968, *FRUS 1964–1968,* 7: Document 60.

8. For the official explanation of why Hanoi's bargaining position shifted, see Loi and Vu, *Le Duc Tho,* 43–46. The authors cite military setbacks on the Communist side as well as a growing awareness in Hanoi that the United States nevertheless could not win the war: "Although compelled to end the war, the US had to defend its interests and those of its agents and to keep SVN within the US sphere of influence. That was the point of agreement among the ruling circles in the US, between the Republican Party and the Democratic Party, between Humphrey and Nixon. Hanoi also realized that there was hardly any possibility for Humphrey to win the election. Since Humphrey's failure was Johnson's, Johnson, therefore, had to further de-escalate the war to help Humphrey win the election and to maintain his reputation of being 'a great President' of the US." See also Lien-Hang T. Nguyen, *Hanoi's War: An International History of the War*

*for Peace in Vietnam* (Chapel Hill: University of North Carolina Press, 2012), Kindle edition, chap. 4, "Phase 3: Toward Dam Va Danh."

9. Helms to Kissinger, "October–November 1968 Vietnam Intelligence Data," 19 March 1970, attached to Haldeman to Ehrlichman, "Documents on 1968 Bombing Halt Decision," 21 October 1971, "H. R. Haldeman—Chron—Oct 1971, A–L" folder, WHSF-SMOF Haldeman Box 197, RMNL, www.nixonlibrary.gov /virtuallibrary/releases/dec10/53.pdf.

10. Homer Bigart, "Bundy Proposes Troop Reduction and Bombing Halt," *New York Times,* 13 October 1968, www.proquest.com.

11. "I would not undertake a unilateral withdrawal," Humphrey said ("Transcript of Speech by the Vice President on Foreign Policy," *New York Times,* 1 October 1968, www.proquest.com; John W. Finney, "Plank on Vietnam Devised by Doves," *New York Times,* 24 August 1968, www.proquest.com).

12. "Editorial Note," *FRUS 1964–1968,* 7: Document 63.

13. Van Dyk, *Heroes, Hacks, and Fools,* 69.

14. Rostow to Johnson, "Meeting with Thieu October 8 [*sic*]," 14 October 1968, "Memos to the President re Bombing Halt 9/30–10/22/68" folder, Box 137, National Security File, Country File: Vietnam, LBJL, http://gateway.proquest.com/openurl ?url_ver=Z39.88-2004&res_dat=xri:dnsa&rft_dat=xri:dnsa:article:CVI02177. See also "Telegram from the Embassy in Vietnam to the Department of State," 13 October 1968; and "Telegram from the Department of State to the Embassy in France," 14 October 1968, *FRUS 1964–1968,* 7: Document 64 and Document 65.

15. "Draft Notes of Meeting," 14 October 1968, *FRUS 1964–1968,* 7: Document 67.

16. "Notes of Meeting," 14 October 1968, *FRUS 1964–1968,* 7: Document 68.

17. Ibid., Document 70. For the "political trick" charge, see "Notes on the President's Meeting with the Tuesday Lunch Group," 15 October 1968, ibid.: Document 73.

18. Harriman to State, 15 October 1968, "Memos to the President re Bombing Halt 9/30–10/22/68" folder, Box 137, National Security File, Country File: Vietnam, LBJL, http://gateway.proquest.com/openurl?url_ver=Z39.88-2004&res _dat=xri:dnsa&rft_dat=xri:dnsa:article:CVI02184. For the conditions as Harriman and Vance stated them to the North Vietnamese, see "Telegram from the Department of State to the Embassy in France," 14 October 1968, *FRUS 1964–1968,* 7: Document 65.

19. "Notes on Meeting," 15 October 1968, *FRUS 1964–1968,* 7: Document 73.

20. Conversation WH6810-04-13546, 15 October 1968, 9:34 a.m., Mansion. For Humphrey's "period, not comma or semi-colon" comment, see John W. Finney, "Humphrey Taunts Nixon as 'Chicken,'" *New York Times,* 16 October 1968, www .proquest.com. Humphrey did mention, once again, that he would look for evidence regarding North Vietnamese restoration of the DMZ.

21. Conversation WH6810-04-13547, 16 October 1968, 11:41 a.m., Oval Office.

22. See summaries for *CBS Evening News, NBC Evening News,* and *ABC Evening News,* 16 October 1968, http://tvnews.vanderbilt.edu.

23. "Telegram from the Department of State to the Embassy in Vietnam," 17 October 1968, *FRUS 1964–1968*, 7: Document 85.

24. "Notes of Meeting" and "Telegram from the Embassy in France to the Department of State," 17 October 1968, *FRUS 1964–1968*, 7: Document 83 and Document 84.

25. "Memorandum of Conversation between the Vietnamese Ambassador (Bui Diem) and the President's Special Assistant (Rostow)," 18 October 1968, *FRUS 1964–1968*, 7: Document 89.

26. "Telegram from the Embassy in Vietnam to the Department of State," 18 October 1968, *FRUS 1964–1968*, 7: Document 87.

27. "Situation Report by the Executive Secretary of the Department of State (Read)," 21 October 1968, *FRUS 1964–1968*, 7: Document 95.

28. "Information Memorandum from the President's Special Assistant (Rostow) to President Johnson," 24 October 1968, *FRUS 1964–1968*, 7: Document 116.

29. R. W. Apple Jr., "Nixon Again Backs a Bombing Pause If It Costs No Lives," *New York Times*, 18 October 1968, www.proquest.com; Carroll Kilpatrick, "Nixon Backs Quest for Bomb Halt," *Washington Post*, 18 October 1968, www .proquest.com.

30. Harry Kelly, "Humphrey Bars Thieu Veto on Bombs," *Washington Post*, 21 October 1968, www.proquest.com. For Johnson's unhappiness with Humphrey's comment, see Conversation WH6810-10-13612-13613, 30 October 1968, 10:25 a.m., President's Little Office.

31. Conversation WH6810-07-13581-13582-13583, 23 October 1968, 10:05 a.m., Mansion.

32. Ibid.

33. "Memorandum for the Record," 23 October 1968, *FRUS 1964–1968*, 7: Document 110.

34. Nixon, *RN*, 326.

35. Transcript, Bryce N. Harlow Oral History Interview II, 6 May 1979, Michael L. Gillette, Internet Copy, LBJL, p. 62, http://web2.millercenter.org/lbj /oralhistory/harlow_bryce_1979_0506.pdf.

36. Conversation WH6810-11-13614-13615-13616-13617, 31 October 1968, 4:09 p.m., Mansion.

37. Conversation WH6810-07-13587, 23 October 1968, 6:02 p.m., Oval Office.

38. See the 17–21 October 1968 results in George Gallup, "HHH Gains 4 Points, Trails Nixon 44-36; Wallace Dips to 15," *Washington Post*, 27 October 1968, www.proquest.com.

39. Robert B. Semple Jr., "Nixon Denounces Welfare Inequity, Calls for National Standards—Repudiates Criticism of Johnson Peace Efforts," *New York Times*, 26 October 1968, www.proquest.com; Peter H. Silberman, "Nixon Reports Cease-Fire Hint," *Washington Post*, 26 October 1968, www.proquest.com. Nixon's baseless claim about a possible cease-fire inflated voter expectations in a way that the announcement of a mere bombing halt could not fulfill.

40. "Remarks in New York City at a Luncheon of the All Americans Council of the Democratic National Committee," 27 October 1968, *PPPUS: Johnson, 1968*, www.presidency.ucsb.edu/ws/?pid=29213.

41. "Telegram from the Embassy in France to the Department of State," 27 October 1968, *FRUS 1964–1968*, 7: Document 128. On the day that LBJ announced the bombing halt, the North Vietnamese dropped their demand for a secret minute altogether (see "Telegram from the Embassy in France to the Department of State," 31 October 1968, *FRUS 1964–1968*, 7: Document 158).

42. Rusk's "vodka and caviar" remark indicated that he thought Russian influence was behind the deal (see "Notes on President's Meeting with Group of Foreign Policy Advisers on Sunday, October 27, 1968," *FRUS 1964–1968*, 7: Document 129).

43. "Information Memorandum from the President's Special Assistant (Rostow) to President Johnson," 27 October 1968, *FRUS 1964–1968*, 7: Document 130.

44. "Memorandum from the President's Special Assistant (Rostow) to President Johnson," 28 October 1968, *FRUS 1964–1968*, 7: Document 131.

45. "Information Memorandum from the President's Special Assistant (Rostow) to President Johnson," 28 October 1968, *FRUS 1964–1968*, 7: Document 138.

46. Clifford and Holbrooke, *Counsel to the President*, 585.

47. Lady Bird Johnson, *A White House Diary* (New York: Holt, Rinehart and Winston, 1970), 728.

48. LBJ recalled this in a phone call to Russell: "he says, from a strictly military standpoint, that this military power is no good for 90 days on account of your weather [in North Vietnam]—that it is needed and will be used. Now, you either get something for it or you don't, because he's going to use it anyway—90 percent of it, in Laos and South Vietnam, even if I didn't issue an order here. He would do it there because he says it's unlikely that you'll get more than one or two days a month that you can do anything" (Conversation WH6810-10-13612-13613, 30 October 1968, 10:25 a.m., President's Little Office).

49. "Notes of Meeting," 29 October 1968, *FRUS 1964–1968*, 7: Document 140.

50. Johnson, *A White House Diary*, 729.

### On the Case

1. "The diplomatic information previously received plus the information from New York took on new and serious significance," Rostow later wrote (see his "Memorandum for the Record," Document 39, 14 May 1973, Reference File: Anna Chennault, South Vietnam and US Politics, LBJL).

2. "Delays Improve South Vietnam's Position," 28 October 1968, National Security Agency Director to White House, Memos to the President, National Security Files, Vol. 101, Box 41, LBJL. The federal government made odd excisions from the cable before declassifying it, omitting words that Ambassador Diem had already published in his memoirs. Diem also wrote that the cable referred to Chennault, Mitchell, and Sen. John G. Tower, R-Texas (Diem, *In the Jaws of History*, 244). One of the other blanks was filled in by former assistant secretary of state for East Asian and Pacific affairs William P. Bundy, who somehow managed in 1992 to get his hands on notes written by someone who read the (uncensored) intercept, Benjamin H. Read, the executive secretary of the Department of State under LBJ (Bundy, *A Tangled Web*, 42, 550n88).

3. Conversation WH6810-10-13609, 29 October 1968, 10:30 a.m., Mansion.

4. Conversation WH6810-10-13610, 29 October 1968, 10:37 a.m., Mansion.

5. "Information Memorandum from the President's Special Assistant (Rostow) to President Johnson," 29 October 1968, *FRUS 1964–1968,* 7: Document 145.

6. The Logan Act states: "Any citizen of the United States, wherever he may be, who, without authority of the United States, directly or indirectly commences or carries on any correspondence or intercourse with any foreign government or any officer or agent thereof, in relation to any disputes or controversies with the United States, or to defeat the measures of the United States, shall be fined under this title or imprisoned not more than three years, or both" (US Library of Congress, Congressional Research Service, *Conducting Foreign Relations without Authority: The Logan Act,* by Michael V. Seitzinger, CRS Report RL 33265 [Washington, DC: Office of Congressional Information and Publishing, 1 February 2006]). See also *FRUS 1964–1968,* 7: Document 161n10.

7. Cartha D. "Deke" DeLoach, *Hoover's FBI: The Inside Story by Hoover's Trusted Lieutenant* (Washington, DC: Regnery, 1995), 396–97.

8. The FBI did not place a wiretap on Chennault's home phone. Many writers think the bureau did tap Chennault's home line for the simple reason that former deputy FBI director Cartha D. "Deke" DeLoach testified that it did and repeated the error in his autobiography (Senate Select Committee to Study Governmental Operations with Respect to Intelligence Activities, *Hearings: Volume 6: Federal Bureau of Investigation* [Washington, DC: GPO, 1976], 195–96; DeLoach, *Hoover's FBI,* 397). But DeLoach was clearly mistaken in his testimony and later recollection, as the Senate Select Committee found. DeLoach can even be heard on the Johnson tapes stating that the FBI did not tap Chennault's telephone.

President Johnson: Well, don't—didn't you have her house . . . weren't you looking after her, too?

DeLoach: No, we had a physical surveillance on her and we had a wiretap on the South Vietnamese embassy.

President Johnson: But you didn't have one on her.

DeLoach: No, sir. We can still put it on if—

President Johnson: No, no, no, no, no.

(Conversation WH6811-04-13730, 12 November 1968, 8:30 p.m., Oval Office)

Moreover, the US government has declassified all the FBI reports on the Chennault Affair, and none of them contain any information from or about a wiretap on Chennault's telephone (Reference File: Anna Chennault, South Vietnam and US Politics, LBJL).

Why didn't the FBI tap Chennault's phone? It "was widely known that she was involved in Republican political circles," Deputy FBI Director Cartha D. "Deke" DeLoach wrote to Associate FBI Director Clyde A. Tolson, "and, if it became known that the FBI was surveilling her, this would put us in a most untenable and embarrassing position" (DeLoach to Tolson, 30 October 1968, quoted in Senate Select Committee on Governmental Operations with Respect to Intelligence Activities, *Intelligence Activities and the Rights of Americans: Book 2: Final Report* [Washington, DC: GPO, 1976], 228n10).

One final reason why people think the FBI tapped Chennault's phone is that they recall reading quotes of conversations between her and Mitchell. Those quotes come from Chennault's memoirs and interviews, not from any FBI wiretap reports.

9. "Notes of Meeting," 29 October 1968, *FRUS 1964–1968, 7*: Document 148. For the general's anger, see Clifford and Holbrooke, *Counsel to the President,* 588.

10. "(Secret—No Foreign Dissemination) Embassy of [South] Vietnam, Internal Security—Vietnam," Document 36, 30 October 1968, Reference File: Anna Chennault, South Vietnam and US Politics, LBJL.

11. Ibid.

12. "Telegram from the Department of State to the Embassy in Vietnam," 30 October 1968, *FRUS 1964–1968, 7*: Document 151.

13. "Notes on Foreign Policy Meeting," 30 October 1968, *FRUS 1964–1968, 7*: Document 153.

14. Conversation WH6810-11-13614-13615-13616-13617, 31 October 1968, 4:09 p.m., Mansion.

15. Ibid.

16. "Transcript of Telephone Conversation among President Johnson, Vice President Humphrey, Richard Nixon, and George Wallace," 31 October 1968, *FRUS 1964–1968, 7*: Document 166. According to the LBJL, there is no recording of this conversation.

17. Conversation WH6810-11-13620-13621, 31 October 1968, 6:52 p.m., Cabinet Room.

18. "The President's Address to the Nation upon Announcing His Decision to Halt the Bombing of North Vietnam," 31 October 1968, *PPPUS: Johnson, 1968,* www.presidency.ucsb.edu/ws/?pid=29218.

19. Robert B. Semple, "Nixon Hopes Johnson Step Will Aid the Talks in Paris," *New York Times,* 1 November 1968, www.nytimes.com. An hour of the rally aired on 247 ABC television stations at a cost to the Republicans of about $200,000.

20. Ibid.

21. Chet Huntley, "Introduction"; Jim Bennett, "Vietnam/Halt/South Vietnam Reaction/Soldiers"; and David Brinkley, "Halt," three segments on *NBC Evening News,* aired 1 November 1968, http://tvnews.vanderbilt.edu.

22. Jack Perkins, "Vietnam/Halt/Candidates Reactions," *NBC Evening News,* aired 1 November 1968, http://tvnews.vanderbilt.edu; John W. Finney, "Doves and Hawks Divided on Johnson's Move," *New York Times,* 1 November 1968, www.nytimes.com.

23. Conversation WH6811-01-13704, 1 November 1968, 1:57 p.m., Oval Office.

24. Carl Solberg, *Hubert Humphrey: A Biography* (New York: Norton, 1984), 397, 524–25n. Rowe later fabricated Johnson quotes from this conversation, such as: "I want you to tell Hubert we've got a problem. I'm not going to work out this Vietnam peace negotiation early enough to help him."

25. Bundy, *A Tangled Web*, 551n92. Bundy writes: "Solberg also gives an accurate account of a meeting between Humphrey and me on Sunday morning, November 3, at which I summarized the intelligence information (using what I had been told, since I never saw the actual messages). I advised against going public." Although Solberg wrote that Bundy briefed Humphrey at "the president's direction," Bundy himself is silent on the question of whether he acted on LBJ's authorization or was, once again, providing the Humphrey campaign classified information that Johnson had denied it (Solberg, *Hubert Humphrey*, 398; Van Dyk, *Heroes, Hacks, and Fools*, 69).

26. Conversation WH6810-11-13620-13621, 31 October 1968, 6:52 p.m., Cabinet Room. Theodore White wrote that Humphrey had been fully "informed of the sabotage of the negotiations" in "the last four days of the campaign" (White, *The Making of the President 1968*, Kindle edition, chap. 11, "October: All Passion Spent," 445). White's account is only a slight exaggeration; Humphrey had been partially informed by Rowe and Bundy, who both had very limited information. Humphrey doesn't address the question of how he found out about the Chennault Affair in *The Education of a Public Man*, 8–9. Other writers cast LBJ as an active participant in informing Humphrey. Califano, relying on a 1975 oral history by LBJ secretary Victoria McCammon, writes, "Johnson was furious [at Humphrey], thinking it was 'the dumbest thing in the world not to do it.'" Walter LaFeber embellishes the story by writing that LBJ "did, however turn some of the material [on the Chennault Affair] over to Humphrey" (LaFeber, *The Deadly Bet: LBJ, Vietnam, and the 1968 Election* [Lanham, MD: Rowman and Littlefield, 2005], 163). Neither Rowe nor Bundy claimed LBJ turned over any material to Humphrey; in fact, neither man saw the NSA, CIA, or FBI reports. The notion that LBJ gave Humphrey the option of exposing the Chennault Affair is at odds with his Election Eve conference call on the subject with Rusk, Rostow, and Clifford, in which LBJ kept that decision to himself. Nothing in the conversation suggests that Johnson gave Humphrey the option of exposing the affair (Conversation WH6811-03-13713-13714, 4 November 1968, 12:27 p.m., LBJ Ranch). According to Clifford, LBJ directed his three advisers not to consult Humphrey on the question (Clifford and Holbrooke, *Counsel to the President*, 583).

### "Hold On"

1. Gene Roberts, "Thieu Says Saigon Cannot Join Paris Talks under Present Plan; NLF Is Top Issue; South Vietnam Bars Any Separate Seat for the Vietcong," *New York Times*, 2 November 1968, www.nytimes.com.

2. United Press International, "Halt Seen by Nixon as Hastily Contrived," *Washington Post*, 3 November 1968, www.proquest.com; "Transcript of Telephone Conversation among President Johnson, Vice President Humphrey, Richard Nixon, and George Wallace," 31 October 1968, *FRUS 1964–1968*, 7: Document 166.

3. Rostow to Johnson, Document 30, 2 November 1968, Reference File: Anna Chennault, South Vietnam and US Politics, LBJL.

4. Ibid.

5. Conversation WH6811-01-13706, 2 November 1968, 9:18 p.m., LBJ Ranch.

6. Ibid.

7. Ibid.

8. Ibid.

9. Robert B. Semple Jr., "Nixon Willing to Go to Saigon or Paris," *New York Times,* 4 November 1968, www.proquest.com.

10. John W. Finney, "Doves and Hawks Divided on Johnson's Move," *New York Times,* 1 November 1968, www.proquest.com.

11. Conversation WH6811-02-13708, 3 November 1968, 1:25 p.m., LBJ Ranch.

12. Conversation WH6811-02-13710, 3 November 1968, 1:54 p.m., LBJ Ranch.

13. Ibid.

14. Robert Dallek, *Nixon and Kissinger: Partners in Power* (New York: HarperCollins, 2007), 76. In *The Deadly Bet,* Walter LaFeber likewise writes that that the "Republican nominee predictably denied that he had any knowledge of her attempts to back-stab the peace talks" (163).

15. Merriam-Webster's online dictionary defines credibility as "the quality or power of inspiring belief" (www.merriam-webster.com/dictionary/credibility). A secondary definition of credibility, "capacity for belief," offers another way to interpret Nixon's statement as something other than a denial of involvement in the Chennault Affair. Either way, credibility is a very different thing from truth.

16. For example, it can be interpreted as (1) his agreeing that it was without his knowledge that the cable traffic went to Thieu saying that Nixon would do better by the South Vietnamese president, or (2) his agreeing that *Johnson had said the other day* that it was without Nixon's knowledge that the cable traffic went out to Thieu saying that Nixon would do better by the South Vietnamese president. Another possible interpretation is that Nixon was simply denying knowledge of what was in the cable traffic to Thieu; unlike LBJ, he didn't get to read the NSA intercepts of communications from the South Vietnamese embassy to Saigon, so he truly didn't have direct knowledge of what the cable traffic said.

17. To put it another way, Nixon could, without lying, accurately state that he never *would* do a certain thing (agree to debate JFK on TV, tell reporters they won't have him to kick around anymore, tape-record his conversations, order a break-in at Brookings) even after he *had* done that very thing. Josephine Turck Baker gives many examples of contingent uses of "would" in *Correct English, How to Use It: A Complete Grammar* (Baltimore: H. M. Rowe, 1907), 184–90.

18. Carl Bernstein and Bob Woodward, *All the President's Men* (New York: Touchstone, 1974), Kindle edition, chap. 5. Merriam-Webster's online dictionary lacks a definition of "non-denial denial," but Wikipedia is helpful: "a statement that seems direct, clear-cut and unambiguous at first hearing, but when carefully parsed is revealed not to be a denial at all, and is thus not untruthful" (see "Non-Denial Denial," Wikipedia, last modified 13 February 2014, http://en .wikipedia.org/wiki/Non-denial_denial).

19. Conversation WH6811-02-13710, 3 November 1968, 1:54 p.m., LBJ Ranch.

20. Lewis Chester, Godfrey Hodgson, and Bruce Page, *An American Melodrama: The Presidential Campaign of 1968* (New York: Viking, 1969), 734.

21. Conversation WH6811-02-13711, 3 November 1968, 2:18 p.m., LBJ Ranch.

22. George Gallup, "Polls Say Election Is Tossup," *Washington Post,* 4 November 1968, www.proquest.com.

### Election Eve

1. FBI Director to Smith, "Embassy of Vietnam; Internal Security—Vietnam," Document 90, 4 November 1968, Reference File: Anna Chennault, South Vietnam and US Politics, LBJL.

2. Typewritten note to Rostow, "Saville Davis of the *Christian Science Monitor* Is Upstairs," Document 91a, 4 November 1968, Reference File: Anna Chennault, South Vietnam and US Politics, LBJL.

3. White House Daily Diary, 4 November 1968.

4. One of LBJ's properties was actually named the Reagan Ranch—obviously not after *Ronald* Reagan.

5. United Press International, "Two GOP Leaders Criticize Johnson," 5 November 1968, www.proquest.com. Although this story ran in Election Day newspapers, Johnson clearly saw it the day before, since he referred to Tower's comment in his forthcoming conference call.

6. "Notes of Meeting," 4 November 1968, *FRUS 1964–1968,* 7: Document 191.

7. Rostow to Johnson, "Embassy of Vietnam; Internal Security—Vietnam," Document 91, 4 November 1968, Reference File: Anna Chennault, South Vietnam and US Politics, LBJL.

8. Conversation WH6811-03-13713-13714, 4 November 1968, 12:27 p.m., LBJ Ranch.

9. Robert B. Semple Jr., "Nixon Urges Fresh Ideas; Republican Stresses Paris," *New York Times,* 5 November 1968, www.nytimes.com.

10. "Humphrey Assails Nixon War Report in Remote 'Debate,'" *New York Times,* 5 November 1968, www.nytimes.com.

### "I Let You Down"

1. "Last-Minute Appeal by Ike: Elect Nixon," *Chicago Tribune,* 5 November 1968, www.proquest.com.

2. Louis Harris, "HHH Overtakes Nixon in Final Harris Survey," *Washington Post,* 5 November 1968, www.proquest.com.

3. White, *The Making of the President 1968,* Kindle edition, chap. 12, "The Election: Passage in the Night," 462.

4. Conversation WH6811-03-13718, 6 November 1968, 11:32 p.m., LBJ Ranch.

### "Time to Blow the Whistle"

1. FBI Director to Smith, "Embassy of Vietnam; Internal Security—Vietnam," Document 86a, 7 November 1968, Reference File: Anna Chennault, South Vietnam and US Politics, LBJL.

2. Beverly Deepe, "Saigon Short Circuit? Diplomatic Pandemonium in South Vietnam; U.S. Accused of Bobbling Peace Package," *Christian Science Monitor,* 8 November 1968, www.proquest.com.

3. Robert B. Semple Jr., "Nixon Leaves Bid to Visit Vietnam Up to President," *New York Times,* 8 November 1968, www.proquest.com.

4. FBI Director to Smith, Document 22, 8 November 1968, Reference File: Anna Chennault, South Vietnam and US Politics, LBJL.

5. Rostow to Johnson, Document 21, 8 November 1968, Reference File: Anna Chennault, South Vietnam and US Politics, LBJL.

6. This was the second time Nixon pointed Johnson in the direction of Sen. John G. Tower, R-Texas. On both occasions that Nixon raised Tower's name, LBJ didn't take the bait.

7. Conversation WH6811-04-13723-13724-13725, 8 November 1968, 9:23 p.m., Mansion.

8. Ibid.

9. It is hard to escape the suspicion that Nixon was testing to see whether LBJ knew about his secret 12 July 1968 meeting in New York with Chennault, Ambassador Diem, and Campaign Chairman Mitchell. President Johnson shows no awareness of that meeting in this conversation or on any other tape. This suggests that either the NSA had not yet begun intercepting communications from the South Vietnamese embassy to Saigon at that point or Ambassador Diem had reported the meeting to his home government through another channel.

10. Conversation WH6811-04-13723-13724-13725, 8 November 1968, 9:23 p.m., Mansion.

11. "The United States channeled its dollars into the Vietnamese economy primarily through the Commercial Import Program (CIP). Modeled on the Marshall Plan in Europe, the CIP provided U.S. funds for the purchase of products in the United States and elsewhere in the currency of the country of origin. Vietnamese importers with special licenses obtained these goods by depositing piasters into a 'counterpart' fund in Saigon. [South Vietnam] also collected tariffs on these U.S. subsidized imports. The counterpart fund and customs duties paid almost all the costs of the South's military establishment and civil administration," wrote David L. Anderson in *Trapped by Success: The Eisenhower Administration and Vietnam, 1953–1961* (New York: Columbia University Press, 1991), 155–56. The overwhelming majority of the South Vietnamese budget went to its military and civilian administration (William Tuohy, "U.S. and Saigon Disagree over Vietnam Budget," *Los Angeles Times,* 12 January 1967, www.proquest.com).

12. Pentagon Papers, *Report of the Office of the Secretary of Defense Vietnam Task Force: United States–Vietnam Relations, 1945–1967,* part IV, A.3, p. 38, www.archives.gov/research/pentagon-papers. Fredrik Logevall quotes Hinh as saying that "the country cannot survive without American help" in *Embers of War: The Fall of an Empire and the Making of America's Vietnam* (New York: Random House, 2012), Kindle edition, chap. 25, "We Have No Other Choice but to Win Here," sec. 5.

13. "Telegram from the Central Intelligence Agency Station in Saigon to the Agency," 5 October 1963, *Foreign Relations of the United States (FRUS), 1961–1963: Vietnam, August–December 1963,* ed. Edward C. Keefer (Washington, DC: GPO, 1991), 4: Document 177 and Document 192. President John F. Kennedy personally oversaw the drafting of and approved the cable giving General Minh assurances

that US aid would continue under the new South Vietnamese regime (Tape 114/A50, 8 October 1963, 5:30–6:15 p.m., Oval Office, John F. Kennedy Library, President's Office Files, Presidential Recordings Collection). The CIA agent who acted as liaison between the US government and the coup plotters, Lucien E. Conein, testified, "I have it on very good authority of very many people that Big Minh gave the order" to murder Diem (see Conein's 20 June 1975 testimony in executive session before the Senate Select Committee to Study Governmental Operations with Respect to Intelligence Activities [SSCIA], p. 61, Assassination Records Review Board [ARRB] Record Number 157-10014-10094).

One could argue that Diem's defiance of the Kennedy administration shows the limits of the power of the threat to cut off American aid. But the US government was demanding that Diem send his brother Nhu, who was both the head of South Vietnam's secret police and Diem's closest adviser, out of the country. Both of Diem's alternatives—losing American aid and losing the person he depended on most to retain control of South Vietnam—threatened his survival in power. Diem faced a dilemma. He tried to resolve it by keeping his brother close by in Saigon while attempting to persuade the Kennedy administration to restore American aid.

14. Conversation WH6811-04-13723-13724-13725, 8 November 1968, 9:23 p.m., Mansion.

15. Conversation WH6811-04-13726, 9 November 1968, 8:13 a.m., Mansion.

16. Chennault, *The Education of Anna,* 176.

17. See memo quoted in Safire, *Before the Fall,* 112.


### The United Front

1. "Telegram from the Director of the Federal Bureau of Investigation (Hoover) to the Executive Secretary of the National Security Council (Smith)," 10 November 1968, *FRUS 1964–1968,* 7: Document 209. Former South Vietnamese vice president Nguyen Cao Ky acknowledged that preference for Nixon over Humphrey was one of the factors behind the boycott in his memoir (Nguyen Cao Ky and Marvin J. Wolf, *Buddha's Child: My Fight to Save Vietnam* [New York: St. Martin's Press, 2002], 290–91).

2. "Telegram from the Department of State to the Embassy in Vietnam," 10 November 1968, *FRUS 1964–1968,* 7: Document 210.

3. "Telegram from the Director of the Federal Bureau of Investigation (Hoover) to the Executive Secretary of the National Security Council (Smith)," 10 November 1968, *FRUS 1964–1968,* 7: Document 209n1.

4. Dallek, *Nixon and Kissinger,* 77. Kissinger wrote that "Thieu was bound to dig in, whatever Nixon urged" (Kissinger, *Ending the Vietnam War,* 53). See also Chennault, *The Education of Anna,* 190–91; and Lewis L. Gould, *1968: The Election That Changed America* (Chicago: Ivan R. Dee, 2010), 146.


### "Candid and Forthright"

1. John Chancellor, "Nixon-Johnson Meeting," *NBC Evening News,* aired 11 November 1968, http://tvnews.vanderbilt.edu.

2. "Notes of the President's Meeting with the President-Elect Richard Nixon," 11 November 1968, *FRUS 1964–1968,* 7: Document 211.

3. "Remarks to the Press with President-Elect Nixon Following Their Luncheon Meeting at the White House," 11 November 1968, *PPPUS: Johnson, 1968*, www.presidency.ucsb.edu/ws/?pid=29232.

4. DeLoach exaggerated slightly; Hoover wouldn't turn seventy-four until New Year's Day 1969.

5. Conversation WH6811-04-13730, 12 November 1968, 8:30 p.m., Oval Office.

6. Ibid.

7. Conversation WH6811-04-13733, 13 November 1968, 5:15 p.m., Mansion. According to DeLoach, the first call was from Agnew to Secretary of State Rusk. LBJ knew about their conversation already. Also, staff member Kent Crane called a Cal Purdy in Harlingen, Texas, and a Bruce Friedle in New York City. A fourth call was made to a Jim Miller in New York City. The fifth and final call was from Crane to "a Mr. Hitt at Nixon Agnew campaign headquarters" at the Willard Hotel. Robert J. Hitt was the husband of Patricia Reilly Hitt, the cochairman of the Nixon campaign. Mrs. Hitt had named Chennault along with former First Lady Mamie G. Eisenhower as cochairs of the Women for Nixon-Agnew Advisory Committee (Howard Seelye, "Times Woman of the Year: Political Worker Who Works for Winners," *Los Angeles Times*, 16 December 1968, www.proquest.com).

### The Man Who Knew Too Little

1. H. R. Haldeman, *The Ends of Power*, with Joseph DiMona (New York: Dell, 1978), 118; John Ehrlichman, *Witness to Power: The Nixon Years* (New York: Simon and Schuster, 1982), 156.

2. Haldeman, *The Ends of Power*, 118.

3. DeLoach to Tolson, 30 October 1968, quoted in Senate Select Committee on Governmental Operations with Respect to Intelligence Activities, *Intelligence Activities and the Rights of Americans: Book 2: Final Report*, 228n10.

4. "In fact, I discovered that Hoover—embellishing the Chennault episode—had told President Nixon that I had once planted a bug on his campaign plane. Eventually this story would find its way into FBI folklore. Indeed, from time to time I still run across it in accounts of the Johnson years. I'm always surprised that anyone could believe such a tale, because the bugging of a campaign plane would have to be categorized as 'Mission: Impossible.' No one could have approached such an aircraft without being apprehended and questioned by the Secret Service. You might as well try to put a bomb aboard" (DeLoach, *Hoover's FBI*, 407). Hoover's deception about the bugging cast DeLoach as LBJ's spy on the Nixon campaign. For DeLoach's perception that the Nixon administration viewed him as "Johnson's man," see ibid., 406–7.

### "All the Documents"

1. Haldeman, *The Ends of Power*, 286.

2. At the time, there was no law to stop any ex-president from treating the documents created during his administration as if they were his private property. Many of Johnson's predecessors did the same. Passage of the 1978 Presidential Records Act established by law that these documents, created at public

expense by the executive branch while carrying out the public business, are indeed public property.

3. Rostow to Harry Middleton, Director, LBJ Library, 26 June 1973, Reference File: Anna Chennault, South Vietnam and US Politics, LBJL.

4. Conversation 525-001, 17 June 1971, 5:15–6:10 p.m., Oval Office.

5. According to White, JFK had "two four-minute eggs, a rasher of broiled bacon, orange juice and milk" every morning (White, *The Making of the President 1960,* Kindle edition, chap. 6, "Rendezvous at Los Angeles: The Democratic Convention," 168).

6. White, *The Making of the President 1968,* Kindle edition, chap. 11, "October: All Passion Spent," 443–44.

7. Ibid., 444. Jules Witcover left open the question of whether the Nixon campaign knew what Chennault was up to in *The Resurrection of Richard Nixon* (New York: Putnam's Sons, 1970), 440–42.

8. White, *The Making of the President 1968,* Kindle edition, chap. 11, "October: All Passion Spent," 445.

9. Dick Allen, the foreign policy adviser who informed Nixon that Chennault wanted to introduce him to Ambassador Diem, "says he thought about it a lot but decided a meeting would be a mistake," Safire wrote in *Before the Fall,* 112. Allen later said that Chennault acted without authorization: "we had Anna Chennault, who was interfering with Diem in South Vietnam, urging the South Vietnamese not to go to the peace table, saying they'd get a better deal with Nixon. That eventually led to a lot of confusion. She had no authority, no brief" (Transcript, Richard V. Allen, Oral History Interview, 28 May 2002, by Stephen F. Knott, Russell L. Riley, and James Sterling Young, Miller Center, http://millercenter.org/president/reagan/oralhistory/richard-allen).

10. Huston to Haldeman, "Vietnam Bombing Halt," 25 February 1970, "John Dean Demon. Memos" folder, Haldeman Box 205, White House Special Files— Staff Member and Office Files, RMNL, www.nixonlibrary.gov/virtuallibrary /releases/jan10/069.pdf.

11. Huston to Haldeman, "Vietnam Bombing Halt," 13 March 1970, "Misc. Memos" folder, RG 460 Records of the Watergate Special Prosecution Force, Plumbers Task Force, Gray/Wiretap Investigation, Documentary Evidence, National Security Wiretaps to White House Documents, Box 17, National Archives and Records Administration, College Park, Maryland (hereafter NARA-CP).

12. Conversation 537-002, 2 July 1971, 2:50–4:02 p.m., Oval Office. Haldeman described the phone call to Nixon: "I just called Huston to track him back down on it. He said, 'Well, somebody'—can't remember his name—'told me it was there.' I say, well, call Blank and tell him that we've now found it isn't there and ask him how he explains that. And he said, 'I can't, they've shipped him out to sea.' He was in the Navy and they moved him out." I wrote Huston in 2000 and 2011 asking about it as well. In 2000, he replied, "I do not choose to discuss the matter." In 2011, he wrote that he couldn't remember the name, but provided some more details. "This information, faulty or sketchy as it may have been, was provided to me by a Navy captain whose name after 40 years I no longer recall who was the military assistant to Assistant Secretary (ISA) [G. Warren] Nutter at

the time of my inquiry and who had previously served as military assistant to Assistant Secretary (ISA) Warnke during the Johnson administration. I knew him as a result of my service at the Pentagon from the fall of 1967 to January of 1969. I reported to Haldeman what he told me. I had no way to confirm the accuracy of what he told me, but had no reason to doubt that it was accurate," Huston wrote. The United States Government Organization Manuals for the relevant years list many military assistants, but none for either Warnke or Nutter (for Warnke, see *United States Government Organization Manual 1968–1969* [Washington, DC: GPO, 1968], 128; for Nutter, see *United States Government Organization Manual 1969–1970* [Washington, DC: GPO, 1969], 109).

13. Helms to Kissinger, "October–November 1968 Vietnam Intelligence Data," 19 March 1970, attached to Haldeman to Ehrlichman, "Documents on 1968 Bombing Halt Decision," 21 October 1971, "H. R. Haldeman—Chron—Oct 1971, A–L" folder, WHSF-SMOF Haldeman Box 197, RMNL, www.nixonlibrary .gov/virtuallibrary/releases/dec10/53.pdf.

14. Haldeman, *The Ends of Power,* 287.

## The Huston Plan

1. Douglas Robinson, "Townhouse Razed by Blast and Fire; Man's Body Found," *New York Times,* 7 March 1970; Mel Gussow, "Tranquility Is Shaken on 11th St.," *New York Times,* 10 March 1970; Thomas R. Brooks, "U.S. 1970: The Radical Underground Surfaces with a Bang," *New York Times,* 15 March 1970, www.nytimes.com; Richard Reeves, *President Nixon: Alone in the White House* (New York: Simon and Schuster, 2001), 175.

2. Homer Bigart, "Many Buildings Evacuated Here in Bomb Scares," *New York Times,* 13 March 1970, www.nytimes.com.

3. Steven V. Roberts, "Bombings on Rise over the Nation; Police Say Most Are Caused by Left-Wing Militants, Both Black and White," *New York Times,* 13 March 1970, www.nytimes.com.

4. Quoted in Reeves, *President Nixon: Alone in the White House,* 175.

5. *Supplemental Detailed Staff Reports on Intelligence Activities and the Rights of Americans: Book 3: Final Report* (Washington, DC: GPO, 1976), 934.

6. Ibid., 934–38.

7. Exhibit 1, "Special Report Interagency Committee on Intelligence (Ad Hoc)," *Hearings before the Senate Select Committee on Governmental Operations With Respect to Intelligence Activities (SSCIA),* vol. 2, *Huston Plan,* 94th Cong., 1st Sess., 168.

8. Ibid., 171, 175, 178.

9. Ibid., 173.

10. Ibid., 176.

11. Ibid., 178.

12. Ibid., 187–88.

13. It is hard to tell, since censors blanked out that entire section of the interagency report except for the subheads, but Huston responded to each of Hoover's objections in his recommendations to the president and mentioned none on this point (ibid., 168–70, 193).

14. Huston to Haldeman, "Domestic Intelligence Gathering Plan: Analysis and Strategy," July 1970, quoted ibid., 189.

15. Ibid., 194.

16. Ibid.

17. Ibid., 194–95.

18. Ibid., 191–92.

19. Fred Emery, *Watergate: The Corruption of American Politics and the Fall of Richard Nixon* (New York: Touchstone, 1994), 25–26. In a 17 December 2013 letter, I asked Huston, "Did you suggest to Haldeman or any other White House official having someone break into Brookings to get the classified material you believed was there?" Huston did not answer the question directly when he responded in a 27 January 2014 e-mail. "Mr. Emery is a hatchet man who jumped to every conclusion that would be damaging to President Nixon and his aides, and there is simply no truth to his assertions," Huston wrote. "If it had been up to me, DoD security men would have waltzed into Brookings at high noon and cleared out their safe of any classified documents." While Huston did not directly address the question of whether he suggested a break-in, he did write that a "number of means of recovery were discussed."

20. Huston to Haldeman, 16 July 1970, quoted in Bruce Oudes, *From: The President: Richard Nixon's Secret Files* (New York: Harper and Row, 1988), 147–48.

21. Haldeman to Huston, "Domestic Intelligence Review," 14 July 1970, quoted in Oudes, *From: The President*, 198; Nixon, *RN*, 474.

22. Huston to Helms, 23 July 1970, quoted in Oudes, *From: The President*, 199–202.

23. Senate Select Committee on Governmental Operations with Respect to Intelligence Activities, *Supplemental Detailed Staff Reports on Intelligence Activities and the Rights of Americans: Book 3: Final Report*, 956.

24. Ibid., 956–57.

25. Hoover to Mitchell, 25 July 1970, quoted ibid., 957.

26. "Chronology of Huston Plan and Intelligence Evaluation Committee," ibid., 985.

27. Stephen E. Ambrose, *Nixon: The Triumph of a Politician 1962–1972* (New York: Simon and Schuster, 1989), 369.

28. Anthony Marro, "Former Aide Says Hoover Order to Find Radicals by 'Any Means' Was Relayed to Indicted Agent," *New York Times*, 12 August 1977, www.proquest.com.

29. Ehrlichman, *Witness to Power*, 161–62.

30. Nixon, *RN*, 475.

31. Ibid.

32. J. Anthony Lukas, *Nightmare: The Underside of the Nixon Years* (New York: Bantam, 1973), 41–42.

33. "Chronology of Huston Plan and Intelligence Evaluation Committee," prepared by staff in Senate Select Committee on Governmental Operations with Respect to Intelligence Activities, *Supplemental Detailed Staff Reports on Intelligence Activities and the Rights of Americans: Book 3: Final Report*, 983–86.

34. Frank Martin, "Interview with Tom Charles Huston," 10 August 1973, Box 22, RG 460, Records of the Watergate Special Prosecution Force, Plumbers Task Force, Gray/Wiretap Investigation, NARA-CP.

35. "Chronology of Huston Plan and Intelligence Evaluation Committee," prepared by staff in Senate Select Committee on Governmental Operations with Respect to Intelligence Activities, *Supplemental Detailed Staff Reports on Intelligence Activities and the Rights of Americans: Book 3: Final Report,* 983.

36. Huston to George Bell, 25 January 1971, quoted in Oudes, *From: The President,* 207–8.

37. Senate Select Committee on Governmental Operations with Respect to Intelligence Activities, *Supplemental Detailed Staff Reports on Intelligence Activities and the Rights of Americans: Book 3: Final Report,* 877.

38. "Bob asked that I pass the following along to you," Higby wrote (Higby to Huston, 14 July 1970, quoted in Oudes, *From: The President,* 146).

39. Huston to Haldeman, 16 July 1970, quoted in Oudes, *From: The President,* 147–48.

40. Alfonso A. Narvaez, "Bomb Damages Russian Offices Here," 26 November 1970, www.proquest.com.

41. "Mrs. Meir Assails Anti-Soviet Terrorism Here," 28 November 1970, www.proquest.com.

42. Richard Halloran, "Blast Damages Soviet Building in Washington," *New York Times,* 9 January 1971, www.proquest.com.

43. Murrey Marder, "FBI Probes Anti-Soviet Bombing," *Washington Post,* 10 January 1971, www.proquest.com.

44. Huston to Haldeman, "The Jewish Defense League," 14 January 1971, "USSR (Jewish Defense League) Jan 71" folder, Box 405, NSC Files, RMNL.

45. Jack Rosenthal, "J.D.L. Suing U.S. on Wiretapping," *New York Times,* 8 October 1971, www.proquest.com.

### Nixon Tapes

1. H. R. Haldeman, "The Decision to Record Presidential Conversations," *Prologue* magazine, Summer 1988, www.archives.gov/publications/prologue/1988/summer/haldeman.html.

2. Conversation 450-010, 16 February 1971, 10:28–10:49 a.m., Oval Office.

3. John Powers, "The History of Presidential Audio Recordings and the Archival Issues Surrounding Their Use," CIDS paper, National Archives and Records Administration, 12 July 1996.

4. Haldeman, "The Decision to Record Presidential Conversations."

5. Nixon, *RN,* 500.

6. Haldeman, *The Ends of Power,* 91.

### Tricia's Wedding

1. Nan Robertson, "Tricia Nixon Takes Vows in Garden at White House," *New York Times,* 13 June 1971, www.proquest.com.

2. Nixon, *RN,* 508.

3. Will Swift, *Pat and Dick: The Nixons, an Intimate Portrait of a Marriage* (New York: Threshold Editions, 2014), 30, 229.

4. Conversation 518-008, 12 June 1971, 11:50 a.m.–1:41 p.m., Oval Office.

5. "Around the White House," *Washington Post,* www.proquest.com.

6. Nixon, *RN,* 13–14.

7. Conversation 518-008, 12 June 1971, 11:50 a.m.–1:41 p.m., Oval Office.

### The Pentagon Papers

1. Neil Sheehan, "Vietnam Archive: Pentagon Study Traces 3 Decades of Growing U.S. Involvement," *New York Times,* 13 June 1971, www.proquest.com.

2. "Key Texts from Pentagon's Vietnam Study," and "The Covert War," *New York Times,* 13 June 1971, www.proquest.com. Johnson's own tapes show that he connected the Tonkin Gulf attacks with covert American operations (see Marc Selverstone and David Coleman, "Gulf of Tonkin, 1964: Perspectives from the Lyndon Johnson and National Military Center Tapes," http://millercenter.org /presidentialclassroom/exhibits/gulf-of-tonkin-1964-perspectives). "But there have been some covert operations in that area that we have been carrying on—blowing up some bridges and things of that kind, roads and so forth. So I imagine they wanted to put a stop to it," President Johnson said (Conversation WH6408-03-04632, 3 August 1964, 9:46 a.m., Mansion).

3. Conversation 005-050, 13 June 1971, 12:18–12:42 p.m., White House Telephone. For some unknown reason, the recording was cut off before the conversation ended. Fortunately, a "telcon," a transcript made by NSC secretaries, exists. See also "The President-General Haig," and "Haldeman-Haig," 13 June 1971, 12:20 p.m., "Haig Telcons—1971 [2 of 2]" folder, National Security Council Files Box 998, Alexander M. Haig Chronological File, RMNL.

4. Conversation "Haldeman-Haig" telcon, 13 June 1971, 1:05 p.m., "Haig Telcons—1971 [2 of 2]" folder, National Security Council Files Box 998, Alexander M. Haig Chronological File, RMNL.

5. Conversation 005-059, 13 June 1971, 3:09–3:22 p.m., White House Telephone.

6. Ibid.

### The Secret Bombing of Cambodia

1. Conversation 519-001, 14 June 1971, 8:49–10:04 a.m., Oval Office.

2. Nixon, *RN,* 380–82.

3. *Foreign Relations of the United States (FRUS), 1969–1976: Vietnam, January 1969–July 1970,* ed. Edward C. Keefer and Carolyn Yee (Washington, DC: GPO, 2006), 6: Document 22; William M. Hammond, *Public Affairs: The Military and the Media, 1968–1973,* United States Army in Vietnam (Washington, DC: Center of Military History, United States Army, 1996), 64.

4. Situation Room to Haig, "Casualties Inflicted by Enemy Rocket Attacks since the Start of Current Offensive," 15 March 1969; Kissinger to Nixon, "Breakfast Plan," 16 March 1969, both in "Breakfast Plan" folder, Box 89, NSC Files: Vietnam Subject Files: Top Secret/Sensitive Vietnam Contingency Planning, RMNL. Kissinger explicitly linked the secret bombing of Cambodia

to the attacks on the South Vietnamese cities: "Failure to take action in response to Saigon/Hue shellings—especially after repeated Presidential warnings—would appear to Hanoi as a demonstration of weakness." Kissinger argued that the bombing would also make Saigon more willing to enter private talks with the NLF and "serve as a signal to the Soviets of the Administration's determination to end the war. It would be a signal that things may get out of hand."

5. Hammond, *Public Affairs,* 66.

6. Nixon, *RN,* 381.

7. Nixon did retaliate against the North Vietnamese by launching air and ground strikes *within* the DMZ, but not north of it at this time ("U.S. Armor Fights Enemy in the DMZ for Three Hours," *New York Times,* 17 March 1969, www.proquest.com).

8. Nixon, *RN,* 380.

9. Atta, *With Honor,* Kindle edition, chap. 10, "Off the Menu."

10. Seymour M. Hersh, *The Price of Power: Kissinger in the Nixon White House* (New York: Summit, 1983), 55.

11. Kenton Clymer, *Troubled Relations: The United States and Cambodia since 1870* (DeKalb: Northern Illinois University Press, 2007), 96–98.

12. William Shawcross, *Sideshow: Kissinger, Nixon and the Destruction of Cambodia* (New York: Simon and Schuster, 1979), 390–91. "In sum, Sihanouk was never asked to approve the B-52 bombings, and he never gave his approval," wrote Kenton Clymer in *Troubled Relations,* 98.

13. Nixon, *RN,* 382; Jeffrey Kimball, *Nixon's Vietnam War* (Lawrence: University Press of Kansas, 1998), 132.

14. David R. Derge, Vice President and Dean of Indiana University, to Nixon, "The Public Appraises the Nixon Administration and Key Issues (With Particular Emphasis on Vietnam)," 11 August 1969, "E.O.B. Office Desk—August 10, 1974" folder, Box 185, President's Personal File, Materials Removed from President's Desk, 1969–74, [EOB Office Desk . . . Administration] to [Blank Stationery— . . . August 9, 1974], RMNL.

15. Bundy, *A Tangled Web,* 148.

16. Shawcross, *Sideshow,* 35; Clymer, *Troubled Relations,* 96.

17. Senate Committee on Armed Services, *Hearings on Bombing in Cambodia,* 93rd Cong., 1st Sess., 8 August 1973, p. 356.

18. Shawcross, *Sideshow,* 113; John L. Hess, "Sihanouk Lays Rioting to 'Plot,' " *New York Times,* 12 March 1970, www.proquest.com.

19. John L. Hess, "Sihanouk Issues Warning to Reds," 13 March 1970, www .proquest.com.

20. United Press International, "Cambodia Orders Reds to Get Out by Sunday," *Los Angeles Times,* 14 March 1970, www.proquest.com.

21. Associated Press, "Viet Reds, Cambodians Said to Clash," *Washington Post,* 16 March 1970, www.proquest.com.

22. Henry Kamm, "Sihanouk Reported Out in a Coup by His Premier; Cambodia Airports Shut," *New York Times,* 19 March 1970, www.proquest.com.

23. Bernard Gwertzman, "Sihanouk, Leaving Moscow for Peking, Speaks of a Possible Government in Exile," *New York Times,* 19 March 1970, www.proquest.com.

24. Wilfred P. Deac, *Road to the Killing Fields: The Cambodian War of 1970–1975* (College Station: Texas A&M University Press, 1997), 60–61.

25. Shawcross, *Sideshow,* 126–27.

26. Agence France-Presse, "Sihanouk, in Peking, Plans an 'Army of Liberation,'" *New York Times,* 24 March 1970, www.proquest.com.

27. Tad Szulc, "U.S. Feels Sihanouk's Bloc Includes Reds, Leftists, and Guerrillas," *New York Times,* 18 May 1970, www.proquest.com.

28. Joseph P. Sterba, "North Vietnamese Reported Recruiting Guerrillas in Cambodia," *New York Times,* 29 May 1970, www.proquest.com; Deac, *Road to the Killing Fields,* 63.

29. United Press International, "Arms Curb Reported," *New York Times,* 26 May 1970, www.proquest.com.

30. Henry Kamm, "Cambodia Warns That Red Troops Step Up Invasion," 30 March 1970, www.proquest.com.

31. Laurence Stern, "Reds' Gains Peril Regime in Cambodia," *Washington Post,* 22 April 1970, www.proquest.com.

32. Nixon, *RN,* 448.

33. "Address to the Nation on the Situation in Southeast Asia," 30 April 1970, *PPPUS: Johnson, 1968,* www.presidency.ucsb.edu/ws/?pid=2490. Kissinger wrote that Nixon "added a sentence that was as irrelevant to his central thesis as it was untrue, that we had heretofore not moved against the sanctuaries—overlooking the secret bombing" (Kissinger, *White House Years,* 505).

34. Nixon, *RN,* 449–50.

35. Linda Charlton, "Big Rallies Are Planned," *New York Times,* 2 May 1970, www.proquest.com.

36. United Press International, "Violence on Campuses," *New York Times,* 3 May 1970, www.proquest.com.

37. Michael T. Kaufman, "Campus Unrest over War Spreads with Strike Calls," *New York Times,* 4 May 1970, www.proquest.com.

38. *Haldeman Diaries,* 4 May 1970.

39. Ibid., 1 May 1970.

40. Ibid., 4 May 1970.

41. Ibid., 7 May 1970. See also Max Frankel, "Hickel, in Note to Nixon, Charges Administration Is Failing Youth," *New York Times;* and Robert C. Maynard, "Reagan Closes State's Colleges As More Campuses Join in Protest," *Washington Post,* both 7 May 1970; and Haynes Johnson, "U.S. Braces As Protests Gain Force," *Washington Post,* 8 May 1970, www.proquest.com.

42. "The President's News Conference," 8 May 1970, *PPPUS: Johnson, 1968,* www.presidency.ucsb.edu/ws/?pid=2496.

43. *Haldeman Diaries,* 8 May 1970.

44. Ibid., 9 May 1970. Nixon expressed "complete frustration" with news reports on his visit to the demonstrators and dictated his own detailed account (Nixon to Haldeman, 13 May 1970, in Oudes, *From: The President,* 127–34).

45. Jeffrey Kimball, *The Vietnam War Files: Uncovering the Secret History of Nixon-Era Strategy*, Modern War Studies (Lawrence: University Press of Kansas, 2004), 25–26, 130.

46. Hersh, *The Price of Power*, 55.

47. Richard M. Nixon, *No More Vietnams* (New York: Arbor House, 1985), 123.

48. Henry Kissinger, *White House Years* (London: Weidenfeld and Nicholson, 1979), 253–54.

49. Conversation 334-044, 4 May 1972, 3:04–5:35 p.m., Executive Office Building.

50. Elizabeth Becker and Seth Mydans, "Norodom Sihanouk, Cambodian Leader through Shifting Allegiances, Dies at 89," *New York Times*, 14 October 2012, www.nytimes.com.

51. Shawcross, *Sideshow*, 390–91.

## Leaks

1. "Sihanouk: U.S. Ally at Last?" *Newsweek*, 10 March 1969.

2. "U.S. Aides Oppose Raids in Cambodia," *New York Times*, 26 March 1969, www.proquest.com.

3. William Beecher, "Raids in Cambodia by U.S. Unprotested," *New York Times*, 9 May 1969, www.proquest.com.

4. Nixon, *RN*, 387–88.

5. Halperin testimony, RG 460 Records of the Watergate Special Prosecution Force, Plumbers Task Force, Fielding Break-In Investigation, Trial Transcripts, US v. Russo and Ellsberg, Box 40, NARA-CP, pp. 16, 754.

6. See Hoover to Tolson, 9 May 1969, in House Committee on the Judiciary, *Statement of Information: Book 7, Part 1: White House Surveillance Activities and Campaign Activities*, 143–45.

7. Halperin affidavit, 30 November 1973, in House Committee on the Judiciary, *Statement of Information: Book 7, Part 1: White House Surveillance Activities and Campaign Activities*, 218–21.

8. House Committee on the Judiciary, *Statement of Information: Book 7, Part 1: White House Surveillance Activities and Campaign Activities*, 9.

9. Halperin affidavit, 30 November 1973, in House Committee on the Judiciary, *Statement of Information: Book 7, Part 1: White House Surveillance Activities and Campaign Activities*, 218–21.

10. House Committee on the Judiciary, *Statement of Information: Book 7, Part 1: White House Surveillance Activities and Campaign Activities*, 8.

11. Hoover to Nixon, 29 December 1969; and undated handwritten notes between Ehrlichman and Haldeman, ibid., 359–68. While the FBI didn't know the identity of Halperin's caller, Clifford identified him as Gelb in Clifford and Holbrooke, *Counsel to the President*, 615.

12. Clark M. Clifford, "Set a Date in Vietnam. Stick to It. Get Out," *Life* magazine, 22 May 1970.

## The Wrong Men

1. "McGovern-Nixon Link: Paul Culliton Warnke," *New York Times*, 16 August 1972, www.nytimes.com.

2. Halperin testimony, RG 460 Records of the Watergate Special Prosecution Force, Plumbers Task Force, Fielding Break-In Investigation, Trial Transcripts, US v. Russo and Ellsberg, Box 40, NARA-CP, p. 16,739.

3. Clifford and Holbrooke, *Counsel to the President,* 490.

4. Ibid., 490–91.

5. Halperin testimony, RG 460 Records of the Watergate Special Prosecution Force, Plumbers Task Force, Fielding Break-In Investigation, Trial Transcripts, US v. Russo and Ellsberg, Box 40, NARA-CP, pp. 16,766–16,767.

6. Ibid., p. 16,763.

7. David Rudenstine, *The Day the Presses Stopped: A History of the Pentagon Papers Case* (Berkeley: University of California Press, 1996), 20; Halperin testimony, RG 460 Records of the Watergate Special Prosecution Force, Plumbers Task Force, Fielding Break-In Investigation, Trial Transcripts, US v. Russo and Ellsberg, Box 40, NARA-CP, p. 16,770.

8. Halperin testimony, RG 460 Records of the Watergate Special Prosecution Force, Plumbers Task Force, Fielding Break-In Investigation, Trial Transcripts, US v. Russo and Ellsberg, Box 40, NARA-CP, p. 16,774.

9. Ibid., pp. 16,807–16,810.

10. Rudenstine, *The Day the Presses Stopped,* 20.

11. Halperin testimony, RG 460 Records of the Watergate Special Prosecution Force, Plumbers Task Force, Fielding Break-In Investigation, Trial Transcripts, US v. Russo and Ellsberg, Box 40, NARA-CP, pp. 16,772–16,774.

12. John Prados and Margaret Pratt Porter, *Inside the Pentagon Papers* (Lawrence: University Press of Kansas, 2004), 4–5; Rudenstine, *The Day the Presses Stopped,* 35–37.

13. Rudenstine, *The Day the Presses Stopped,* 69.

14. "Kissinger Conducts His Last Seminar in Government before Joining It," *New York Times,* 17 December 1968, www.nytimes.com.

15. Daniel Ellsberg, *Secrets: A Memoir of Vietnam and the Pentagon Papers* (New York: Viking, 2002), 186.

16. Ibid., 228.

17. Halperin testimony, RG 460 Records of the Watergate Special Prosecution Force, Plumbers Task Force, Fielding Break-In Investigation, Trial Transcripts, US v. Russo and Ellsberg, Box 40, NARA-CP, pp. 16759, 16,935. See also Ellsberg, *Secrets,* 231–35.

18. Halperin testimony, RG 460 Records of the Watergate Special Prosecution Force, Plumbers Task Force, Fielding Break-In Investigation, Trial Transcripts, US v. Russo and Ellsberg, Box 40, NARA-CP, p. 16,760.

19. Sanford J. Ungar, *The Papers & the Papers: An Account of the Legal and Political Battle over the Pentagon Papers* (New York: Dutton, 1972), 56. See also Ellsberg, *Secrets,* 235–37.

20. Halperin testimony, RG 460 Records of the Watergate Special Prosecution Force, Plumbers Task Force, Fielding Break-In Investigation, Trial Transcripts, US v. Russo and Ellsberg, Box 40, NARA-CP, p. 16,838.

21. Ibid., pp. 16,842–16,844.

22. Ibid., pp. 16,850–16,851.

23. Ibid., p. 16,851.

24. There was an exception to this rule for the Pentagon Papers covering the period before the Kennedy and Johnson administrations; RAND could distribute those to its employees as it saw fit (ibid., pp. 16,876–16,877).

25. Ibid., pp. 16,877–16,879; Martin Arnold, "Former U.S. Aide Rebuts Ellsberg," *New York Times,* 21 April 1973, www.nytimes.com.

26. Ungar, *The Papers & the Papers,* 56; Rudenstine, *The Day the Presses Stopped,* 39; Hersh, *The Price of Power,* 50.

27. Ellsberg, *Secrets,* 241–42.

28. Halperin testimony, RG 460 Records of the Watergate Special Prosecution Force, Plumbers Task Force, Fielding Break-In Investigation, Trial Transcripts, US v. Russo and Ellsberg, Box 40, NARA-CP, pp. 16,865–16,868.

29. "McGovern-Nixon Link: Paul Culliton Warnke," *New York Times,* 16 August 1972, www.nytimes.com; Clifford and Holbrooke, *Counsel to the President,* 490, 611.

30. Halperin testimony, RG 460 Records of the Watergate Special Prosecution Force, Plumbers Task Force, Fielding Break-In Investigation, Trial Transcripts, US v. Russo and Ellsberg, Box 40, NARA-CP, p. 16,732.

31. Clifford and Holbrooke, *Counsel to the President,* 615.

### "Charge Gelb"

1. Conversation 519-001, 14 June 1971, 8:49–10:04 a.m., Oval Office.

### LBJ Cracks the Case

1. Conversation 519-007, 14 June 1971, 12:26–1:09 p.m., Oval Office. An account written before the government declassified this tape portrayed Haig as providing Ellsberg's name to Rostow (Harrison E. Salisbury, *Without Fear or Favor: The New York Times and Its Times* [New York: Ballantine, 1980], 210).

### Ellsberg's Decision

1. Ellsberg, *Secrets,* vii.

2. Ted Sell, "Green Beret Case Charges Dropped; Army Acts after CIA Refuses to Give Testimony," *Los Angeles Times,* 30 September 1969, www.proquest.com.

3. Ibid.

4. *Haldeman Diaries,* 12 September 1969.

5. Ibid., 18 and 25 September 1969.

6. Ibid., 29 September 1969.

7. Ellsberg, *Secrets,* 289.

8. Ibid., 230.

9. Jeffrey Kimball, *The Vietnam War Files: Uncovering the Secret History of Nixon-Era Strategy,* Modern War Studies (Lawrence: University Press of Kansas, 2004), 187.

10. "Memorandum of Conversation," 9 July 1971, 4:35–11:20 p.m., attached to Lord to Kissinger, "Memcon of Your Conversations with Chou En-lai," 29 July 1971, NSCF Box 1033, RMNL.

11. Conversation 760-006, 3 August 1972, 8:28–8:57 a.m., Oval Office.

12. "Memorandum of Conversation," 31 May 1971, 10:00 a.m.–1:30 p.m., "Camp David—Vol. VII" folder, NSCF Box 853, RMNL.

13. NSC to Vice President's Office, "Revised Summary of Responses to NSSM-1: The Situation in Vietnam," 22 March 1969, http://gateway.proquest.com /openurl?url_ver=Z39.88-2004&res_dat=xri:dnsa&rft_dat=xri:dnsa:article: CPD01323.

14. "Address to the Nation on the War in Vietnam," 3 November 1969, *Public Papers of the Presidents of the United States: Richard M. Nixon, 1969* (Washington, DC: GPO, 1971), www.presidency.ucsb.edu/ws/?pid=2303.

15. Ibid.

16. Conversation 507-004, 29 May 1971, 8:13–10:32 a.m., Oval Office.

17. Conversation 760-006, 3 August 1972, 8:28–8:57 a.m., Oval Office.

18. I made a series of web videos using the Nixon tapes to show how he prolonged the war and faked peace for political gain. Go to www.fatalpolitics.com.

19. Ellsberg, *Secrets*, 293.

### Fear of a Damaging Disclosure

1. Conversation 520-004, 15 June 1971, 10:39–10:59 a.m., Oval Office.

2. Henry Kissinger, *Years of Upheaval* (Boston: Little, Brown, 1982), 429; Henry Kissinger, *Years of Renewal* (New York: Touchstone, 1999), 497.

3. Seymour M. Hersh, "Cambodian Raids Reported Hidden before '70 Foray," *New York Times*, 15 July 1973, www.proquest.com.

4. Conversation 334-044, 4 May 1972, 3:04–5:35 p.m., Executive Office Building.

### Legal Action

1. Conversation 521-012, 15 June 1971, 4:40-5:13 p.m., Oval Office.

2. "The Hour Approaches," *New York Times*, 14 June 1971, www.proquest.com.

3. Conversation 005-068, 14 June 1971, 7:13-7:15 p.m., White House Telephone.

4. Conversation 006-070, 14 June 1971, 7:19-7:22 p.m., White House Telephone.

5. Max Frankel, "Court Step Likely; Return of Documents Asked in Telegram to Publisher," *New York Times*, 15 June 1971, www.proquest.com.

6. Rudenstine, *The Day the Presses Stopped*, 9.

7. Conversation 005-086, 15 June 1971, 6:35–6:38 p.m., White House Telephone; Richard Dougherty, "Judge Refuses to Silence N.Y. Times," 20 June 1971, www .proquest.com.

8. Linda Mathews, "Attorney for Paper Calls Restraint Order 'First,'" *Los Angeles Times*, 16 June 1971, www.proquest.com.

9. Chalmers Roberts, "Documents Reveal U.S. Effort in '54 to Delay Viet Election," *Washington Post*, 18 June 1971, www.proquest.com.

10. James Naughton, "*Washington Post* Restrained: Appeals Court Reverses Decision Favoring Paper," *New York Times*, 19 June 1971, www.proquest.com.

11. Richard Dougherty, "Judge Refuses to Silence N.Y. Times," 20 June 1971, www.proquest.com.

12. Conversation 527-012, 22 June 1971, 5:09–6:46 p.m., Oval Office.

13. Associated Press, "205 Reds on Job in State Dept., McCarthy Says," *Chicago Tribune,* 10 February 1950, www.proquest.com. For a side-by-side comparison of two nearly identical passages from Nixon's and McCarthy's speeches, see Fawn McKay Brodie, *Richard Nixon: The Shaping of His Character* (New York: Norton, 1981), 292–93; or David M. Oshinsky, *A Conspiracy So Immense: The World of Joe McCarthy* (Oxford: Oxford University Press, 2005), 108.

14. Associated Press, "Senator Says 57 Reds in State Dept.," *Los Angeles Times,* 11 February 1950, www.proquest.com.

15. United Press International, "'20 Years of Treason' Charged," *New York Times,* 6 February 1954, www.proquest.com; 97 Cong. Rec. 6602 (daily ed. 14 June 1951) (statement of Senator McCarthy).

16. It was a lesson Nixon drew for his aides on more than one occasion: "I got Joe out and I could have saved his life. I saw him in California. He made that silly speech in West Virginia with the names of 57 Communists. I said, 'Joe,' I said, 'There are some there,' [*unclear*] of course, I said, 'You're stuck on a number and you must not be stuck on a number. They'll kill you with that number'" (see Conversation 246-005, 7 April 1971, 10:55–12:15, Executive Office Building).

17. Conversation 527-012, 22 June 1971, 5:09–6:46 p.m., Oval Office.

18. Buchanan to Nixon, 4 August 1971, "HRH. Patrick J. Buchanan, August 1971, Box 83" folder, Haldeman Contested Folder 8, RMNL.

### The Diem Chapter

1. Conversation 521-009, 15 June 1971, 3:45–4:30 p.m., Oval Office.

2. "Divergent Views at Home," *New York Times,* 15 June 1971, www.proquest.com.

3. Conversation 522-001, 16 June 1971, 9:05–10:38, Oval Office.

4. Conversation 523-6, 16 June 1971, 5:16–6:05 p.m., Oval Office.

5. Conversation 525-001, 17 June 1971, 5:15–6:10 p.m., Oval Office.

6. Jonathan Aitken, *Charles W. Colson: A Life Redeemed* (New York: Doubleday, 2005), 160.

7. Conversation 458-11, 25 February 1971, 5:44–6:30 p.m., Oval Office.

8. Ibid.

9. Haldeman, *The Ends of Power,* 92.

10. Aitken, *Charles W. Colson,* 161.

11. Lukas, *Nightmare,* 15–17.

12. Conversation 005-113, 17 June 1971, 6:38–6:45 p.m., White House Telephone.

13. Spencer Rich, "McCloskey Says Documents Show U.S. 'Encouraged' Ouster of Diem," *Washington Post,* 22 June 1971, www.proquest.com.

14. Conversation 528-001, 23 June 1971, 11:04 a.m.–12:45 p.m., Oval Office.

### "Destroy the *Times*"

1. Conversation 524-027, 17 June 1971, 2:42–3:33 p.m., Oval Office. This wasn't a momentary outburst, but a repeated instruction. "Listen, the main thing is just

cast it in terms of doing something disloyal to the country," he told Colson on June 15, 1971. "This risks our men, you know, just all that sort of thing. Secret things that [give] aid and comfort to the enemy" (see Conversation 005-081, 15 June 1971, 6:21–6:27 p.m., White House Telephone).

2. Conversation 525-001, 17 June 1971, 5:15–6:10 p.m., Oval Office.

3. Conversation 519-001, 14 June 1971, 8:49–10:04 a.m., Oval Office.

4. Nixon to Haldeman, 15 June 1971, in Oudes, *From: The President,* 270–71.

5. Conversation 005-131, 22 June 1971, 10:31–10:38 p.m., White House Telephone.

6. Conversation 528-001, 23 June 1971, 11:04 a.m.–12:45 p.m., Oval Office.

7. Conversation 521-009, 15 June 1971, 3:45–4:30 p.m., Oval Office.

8. The other 12 percent had no opinion (see George Gallup, "58% Favor Papers Printing War Study," *Washington Post,* 5 July 1971, www.proquest.com).

### Illegal Action

1. Conversation 527-012, 22 June 1971, 5:09–6:46 p.m., Oval Office.

2. Ellsberg, *Secrets,* 306–9.

3. See Rule 6(e)(2)(B) of the Federal Rules of Criminal Procedure.

4. Conversation 527-012, 22 June 1971, 5:09–6:46 p.m., Oval Office.

5. Conversation 528-001, 23 June 1971, 11:04 a.m.–12:45 p.m., Oval Office.

### "A Natural Enemy"

1. Keith W. Olson, *Watergate: The Presidential Scandal That Shook America* (Lawrence: University Press of Kansas, 2003), 18.

2. Conversation 530-003, 29 June 1971, 8:32–10:07 a.m., Oval Office.

3. Gene Blake and Jack Nelson, "Ellsberg Indicted in Pentagon Documents Theft, Surrenders," *Los Angeles Times,* 29 June 1971, www.proquest.com; Conversation 529-020, 28 June 1971, 10:23–10:51 a.m., Oval Office; Ellsberg, *Secrets,* 406–8, 430.

4. Conversation 531-024, 28 June 1971, 6:50–7:25 p.m., Oval Office.

### Lord High Executioner

1. Conversation 063-003, 29 June 1971, 8:05–10:07 a.m., Cabinet Room; *Haldeman Diaries,* 29 June 1971.

2. Conversation 530-003, 29 June 1971, 8:32–10:07 a.m., Oval Office.

### Supreme Court Rules

1. "Texts of the Supreme Court Decision, Opinions and Dissents in Times-Post Case," *New York Times,* 1 July 1971, www.proquest.com; Fred P. Graham, "Burger Dissents; First Amendment Rule Held to Block Most Prior Restraints," *New York Times,* 1 July 1971, www.proquest.com.

2. Erwin N. Griswold, "Secrets Not Worth Keeping: The Courts and Classified Information," *Washington Post,* 15 February 1989, www.proquest.com.

### 1969 Documents

1. Conversation 532-023, 30 June 1971, 2:31–3:07 p.m., Oval Office.

### "Break In and Take It Out"

1. Charles M. Cooke told me this in an interview on 11 March 2000.

2. Conversation 533-001, 30 June 1971, 5:14–6:23 p.m., Oval Office; Kutler, *Abuse of Power,* 6; Christopher Matthews, "Nixon Personally Ordered Break-In," *San Francisco Examiner,* 21 November 1996, www.sfgate.com/news/article/Nixon -personally-ordered-break-in-3112881.php.

3. Conversation 006-062, 30 June 1971, 7:22–7:27 p.m., White House Telephone.

### "Rumors and Reports of a Conspiracy"

1. Nixon, *RN,* 512.

2. Conversation 520-003, 15 June 1971, 9:56–10:37 a.m., Oval Office.

3. Conversation 521-013, 15 June 1971, 5:13–6:03 p.m., Oval Office.

4. John M. Lee, "Sweden Defends Stand on Vietnam," *New York Times,* 17 March 1968, www.proquest.com.

5. Conversation 537-004, 5 July 1971, 4:03–6:15 p.m., Oval Office.

6. Conversation 534-002, 1 July 1971, 8:45–9:52 a.m., Oval Office.

7. David Greenberg, "Nixon and the Jews. Again," *Slate,* 12 March 2002, www .slate.com/articles/news_and_politics/history_lesson/2002/03/nixon_and_the_ jews_again.single.html.

8. Conversation 536-016, 3 July 1971, 10:41–11:53 a.m., Oval Office.

9. Arthur M. Schlesinger Jr., *The Coming of the New Deal: 1933–1935* (Boston: Houghton Mifflin, 1958), Kindle edition, chap. 3, sec. 5. Schlesinger was characterizing the views of the farm specialists, not his own. He had a Jewish grandparent, a Harvard degree, and a reputation as one of America's leading liberal intellectuals.

10. See Sam Tanenhaus's chapter on the Pumpkin Papers in *Whittaker Chambers: A Biography* (New York: Random House, 1997), 290–317; and Allen Weinstein, *Perjury: The Hiss-Chambers Case* (1978; repr., New York: Random House, 1997), 167.

11. William Conklin, "Hiss Guilty on Both Perjury Counts; Betrayal of U.S. Secrets Is Affirmed," *New York Times,* 22 January 1950, www.proquest.com.

12. 96 Cong. Rec. 1,002 and 1,007 (daily ed., 26 January 1950) (statement of Rep. Nixon).

13. Ibid., 1,007.

14. "Nixon Is Youngest of G.O.P. in the Senate," *New York Times,* 12 July 1952, www.proquest.com.

15. "Texts of Eisenhower and Nixon Addresses to the Convention," *New York Times,* 12 July 1952, www.proquest.com.

16. Conversation 524-027, 17 June 1971, 2:42–3:33 p.m., Oval Office.

### Imitation of the Enemy

1. Conversation 534-002, 1 July 1971, 8:45–9:52 a.m., Oval Office.

2. Richard Hofstadter, *The Paranoid Style in American Politics and Other Essays* (Cambridge: Harvard University Press, 1964), 32.

3. Conversation 534-002, 1 July 1971, 8:45–9:52 a.m., Oval Office.

4. Conversation 534-005, 1 July 1971, 10:27–11:49 a.m., Oval Office.

5. Hofstadter, *The Paranoid Style in American Politics,* 32.

6. Under federal law, a conspiracy exists if two or more people agree to commit a crime—regardless of whether the crime takes place. "The crime is complete upon agreement, although some statutes require prosecutors to show that at least one of the conspirators has taken some concrete step or committed some overt act in furtherance of the scheme," writes Charles Doyle, senior specialist in American public law with the Congressional Research Service (see US Library of Congress, CRS, *Federal Conspiracy Law: A Brief Overview,* by Charles Doyle, CRS Report R41223 [Washington, DC: Office of Congressional Information and Publishing, 30 April 2010], 3). Nixon took such "concrete steps" with his aides when he created the SIU to commit crimes such as the leak of grand jury testimony and a break-in at Brookings.

### Special Investigations Unit

1. Conversation 534-005, 1 July 1971, 10:27–11:49 a.m., Oval Office.

2. Conversation 534-002, 1 July 1971, 8:45–9:52 a.m., Oval Office. Later that day, Nixon said, "Huston would die before he'd rat on us" (Conversation 534-005, 1 July 1971, 10:27–11:49 a.m., Oval Office).

3. Conversation 534-005, 1 July 1971, 10:27–11:49 a.m., Oval Office.

4. Conversation 534-012, 1 July 1971, 1:38–2:05 p.m., Oval Office.

5. Conversation 534-002, 1 July 1971, 8:45–9:52 a.m., Oval Office.

6. Ibid.

7. Don Oberdorfer, "U.S. Supported Coup against Diem," *Washington Post,* 1 July 1971, www.proquest.com.

8. Conversation 519-001, 14 June 1971, 8:49–10:04 a.m., Oval Office. See also Viren Swami et al., "Conspiracist Ideation in Britain and Austria: Evidence of a Monological Belief System and Associations between Individual Psychological Differences and Real-World and Fictitious Conspiracy Theories," *British Journal of Psychology* 102, no. 3 (2011): 443–63, doi: 10.1111/j.2044-8295.2010.02004.x.

9. Conversation 524-008, 17 June 1971, 9:58–10:34 a.m., Oval Office.

10. Conversation 528-004, 24 June 1971, 9:10–10:45 a.m., Oval Office.

11. Conversation 534-005, 1 July 1971, 10:27–11:49 a.m., Oval Office.

12. Evan Thomas, *The Very Best Men: Four Who Dared: The Early Years of the CIA* (New York: Simon and Schuster, 1995), 114–15, 155, 312.

13. House Committee on the Judiciary, *Statement of Information: Book 7, Part 2: White House Surveillance Activities and Campaign Activities* (Washington, DC: GPO, 1974), 814.

14. Ibid., 795.

15. Olson, *Watergate,* 18.

16. Lukas, *Nightmare,* 100–101.

17. Theodore H. White, *Breach of Faith: The Fall of Richard Nixon* (New York: Atheneum, 1975), 149.

18. Krogh to Haldeman, "Internal Security," 26 January 1970, "Internal Security [1969–71] Box #14 Nixon Withdrawals" folder, Krogh Contested Folder 1, RMNL.

19. Krogh to Haldeman, "Internal Security Organization," 23 February 1970, "Memos, February 1970] Box #2 Nixon Withdrawal" folder, Krogh Contested Folder 1, RMNL.

20. Lukas, *Nightmare,* 100.

21. House Committee on the Judiciary, *Statement of Information: Book 7, Part 2: White House Surveillance Activities and Campaign Activities,* 815.

22. Lukas, *Nightmare,* 118–19; Emery, *Watergate,* 55–56.

23. Emery, *Watergate,* 56.

24. House Committee on the Judiciary, *Statement of Information: Book 7, Part 2: White House Surveillance Activities and Campaign Activities,* 829. See also "Summary of Interview with Egil Krogh," 3 April 1974, RG 460 Records of the Watergate Special Prosecution Force, Plumbers Task Force, Fielding Break-In Investigation, Box 20.

### "All These Harvard People"

1. Ralph Blumenthal, "Saigon Deputy Seized in Assembly," *New York Times,* 27 February 1970; James Doyle, "Pressure Grows: Bunker in the Middle of the Chau Affair," *Washington Star,* 26 March 1970. Cooke provided details in an 11 March 2000 interview with me.

2. Conversation 534-002, 1 July 1971, 8:45–9:52 a.m., Oval Office, and Conversation 534-005, 1 July 1971, 10:27–11:49 a.m., Oval Office.

3. Nixon, *RN,* 512–13.

4. Conversation 534-002, 1 July 1971, 8:45–9:52 a.m., Oval Office.

### The Economic Conspiracy Theory

1. Conversation 006-068, 30 June 1971, 7:44–7:46 p.m., White House Telephone.

2. The BLS conducted its employment survey during the week that included the 12th of the month. In June 1971, the 12th fell on a Saturday, so the survey week, June 6–12, was relatively early in the month. The seasonal adjustment to the unemployment rate "is essentially based upon the average experience of the previous eight years," according to the Labor Department (US Department of Labor, "The Employment Situation: June 1971," news release, 2 July 1971, attached to Colson to Haldeman, "CEA," 7 July 1971, WHSF-SMOF Haldeman Box 81, RMNL).

3. Conversation 534-002, 1 July 1971, 8:45–9:52 a.m., Oval Office.

4. Conversation 535-004, 2 July 1971, 9:15–10:39 a.m., Oval Office. Nixon would appoint Stein chairman of the CEA in November 1971.

5. Edwin L. Dale, "Jobless Rate off Sharply, But Doubt Is Cast on Data," *New York Times,* 3 July 1971.

6. Norman Kempster, "Jobless Rate Declines to 5.6%," *Washington Evening Star,* 2 July 1971.

7. Conversation 006-093, 2 July 1971, 4:14–4:22 p.m., White House Telephone.

8. Since the 12th of the month fell on a Saturday in September 1970, the survey week was September 6–12, relatively early in the month. See the explanation of the survey week in note 2 above.

9. "Nixon Hopes Dashed; Rise in September Jobless Rate to 5.5% Sharpens Election Issue," *Wall Street Journal,* www.proquest.com.

10. Frank C. Porter, "Jobless Rate Leaps to 5½%, 6-Year High," *Washington Post,* 3 October 1970.

11. "Jobless Rate Rises in July to 3.6 Pct.," *Washington Post*, 5 August 1969.

12. Jan Nugent Pearce, "Jobless Rate Hits 5% Mark," *Washington Post*, 6 June 1970.

13. Eileen Shanahan, "Jobless Rate Up to 6% in Nation; Highest Since '61," *New York Times*, 9 January 1971.

14. Eileen Shanahan, "Unemployment Rate Down for First Time in 7 Months," *New York Times*, 6 February 1971.

15. *Haldeman Diaries*, 6 February 1971.

16. Edwin L. Dale Jr., "Rate of Jobless Fell in February for a 2d Month," *New York Times*, 6 March 1971.

17. Allen J. Matusow, *Nixon's Economy: Booms, Busts, Dollars, & Votes* (Lawrence: University Press of Kansas, 1998), 96.

18. Ehrlichman to Haldeman, 6 March 1971, "Frederic Malek March 1971, Box 75" folder, Haldeman Contested Folder 7, RMNL.

19. Murray Seeger, "Briefings Posed PR Problem," *Washington Post*, 20 March 1971, www.proquest.com.

20. "Proxmire Acts to Offset Labor Unit's Briefings Halt," *Wall Street Journal*, 29 March 1971.

21. Conversation 063-003, 29 June 1971, 8:05–10:07 a.m., Cabinet Room; *Haldeman Diaries*, 29 June 1971.

22. *Haldeman Diaries*, 2 July 1971.

### "Are They All Jews?"

1. Conversation 536-004, 3 July 1971, 8:00–9:55 a.m., Oval Office.

2. Ibid.

3. Ibid.

4. Ibid.

5. Conversation 536-010, 3 July 1971, 9:05–9:55 a.m., Oval Office.

### "They're All Over"

1. "Remarks of the President, Chief Justice Warren E. Burger, and Speaker of the House Carl Albert at a Ceremony Opening the American Revolution Bicentennial Era," 3 July 1971, *Public Papers of the Presidents of the United States: Richard M. Nixon, 1971* (Washington, DC: GPO, 1972), www.presidency.ucsb.edu /ws/?pid=3067. See also Associated Press, "Nixon Sets Goal of 'Open World,'" *New York Times*, 4 July 1971, www.proquest.com.

2. Conversation 536-016, 3 July 1971, 10:41–11:53 a.m., Oval Office.

3. Ibid.

4. Ibid.

5. Lawrence M. Higby to Haldeman, 8 July 1971, "Lawrence Higby July 1971" folder, WHSF-SMOF Haldeman Box 82, RMNL, www.nixonlibrary.gov/ virtuallibrary/releases/jun09/070871_Higby.pdf.

### "Somebody Sits on High"

1. Conversation 006-129, 3 July 1971, 4:12–4:22 p.m., White House Telephone.

## Counting Ivy Leaguers

1. "The Outlook," *Wall Street Journal,* 2 February 1970.

2. Hobart Rowen, "Nixon Presses Burns for Monetary Expansion," *Washington Post,* 10 February 1971.

3. "Burns, Despite Nixon, Asks Firmer Curbs on Inflation and Hopes for Incomes Policy," *Wall Street Journal,* 1 July 1971.

4. Conversation 540-009, 20 July 1971, 11:09 a.m.–1:21 p.m., Oval Office.

## Counting Jews

1. Timothy Noah, "Nixon's Jew Count: the Whole Story!" *Slate,* 26 September 2007, www.slate.com/articles/news_and_politics/chatterbox/2007/09/nixons_jew_count_the_whole_story.html.

2. Conversation 545-001, 24 July 1971, 9:43–10:36 a.m., Oval Office.

3. Conversation 470-018, 19 March 1971, 1:30–2:12 p.m., Oval Office.

4. Edwin L. Dale Jr., "Burns Says Inflation Curb Is Making Scant Progress," *New York Times,* 24 July 1971.

5. Conversation 545-003, 24 July 1971, 12:36–1:03 p.m., Oval Office.

6. Norman Kempster, "Reserve," United Press International, 28 July 1971, attached to Bruce Kehrli to Ehrlichman, 29 July 1971, WHSF-SMOF Haldeman Box 81.

7. Conversation 549-012, 28 July 1971, 11:51 a.m.–12:46 p.m., Oval Office.

8. Haldeman to Malek, 26 July 1971, WHSF-SMOF Haldeman Box 82.

9. Malek to Haldeman, "Bureau of Labor Statistics," 27 July 1971, WHSF-SMOF Haldeman Box 82.

10. Conversation 549-012, 28 July 1971, 11:51 a.m.–12:46 p.m., Oval Office.

11. Conversation 550-001, 28 July 1971, 4:58–5:16 p.m., Oval Office. Nixon would appoint Greenspan chairman of the Council of Economic Advisers in 1974. President Ronald W. Reagan appointed him chairman of the Federal Reserve Board in 1987.

12. The reorganization also removed two other Jewish employees from their BLS posts. "Peter Henle, Associate Commissioner for Economic and Social Research, and Leon Greenberg, Associate Commissioner for Statistical Standards and Operations, will be transferred when the reorganization is announced," Malek wrote (Malek to Haldeman, "Bureau of Labor Statistics," 8 September 1971, "Haldeman, Alpha Name Files, Fred Malek, September 1971, Box #85" folder, Haldeman Contested Folder 8, RMNL).

## Above the Law

1. House Committee on the Judiciary, *Statement of Information: Book 7, Part 2: White House Surveillance Activities and Campaign Activities,* 815; Lukas, *Nightmare,* 101.

2. See Young to Ehrlichman, 26 August 1971, in House Committee on the Judiciary, *Statement of Information: Book 7, Part 2: White House Surveillance Activities and Campaign Activities,* 1215–19.

3. Liddy, *Will,* 236.

4. Ibid., 237. Domestic terrorists like the Weathermen also timed their bombs "to go off at night so as not to endanger lives needlessly," as Liddy put it, but that didn't always work as planned.

### "Pretty Much Carte Blanche"

1. Hoover to Krogh, 3 August 1971, in House Committee on the Judiciary, *Statement of Information: Book 7, Part 2: White House Surveillance Activities and Campaign Activities,* 953.

2. See Partial Transcript of a Telephone Conversation between Cushman and Ehrlichman, 7 July 1971, quoted in House Committee on the Judiciary, *Statement of Information: Book 7, Part 2: White House Surveillance Activities and Campaign Activities,* 728.

3. See House Committee on the Judiciary, *Statement of Information: Book 7, Part 2: White House Surveillance Activities and Campaign Activities,* 897.

4. See CIA Employee Affidavit, 9 May 1973, quoted in House Committee on the Judiciary, *Statement of Information: Book 7, Part 2: White House Surveillance Activities and Campaign Activities,* 900–901.

5. Helms testimony before the Senate Foreign Relations Committee, 21 May 1972, quoted in House Committee on the Judiciary, *Statement of Information: Book 7, Part 2: White House Surveillance Activities and Campaign Activities,* 898–99.

6. CIA Employee Affidavit, 9 May 1973, quoted in House Committee on the Judiciary, *Statement of Information: Book 7, Part 2: White House Surveillance Activities and Campaign Activities,* 902, 1007.

7. "CIA Preliminary Psychological Study," 9 August 1971, in House Committee on the Judiciary, *Statement of Information: Book 7, Part 2: White House Surveillance Activities and Campaign Activities,* 1012–15.

8. Nixon, *RN,* 513.

9. Prosecution memo, "Obstruction of Justice in Connection with the Trial of Daniel Ellsberg," 25 September 1973, RG 460 Records of the Watergate Special Prosecution Force, Plumbers Task Force, Fielding Break-In Investigation, Box 26, NARA-CP.

10. Conversation 538-015, 6 July 1971, 11:47 a.m.–12:15 p.m., Oval Office.

11. House Committee on the Judiciary, *Statement of Information: Book 7, Part 2: White House Surveillance Activities and Campaign Activities,* 1449.

12. Egil "Bud" Krogh, *Integrity: Good People, Bad Choices, and Life Lessons from the White House* (New York: Public Affairs, 2007), 41–42.

13. Liddy, *Will,* 216–18.

14. House Committee on the Judiciary, *Statement of Information: Book 7, Part 2: White House Surveillance Activities and Campaign Activities,* 967–73.

15. Krogh and Young to Ehrlichman, 11 August 1971, in House Committee on the Judiciary, *Statement of Information: Book 7, Part 2: White House Surveillance Activities and Campaign Activities,* 1023–24.

16. Krogh and Young to Ehrlichman, 11 August 1971, in House Committee on the Judiciary, *Statement of Information: Book 7, Part 2: White House Surveillance Activities and Campaign Activities,* 1023–24.

17. House Committee on the Judiciary, *Statement of Information: Book 7, Part 2: White House Surveillance Activities and Campaign Activities,* 1151–77.

18. Ibid., 1186; Liddy, *Will,* 231.

19. House Committee on the Judiciary, *Statement of Information: Book 7, Part 2: White House Surveillance Activities and Campaign Activities,* 1186; Krogh's "Statement of the Defendant on the Offense and His Role," RG 460 Records of the Watergate Special Prosecution Force, Plumbers Task Force, Fielding Break-In Investigation, Box 20, NARA-CP.

20. House Committee on the Judiciary, *Statement of Information: Book 7, Part 2: White House Surveillance Activities and Campaign Activities,* 1186.

21. Krogh, *Integrity,* 74.

22. Colson is quoted in Aitken, *Charles W. Colson,* 157.

### "One Little Operation"

1. House Committee on the Judiciary, *Statement of Information: Book 7, Part 2: White House Surveillance Activities and Campaign Activities,* 981.

2. Conversation 274-044, 8 September 1971, 3:26–5:10 p.m., Executive Office Building.

### The CIA Bluff

1. Ehrlichman to Nixon, 7 October 1971, "Meeting with Director Richard Helms, CIA, Friday, October 8, 1971," "JDE Notes—Meetings with the President, 8/3/71-12/31/71 [3 of 5]" folder, WHSF-SMOF Ehrlichman Box 12, RMNL, www.nixonlibrary.gov/virtuallibrary/releases/dec10/40.pdf.

2. Conversation 587-007, 8 October 1971, 10:58 a.m.–12:12 p.m., Oval Office.

3. "The CIA was closed like a safe, and we could find no one who would give us the combination to open it," Nixon wrote in *RN,* 515.

### The Smoking Gun

1. "Ex-Aide Says Nixon Agreed to Break-In at Watergate," *New York Times,* 27 July 2003, www.nytimes.com/2003/07/27/us/ex-aide-says-nixon-agreed-to-break-in-at-watergate.html.

2. Lawrence R. Meyer and Peter Osnos, "Magruder Testifies Mitchell Helped to Plan Watergate and Its Cover-Up," *Washington Post,* 15 June 1973, www.proquest.com.

3. *Watergate Plus 30: Shadow of History,* DVD, directed by Foster Wiley (Alexandria, VA: PBS Home Video, 2004).

4. Kutler, *Abuse of Power,* 47–49.

5. Ibid., 50–51.

6. Emery, *Watergate,* 188–89.

7. Conversation 741-002, 23 June 1972, 9:41–10:39 a.m., Oval Office, http://whitehousetapes.net/transcript/nixon/smoking-gun.

8. Kutler, *Abuse of Power,* 69.

9. House Committee on the Judiciary, *Statement of Information: Book 7, Part 2: White House Surveillance Activities and Campaign Activities,* 92.

10. Haldeman, *The Ends of Power,* 67.

11. House Committee on the Judiciary, *Statement of Information: Book 2: Events Following the Watergate Break-In* (Washington: GPO, 1974), 402, 472.

12. Emery, *Watergate*, 193–94.

13. Haldeman, *The Ends of Power*, 119.

14. Associated Press, "7 Indicted in Watergate Caper," *Los Angeles Times*, 15 September 1972, www.proquest.com.

15. Louis Harris, "Bugging, Fund Charges Leave Public Apathetic," *Washington Post*, 19 October 1972, www.proquest.com.

16. Theodore H. White, *The Making of the President 1972* (New York: Bantam, 1973), Kindle edition, chap. 13, "Appeal to the People: Verdict in November," 341–42. The only candidate to receive a higher percentage of the popular vote than Nixon in 1972 was Johnson in 1964.

17. *Haldeman Diaries*, 8 January 1973.

18. Conversation 835-008, 8 January 1973, 10:50 a.m.–1:45 p.m., Oval Office.

19. *Haldeman Diaries*, 11 January 1973.

20. Ibid., 12 January 1973.

21. Conversation 858-003, 16 February 1973, 9:08–9:36 a.m., Oval Office.

22. Conversation 852-007, 7 February 1973, 10:23 a.m.–2:21 p.m., Oval Office.

### "I Don't Kiss and Tell"

1. Robert Caro, *The Path to Power: The Years of Lyndon Johnson* (New York: Vintage, 1982), Kindle edition, chap. 23, "Galveston."

2. Judith Viorst, "The Three Faces of Anna Chennault," *Washingtonian*, September 1969, Reference File: Anna Chennault, South Vietnam and US Politics, LBJL.

3. In her memoir, Chennault wrote that on November 13, 1968, Klein called her. "Anna, I'm not going to beat around the bush," Klein said. "You must promise to say to the press that our friend does not know about our arrangement with President Thieu." Klein added, "We know you're a good soldier; we just want to be sure our friend is protected" (Chennault, *The Education of Anna*, 193–94).

4. Conversation 835-003, 8 January 1973, 8:42–9:33 a.m., Oval Office.

5. Conversation 870-002, 6 March 1973, 3:42–4:20 p.m., Oval Office.

### Dean Testifies

1. Senate Watergate Committee, *Watergate and Related Activities: Phase I: Watergate Investigation: Book 3* (Washington: GPO, 1973), 919–20; John W. Dean, *Blind Ambition: The End of the Story* (Palm Springs, Calif.: Polimedia, 2009), 42–46.

2. Senate Watergate Committee, *Watergate and Related Activities: Phase I: Watergate Investigation: Book 6* (Washington: GPO, 1973), 2535.

### The *X* Envelope

1. Rostow to Middleton, "Literally Eyes Only," Document 0, 26 June 1973, Reference File: Anna Chennault, South Vietnam and US Politics, LBJL.

2. Senate Watergate Committee, *Watergate and Related Activities: Phase I: Watergate Investigation: Book 3*, 981.

3. Rostow's "Memorandum for the Record," Document 39, 14 May 1973, Reference File: Anna Chennault, South Vietnam and US Politics, LBJL.

## The White House Tapes

1. Arthur Siddon and Jim Squires, "Nixon Bugged Own Offices," *Chicago Tribune*, 17 July 1973, www.proquest.com.

2. "Article II of Impeachment Resolution," *Washington Post*, 30 July 1974, www.proquest.com. While the Fielding break-in was financed by campaign contributions, most of the SIU's activities were carried out while members were on the federal payroll, so they were financed by taxpayer money.

3. Linda Charlton, "Ehrlichman Is Convicted of Plot and Perjury in Ellsberg Break-in," *New York Times*, 13 July 1974, www.proquest.com.

4. George Lardner Jr., "Krogh Yields, Pleads Guilty in 1971 Ellsberg Burglary," *Washington Post*, 1 December 1973, www.proquest.com.

5. Associated Press, "Immunity Is Granted for Hunt and Young," *New York Times*, 18 June 1974, www.proquest.com.

6. See Bob Woodward and Carl Bernstein, "U.S. Panel Voted 19-0 in March; President Listed as Unindicted Co-Conspirator," *Washington Post*, 6 June 1974, www.proquest.com.

7. Liddy, *Will*, 236–37. Under federal law, the Brookings burglary did not have to take place for the criminal conspiracy to exist. Nixon, Colson, Caulfield, Ulasewicz, Hunt, and Liddy had all taken concrete steps "in furtherance of the scheme" (see US Library of Congress, Congressional Research Service, *Federal Conspiracy Law: A Brief Overview*, by Charles Doyle, CRS Report R41223 [Washington, DC: Office of Congressional Information and Publishing, 30 April 2010]).

8. "Congress Passes Nixon Tapes Bill," *New York Times*, 10 December 1974, www.proquest.com.

9. See "The 'X' envelope," Reference File: Anna Chennault, South Vietnam and US Politics, LBJL. Rostow died in 2003. Two decades after the fact, library officials could not recall why the decision was made to open the material at that time.

10. Christopher Matthews, "Nixon Personally Ordered Break-In," *San Francisco Examiner*, 21 November 1996, www.sfgate.com/cgi-bin/article.cgi?f= /e/a/1996/11/21/NEWS12569.dtl.

11. Kutler, *Abuse of Power*, 3, 6, 8, 10, 17.

12. Ken Hughes, "A Rough Guide to Richard Nixon's Conspiracy Theories," Miller Center website, 24 September 2007, http://millercenter.org /presidentialclassroom/exhibits/a-rough-guide-to-richard-nixons-conspiracy -theories.

13. James Rosen, *The Strong Man: John Mitchell and the Secrets of Watergate* (New York: Doubleday, 2008), 62; Gibbs and Duffy, *The Presidents Club*, Kindle edition, chap. 13, " 'I Want the Break-in': Secrets and Lies," 264; Robert Parry,

*America's Stolen Narrative: From Washington and Madison to Nixon, Reagan and the Bushes to Obama* (Arlington, VA: Media Consortium, 2012), Kindle edition, chap. 4, "On to Watergate."

14. Nixon, *RN*, 512.

15. Huston to Haig, 23 March 1970, "Misc. Memos" folder, RG 460 Records of the Watergate Special Prosecution Force, Plumbers Task Force, Gray/Wiretap Investigation, Documentary Evidence, National Security Wiretaps to White House Documents, Box 17, NARA-CP. It is worth mentioning again that there is no evidence that the report actually existed.

16. "The Foreign Minister discussed the San Antonio formula and said it could not be accepted even in the somewhat diluted form which the new Defense Minister Clifford had given in his meeting with the Senate" (see the 5 April 1968 summary of Norwegian Ambassador Ole Algard's visit to Hanoi in the Pentagon Papers, *Report of the Office of the Secretary of Defense Vietnam Task Force: United States-Vietnam Relations, 1945–1967,* part VI, C.4, p. 127, www.archives .gov/research/pentagon-papers).

17. The historian Stephen E. Ambrose nevertheless believed Nixon "wanted the information to use as political leverage against Clark Clifford and others who were opposing his Vietnam policy" (see Stephen E. Ambrose, *Nixon: The Triumph of a Politician 1962–1972* [New York: Simon and Schuster, 1989], 448).

18. Conversation 525-001, 17 June 1971, 5:15–6:10 p.m., Oval Office.

19. Ibid.; Nixon, *RN*, 510.

20. Conversation 005-117, 17 June 1971, 7:39–7:45 p.m., White House Telephone.

21. "McGovern Adviser Comments," *New York Times,* 17 August 1972, www .nytimes.com.

22. The American Presidency Project website makes it possible to search through all of the public statements of President Nixon at www.presidency.ucsb .edu.

23. David Frost and Robert Zelnick, *Frost/Nixon: Behind the Scenes of the Nixon Interviews* (New York: Harper Perennial, 2007), 303–5.

24. Nixon's use of "at that point" in his answer to Frost also narrows the time frame of his denial.

25. Nixon, *RN*, 322–28, 628–29; Monica Crowley, *Nixon Off the Record* (New York: Random House, 1996), 17. Bundy noted Nixon's pattern of (1) silence about Chennault and (2) attacks on LBJ's advisers as partisan advocates of a bombing halt in *A Tangled Web*, 36.

26. Kissinger, *Ending the Vietnam War,* 53.

27. Kissinger (ibid., 585n3) cites Anatoly Fedorovich Dobrynin, *In Confidence: Moscow's Ambassador to American's Six Cold War Presidents (1962–1986)* (New York: Times Books, 1995), 178–81, 190–91.

28. Victor Lasky, *It Didn't Start with Watergate* (New York: Dial, 1977), 215–18.

29. Safire, *Before the Fall,* 113.

30. Ibid., 111.

31. One laudable exception is Melvin Small, who, in a volume he edited, didn't accept the claim that LBJ halted the bombing to defeat Nixon (Melvin Small, ed., *A Companion to Richard M. Nixon* [Chichester, West Sussex; Malden, MA: Wiley-Blackwell, 2011], 157).

32. LaFeber, *The Deadly Bet*, 162. LaFeber makes a gesture in the direction of fairness, but it, too, is inaccurate: "Or perhaps, as Johnson later claimed, the timing of the announcement had little to do with the election and much to do with the changing North Vietnamese position." Johnson claimed all along (not just "later") that his bombing halt position had nothing (not "little") to do with the election, and the diplomatic record (against which LaFeber neglects to test his assumptions) confirms that Hanoi, not LBJ, changed position on his three bombing halt conditions in October 1968.

33. Catherine Forslund, *Anna Chennault: Informal Diplomacy and Asian Relations* (Wilmington, DE: SR, 2002), 60–61.

34. LaFeber, *The Deadly Bet*, 163, 196n19. LaFeber cites Irwin Unger and Debi Unger, *LBJ: A Life* (New York: Wiley, 1999), 490–91 (LaFeber means page 492, where Unger and Unger claim that "the evidence the president had collected came from illegal wiretaps and other dubious sources," but the authors provide no substantiation for the charge of illegality). Larry Berman, *No Peace, No Honor: Nixon, Kissinger, and Betrayal in Vietnam* (New York: Free Press, 2001). (LaFeber provides no page numbers; on page 33, Berman claims LBJ's "information had been obtained from illegal wiretaps and surveillance" without citing any evidence to support the claim that they were illegal.) Clifford, *Counsel to the President*, 582–96. (Clifford, of course, doesn't claim that any of the intelligence was obtained illegally.) None of LaFeber's sources say anything about the CIA wiretap he alleges. See also Reference File: Anna Chennault, South Vietnam and US Politics, LBJL.

35. Senate Select Committee to Study Governmental Operations with Respect to Intelligence Activities, *Intelligence Activities and the Rights of Americans: Book II: Final Report*, 120, 228. The Church Committee conducted its investigation before the public release of the *X* envelope's contents and mistakenly included the Chennault Affair in a discussion of "political misuse" of the FBI. "Under the Johnson administration, the FBI was used to gather and report political intelligence on the administration's partisan opponents in the last days of the 1964 and 1968 Presidential election campaigns" (ibid., 227–28). LBJ used the FBI to gather evidence that "the administration's partisan opponents" were sabotaging US negotiations, a violation of the Logan Act. The Church Committee report neglected to address the question of Logan Act violations at all. Even though the committee implied the surveillance was politically motivated, it didn't charge illegality. Neither did a separate committee staff report that briefly addressed the subject. Like later historians, the writers of the Church Committee reports suggested that there was *something* wrong with the Chennault surveillance, but failed to come up with a specific violation. The staff report weakly concluded that "a 'foreign' electronic surveillance [the FBI wiretap on the South Vietnamese embassy phone] was

instituted to indirectly target an American citizen, who, it was apparently believed, should not be surveilled directly." The FBI *did* surveil Chennault directly, tailing her for several weeks at LBJ's instruction; DeLoach rejected the wiretap on her as "untenable and embarrassing," not illegal or unethical (see Church Committee, *Book III: Supplementary Detailed Staff Reports on Intelligence Activities and the Rights of Americans* [Washington, DC: GPO 1976], 314–15).

# INDEX

Diego, Felipe de, 149
Diem, Bui: and Bundy's speech on
   bombing halt, 28; Chennault's
   contacts with, 39, 46–48, 57–58, 61,
   185n2; Dirksen delivers message
   from Nixon to, 60–62; FBI monitoring of, 67; Nixon's meeting with,
   9, 59, 62, 168, 178–79nn24–27; and
   Nixon's ultimatum on peace talks,
   62–63; on US elections, 37
Diem, Ngo Dinh, 60, 110–11, 127–28
Dirksen, Everett McKinley: and
   election of 1968, 24, 32, 39; on
   Humphrey's calls for bombing halt,
   23; LBJ's confrontation with, 46–48;
   Nixon's ultimatum to South
   Vietnam delivered by, 60–61, 64;
   and peace talks, 59
DMZ. See Demilitarized Zone
Dobrynin, Anatoly, 34, 169
domestic terrorism, 71, 74–78
Douglas, Helen Gahagan, 125
Douglas, William O., 117
Doyle, Jimmy, 131
Duong Van Minh. See Minh, Duong
   Van

economic conspiracy theory, 133–45,
   209n2
Education of Anna, The (Chennault), 9
Ehrlichman, John D.: conviction of,
   162; and Fielding break-in, 148–49,
   150; on Gelb, 144, 150; on grand jury
   investigation of Pentagon Papers
   leak, 142; on Hoover, 66, 74–75; and
   Nixon's desire to leak information,
   111; and secret bombing of
   Cambodia, 88; and SIU, 129, 148–50;
   testimony of, 160; and Watergate
   cover-up, 155
Eisenhower, Dwight D., 1, 26, 34, 56, 101
Eisenhower, Mamie, 8
election results of 1968, 1, 175n2
Ellsberg, Daniel: and Chau arrest
   documents, 131–33; CIA psychological profile on, 147; LBJ's

suspicions about, 98–99, 203n1;
   legal actions against, 113–14, 115; and
   NSSM-1, 96, 102–4, 119; Pentagon
   Papers access by, 95–96; Pentagon
   Papers leaked by, 99–104; surrenders
   himself, 114–15; and "Vietnam
   Alternatives" paper, 95
Emery, Fred, 73
Ending the Vietnam War (Kissinger),
   168–69
"enemies list," 76
Espionage Act of 1917, 107, 115
Executive Office Building (EOB),
   145–46
executive privilege, 162

Face the Nation, Humphrey's
   appearance on, 31
Federal Bureau of Investigation (FBI):
   and Chennault Affair, 161; Chennault Affair investigation by, 38,
   39, 46, 186–87n8; and domestic
   terrorism threats, 72, 74–76, 77–78;
   and Huston Plan, 73–74; Kahane
   investigation by, 77–78; monitoring
   of South Vietnamese embassy,
   38–39, 46, 52; Watergate break-in
   investigation by, 154–55; wiretaps on
   suspected leak sources, 92–93, 169
Federal Reserve, 142, 143, 144
Fielding, Lewis, 148–49, 150, 160, 215n2
Finch, Robert H., 49, 50, 51
Fish, Hamilton, 130
Flying Tiger Line, 7–8
Ford, Gerald R., 44, 53, 163
Forslund, Catherine, 169
Fortas, Abe, 5
four-party conference, 57
Frankfurter, Felix, 123
Frost, David, 167–68
Fulbright, J. William, 59

Gallup Poll: on election of 1968, 19, 33,
   52; on Pentagon Papers, 113; on
   Wallace's support, 13
Garment, Leonard, 123

LaFeber, Walter, 169, 170, 217n32, 217n34
Laird, Melvin R., 70, 84, 96, 120–21, 125, 127
Lake, Tony, 96, 140
Lansdale, Edward G., 131
Laos, bombing of, 36, 83, 185n48
Lasky, Victor, 148, 169
Liddy, G. Gordon: and Brookings break-in plan, 146, 177n8; conviction of, 162; and Fielding break-in, 149, 163; indictment of, 155; and SIU, 130, 148; and Watergate break-in, 153, 154
*Life* magazine: on Chennault, 7; Clifford article criticizing Nixon published in, 93–94
Logan Act of 1799, 38, 62, 167, 186n6, 217–18n35
Lon Nol. *See* Nol, Lon
*Los Angeles Times,* on Green Berets case, 99
Lukas, J. Anthony, 111

MACV (Military Assistance Command, Vietnam), 14–15
Magruder, Jeb Stuart, 152–53
mail surveillance, 72–74
*Making of the President 1960, The* (White), 68
*Making of the President 1968, The* (White), 68–69
Malek, Frederic V., 139–40, 144–45
Mansfield, Michael J., 30, 59
Mao Zedong, 7
Mardian, Robert C., 141, 142
Marshall, George C., 7, 109
Marshall, Thurgood, 117
Martinez, Eugenio, 149
Mathias, Charles McCurdy "Mac," 118–20, 141
Matthews, Christopher, 164
Matusow, Allen J., 136
McCarthy, Eugene J., 12, 17
McCarthy, Joseph R., 53, 108–9, 205n16
McCloskey, Paul N. "Pete," 111
McGovern, George S., 156

McNamara, Robert S., 70, 81, 94–95
*Meet the Press,* Nixon's appearance on, 49, 51
Meir, Golda, 76
Military Assistance Command, Vietnam (MACV), 14–15
Minh, Duong Van ("Big Minh"), 60
Mitchell, John: and Chennault Affair, 6, 9, 37–38, 67, 178–79nn24–27, 185n2, 186–87n8; and Huston Plan, 73–75; and legal actions against *New York Times,* 106–7; and Mathias papers, 119–20; and peace negotiations delays, 6; on public opinion on Pentagon Papers, 113–14; and Watergate break-in, 152, 154
Momyer, William W., 32
Mossadegh, Mohammad, 151
Muskie, Edmund S., 93, 114

National Liberation Front (NLF), 12, 17, 27–31, 34–35, 41, 43, 45–46, 57, 59–60, 62
National Security Agency (NSA): and Chennault Affair, 37, 45, 53, 59, 62, 66, 68, 70, 161, 169, 170, 185n2; and domestic terrorism threats, 72; and Huston Plan, 72–73, 75; South Vietnam's embassy cables intercepted by, 6, 8, 37, 185n2; on South Vietnam's motivations for peace talk delays, 61
National Security Study Memorandum (NSSM-1), 95–96, 102–4, 119
National Student Association, 87
*Newsweek,* on Cambodia bombing campaign, 92
*New York Times:* on Cambodia bombing campaign, 92–93, 105; on Chennault Affair, 167; on Diem coup, 127–28; on domestic terrorism, 71; on FBI's methods against Weather Underground, 74; on Hiss verdict, 124; on Humphrey's calls for bombing halt, 22, 24–25; on inflation, 143; legal actions against, 105–9;

Nixon's attacks on, 112–13, 205–6n1; on Nixon's daughter's wedding, 79; on Nixon's flip-flop on bombing halt, 25–26; on Nixon's public support of US negotiating position, 43; Pentagon Papers published by, 71, 81–83, 113, 117, 124, 148; on Sachs, 5; on South Vietnam's boycott of peace talks, 45, 49

Ngo Dinh Diem. *See* Diem, Ngo Dinh

Nguyen Cao Ky. *See* Ky, Nguyen Cao

Nguyen Duy Trinh. *See* Trinh, Nguyen Duy

Nguyen Van Hinh. *See* Hinh, Nguyen Van

Nguyen Van Thieu. *See* Thieu, Nguyen Van

Nissen, David, 115

Nixon, Pat, 79–80

Nixon, Richard: and bombing halt, 3, 19–21, 25–37, 43, 46, 49, 67–71, 182–83n8; briefings on US negotiations, 13, 15–16, 17, 40–42; and Chennault Affair, 4–19, 39–40, 50–51, 62, 168, 189nn14–18, 191n9, 194n9; conspiracy theories of, 121–26, 131–42; death of, 164; and "decent interval" exit strategy, 60, 101–2; Bui Diem's meeting with, 9, 62, 168, 178–79nn24–27; as Eisenhower's vice president, 125; election eve campaigning by, 55–56; and election results, 1, 175n2; and Federal Reserve, 144–45; and Hiss case, 123–25; and Huston Plan, 68, 71–75; on Jews, 108–9, 122–23, 125–26, 128, 137–40, 142–45; LBJ's post-election meeting with, 63–65; LBJ's use of Chennault Affair against, 50–51, 58–59; leaks desired by, 110–12; leaks detested by, 92–94, 116–17; and legal action on Pentagon Papers, 105–9; legal battle to keep tapes from public, 164; and Mathias papers (NSSM-1), 118–20; and McCarthy, 108–9, 205n16; and *New*

*York Times,* 106, 112–13, 205–6n1; ordering Brookings Institution break-in, 1–3, 68, 121, 126–27, 208n6, 216n17; Pentagon Papers leak accusations by, 83, 94–97, 104–5, 206–7n1; political rise of, 124–25; public support for US negotiating position, 10, 12, 14, 15–17, 43, 49, 51, 64; on Quakers, 80–81; resignation of, 163; and secret bombing of Cambodia, 83–92, 200n33; tape-recording system installed by, 78–79, 162–64; Thieu's preference for, 6, 10; and ultimatum to Thieu, 60–61, 62–63; and unemployment rate reporting, 133–37, 140–41

Nixon, Tricia, 79–81

*Nixon and Kissinger: Partners in Power* (Kissinger), 63

NLF. *See* National Liberation Front

Nol, Lon, 86, 87

*No More Vietnams* (Nixon), 90

"non-denial denials," 51, 167–68, 189n18, 216n24

North Vietnam: and conditions for bombing halt, 11, 26–27, 29, 182–83n8; and National Liberation Front, 12, 31, 35, 43; and secret minute demand, 34, 185n41; and US bombing of Cambodia, 86–87, 89–90, 198–99n4

NSA. *See* National Security Agency

NSSM-1. *See* National Security Study Memorandum

Oberemko, Valentin, 27

Olson, Keith W., 115

Operation Menu, 83–92, 105, 152

Osborn, Howard J., 147

"our side/your side" formula, 17, 31, 45, 57

Palme, Olof, 122

peace talks: and Chennault Affair, 4–19; and conditions for bombing halt, 11–12, 20–21, 26–30, 35, 41–43,